Schriftenreihe

Schriften zur Existenz- und Unternehmensgründung

Band 10

ISSN 2196-0054 (Print)

Verlag Dr. Kovač

New Venture Performance: Measurement, Determinants, and a Methodological Approach

INAUGURALDISSERTATION

zur Erlangung der Würde eines

Doctor rerum oeconomicarum

der Wirtschafts- und Sozialwissenschaftlichen Fakultät

der Universität Bern

vorgelegt von:

Johann Josef Martin Johannes Brieler

Die Wirtschafts- und Sozialwissenschaftliche Fakultät der Universität Bern hat diese Arbeit am 19. September 2024 auf Antrag der beiden Gutachter Prof. Dr. Artur Baldauf und Prof. Dr. Christian Lüthje als Dissertation angenommen, ohne damit zu den darin ausgesprochenen Auffassungen Stellung nehmen zu wollen.

Johann Josef Martin Johannes Brieler

New Venture Performance: Measurement, Determinants, and a Methodological Approach

Verlag Dr. Kovač

Hamburg
2025

VERLAG DR. KOVAČ GMBH
FACHVERLAG FÜR WISSENSCHAFTLICHE LITERATUR

Leverkusenstr. 13 · 22761 Hamburg · Tel. 040 - 39 88 80-0 · Fax 040 - 39 88 80-55

E-Mail info@verlagdrkovac.de · Internet www.verlagdrkovac.de

Bibliografische Information der Deutschen Nationalbibliothek
Die Deutsche Nationalbibliothek verzeichnet diese Publikation
in der Deutschen Nationalbibliografie;
detaillierte bibliografische Daten sind im Internet
über http://dnb.d-nb.de abrufbar.

ISSN: 2196-0054 (Print)

ISBN: 978-3-339-14352-5
eISBN: 978-3-339-14353-2

Zugl.: Dissertation, Universität Bern, 2024

Inauguraldissertation zur Erlangung der Würde eines *Doctor rerum oeconomicarum* der Wirtschafts- und Sozialwissenschaftlichen Fakultät der Universität Bern.

Die Wirtschafts- und Sozialwissenschaftliche Fakultät der Universität Bern hat diese Arbeit am 19. September 2024 auf Antrag der beiden Gutachter Prof. Dr. Artur Baldauf und Prof. Dr. Christian Lüthje als Dissertation angenommen, ohne damit zu den darin ausgesprochenen Auffassungen Stellung nehmen zu wollen.

Printed in Germany

Gedruckt auf holz-, chlor- und säurefreiem, alterungsbeständigem Papier. Archivbeständig nach ANSI 3948 und ISO 9706.

Acknowledgements

First and foremost, I express my deep gratitude towards Prof. Dr. Artur Baldauf, and thank him for the possibility to write my dissertation at the Department of Management and Entrepreneurship at the Universität Bern. He was an inspiration in many regards. His attitude towards excellence in research as well as his unparalleled integrity in all areas continue to truly impress me. His passion and work towards the fostering of entrepreneurship in the city and canton of Bern and the whole of Switzerland are advancing the region and many people involved. He provides a great amount of support for the doctoral students, in terms of feedback as well as help with the attendance of conferences and research seminars. He works towards a great academic education for all doctoral students.

I am also very grateful to Prof. Dr. Christian Lüthje from the Technische Universität Hamburg for his expertise and willingness to act as a second reviewer. He has dedicated valuable time to read and evaluate my dissertation.

Furthermore, I express my gratitude to my collaborators Prof. Dr. Tatjana Stettler, Dr. Simone Schweiger and Esther Moosauer for fruitful discussions and their input and work in our collaboration. Prof. Dr. Phillip Sieger was also major help in writing this dissertation. His constructive feedback and personality were always appreciated. Beatrice Rüfenacht deserves special thanks for always being cheerful, supportive, and helpful in everything regarding the dissertation and the university. Without her assistance, the doctoral students would miss a big supporting pillar at the chair.

Furthermore, I would like to thank Dr. Ilija Braun. As my first office colleague, roommate, and friend, he has always supported me and helped me navigate the shoals of the Doctorate. Dr. Isabelle Hahn has also been a great support in terms of content and mentality, with her open nature and dissertation experiences. I thank Prof. Dr. Sabrina Schell for her advice and support. I also thank my doctoral co-students for the collaboration, Joëlle Hofer, Dr. Fabian Mändli, Esther Moosauer, Simon Nobs, Lea Raemy, Dr. Jessica Villiger, and Lukas Wieland for the positive collaboration in teaching and research, the joint research trips, conferences, summer schools, exciting talks, entertaining leisure time at fairs and stadiums and for the support through all the ups and downs of our time and collaboration together. I also want to thank everyone from the outreach team. This includes Anna-Leena Marti, Danja Rutschi, Mirjam Viviani and Joëlle Prisi. They all contributed to a great atmosphere at the chair and allowed a link into practice with their work. Furthermore, I want to thank all student assistants who I had the opportunity to work with over the years. Samuel Albrecht, Aylin Atacan, Corsin Derungs, Dominik Fischli, Remo Handl, Claudio Heintze, Alice Huber, Lucas Moseler, Matteo Mosimann, Tim Ogi, Noemi Steiner, Nadine Stiebellehner, and Isabel Stuber. Franz Kölliker was always quick to assist in any technical problem, thank you for that.

Finally, and especially, I would like to thank my family. The completion of academic education with the dissertation is a milestone on the path of lifelong learning. Such a path cannot be taken without great support from family and friends. I would especially like to thank my grandparents, uncles, aunts, cousins, and all others who have supported me. It is always an extraordinary pleasure for me to do and experience all kinds of things with all of you. In particular, I would like to thank Lisa Holder, who has always encouraged and supported me, and with whom I have been able to celebrate the successes along the way. I look forward to a myriad of more adventures together. I would like to thank my sister Katharina. Her work ethic and determination are impressive, and it has helped me to take an example from her. The many wonderful experiences with her have also made me the person I am today. Her positive attitude and character are always a joy. I am proud to have her as a sister. Finally, I would like to thank my parents Martin and Irene. They made it possible for me to pursue my interests and abilities and to complete my studies and dissertation. Their support and example of values was and remains a great help in my professional and private life. They spurred me on to actively influence the fate of life, to take calculated risks and seize opportunities.

Table of Contents

List of Figures

List of Tables

List of Abbreviations

AC	Absorptive Capacity
AMJ	Academy of Management Journal
AOM	Academy of Management
BCERC	Babson College Entrepreneurship Research Conference
BHAR	Buy-and-Hold Abnormal Returns
BV	Book Value
CI	Confidence interval
csQCA	Crisp-set Qualitative Comparative Analysis
CVC	Corporate Venture Capital
Dr.	Doctor
e.g.	Example given
et al.	Among others (et alii)
etc.	Et cetera
ETP	Entrepreneurship: Theory and Practice
fsQCA	Fuzzy-set Qualitative Comparative Analysis
i.e.	That is (id est)
INN	Innovation
IPO	Initial Public Offering
JBV	Journal of Business Venturing
JMS	Journal of Management Studies
JOM	Journal of Management
log	Logarithm
MA	Meta-Analysis
MAQCA	Meta-Analytic Qualitative Comparative Analysis
MARA	Meta-Analytic Regression Analysis
MASEM	Meta-Analytic Structural Equation Modeling
MV	Market Value

n	Sample Size
Prof.	Professor
PSED II	Panel Study of Entrepreneurial Dynamics II
QCA	Qualitative Comparative Analysis
R&D	Research and Development
RoA	Return on Assets
RoE	Return on Equity
RoS	Return on Sales
RP	Research Policy
SEJ	Strategic Entrepreneurship Journal
SMJ	Strategic Management Journal
USD	United States Dollars
VC	Venture Capital

1. Introduction

1.1. Motivations and background

The advancement and increase in prosperity of humankind is based on entrepreneurship and innovation. Entrepreneurs act as creators and changemakers in industries, from which they gain Schumpeterian rents, i.e., rents, earned by innovators between the introduction and diffusion of an innovation (Newbert, 2003; Schumpeter, 1934). The success of new ventures is crucial for the society as a whole and for the prosperity that humankind experiences. Therefore, gaining knowledge of the success of new ventures is a central goal in academic research. To understand this success, it is important to grasp how performance and success are measured. It is further important to recognize which factors affect success and performance. In addition, researchers need to have the right tools to work towards a better understanding of these topics. Therefore, this dissertation focusses on these three issues. Firstly, the multitude of performance measures in research on new ventures is a challenge to overcome (Reese et al., 2020; Söderblom et al., 2015). A collective comprehension of the application of measurement and constructs is essential to advance research. The high pace in the development of new ventures needs to be accounted for, when selecting measurement options. Researchers gain knowledge about new venture performance measurement and are enabled to work more efficiently. The second important field of research in connection with new ventures and their performance is the factors which influence their success. Especially in their initial stages, new ventures experience scarcity in resources. Realizing which factors influence new venture performance positively or negatively is an important challenge for research. It can help with the effective and efficient support for new ventures and therefore, research can provide a service to society and the new ventures. The earliest stage of getting a first idea to the market is especially relevant, given the more pronounced scarcity in resources. An understanding of the factors that affect the entrepreneurial process and its success is essential (Timmons, 1999). Especially, the combinations of elements that affect new venture performance, is a topic that benefits from additional research (Douglas et al., 2020). Ultimately, researchers want to deliver added value to an ongoing discussion in research. Therefore, scholars may work on the consolidation of previous research through meta-analysis. In that case, they will be able to extend the insights from their work, if they utilize a combination of meta-analysis and qualitative comparative analysis. By combining the benefits of both aforementioned methods, researchers may deliver enhanced insights. Overall, this dissertation shall advance research in management and entrepreneurship and provide value to practitioners in new venture ecosystems.

1.2. Research objectives and contributions

This dissertation tackles multiple objectives over the three articles it contains. More specifically, the research on new ventures is the main focus of this thesis, together with qualitative comparative analysis (QCA) as a research method. New ventures and their innovations are integral to the wealth and growth of economies (Schumpeter, 1934). Each article focusses on a different objective. The first article is concerned with the measurement of new venture performance. The second article tackles the question of getting an idea to the market in a new venture. The third article builds on the method of QCA, that is employed in the second article, and provides insights on the benefits of utilizing this method in combination with meta-analysis. All three articles provide added value to research in their own right. The measurement of new venture performance in research is disputed and no consensus has been found (Brush and Vanderwerf, 1992; Reese et al., 2020; Söderblom et al., 2015). Existing frameworks which assess performance measurement do not encompass a comprehensive set of measures of new venture performance. This is rooted in a lack of focus on new venture performance. New ventures differ from established organizations in terms of resource endowment, size, age and performance (Barney, 1991; Henrekson and Sanandaji, 2020; Hult et al., 2008; Richard et al., 2009). In addition, the characteristics of new ventures change over time (Brockner et al., 2004; Hanks et al., 1993; Miller and Friesen, 1984). This effect is especially strong in the first years of existence (Coad, 2018). I find no consensus in the definition and conceptualization of performance and its measurement for new ventures (Reese et al., 2020; Richard et al., 2009; Söderblom et al., 2015). The multitude of performance measurement frameworks, as well as the diversity in new venture performance measures become apparent. I strive to provide guidance for researchers, overcoming this difficulty. I provide information on the use of new venture performance measurement in research, that may assist researchers in choosing new venture performance measures, in a way that takes the development of the new ventures into account.

The successful introduction of an idea to the market is critical for new ventures (Song et al., 2011). However, there are many factors to consider when transferring an idea to the market. Therefore, it is essential to identify which starting

conditions are associated with success to advance research on new ventures and their performance. The issue of having adequate (or inadequate) starting conditions to ensure survival is a crucial aspect of entrepreneurship (Linder et al., 2020). Nevertheless, there is still uncertainty in how different configurations of conditions influence performance (Gruber et al., 2010), and it is necessary to improve our understanding of the configurational issue as new ventures evolve over time (Brockner et al., 2004). Qualitative comparative analysis can be an effective method to enhance our understanding of these issues (Douglas et al., 2020; Fiss, 2007). Additionally, the question of new venture performance is a topic of debate in entrepreneurship research, but a lack of standards for assessing it hinders research findings and theory development (Reese et al., 2020; Söderblom et al., 2015; Wibbens and Siggelkow, 2020). This motivated me to perform QCA on the Timmons' model of entrepreneurial process. The elements are considered to be decisive factors in the potential of a new venture to get an idea to the market.
The findings suggest that there are consistent configurations of conditions that lead to a new venture reaching the market. Furthermore, I provide configurations that lead to high and low speed in getting a product to the market. Multiple paths leading to failure in getting a product to the market and configurations related to high and low speed in terms of getting a product to the market are described. The study confirms the value of Timmons' model in terms of the portrayed elements and suggests that researchers may use it in future evaluations of new venture performance to account for the causal complexity of outcomes.

The combination of meta-analysis and QCA (MAQCA) can balance strengths and weaknesses of both methods (Meuer and Rupietta, 2017b; Moore et al., 2018). Researchers are encouraged to utilize the method and apply it to a variety of problems in research. MAQCA can explain diverging results from differences in research design and unearth the reasons. The MAQCA process can ultimately be condensed into five steps. These are, setting the research question, identifying, and coding of studies, performing meta-analytical and QCA procedures. Ultimately, discussing the results and implications from the MAQCA analysis. I performed this project, in order to provide insights into how researchers can better understand the differences between pieces of research that they assess in meta-studies, given the sometimes sharply differing outcomes in similar research projects.

1.3. Structure of the dissertation

This dissertation comprises three research projects. All three provide a standalone value to research, as well as a combined value in the form of this dissertation project. Table 1 displays an overview over the projects included in this dissertation. Chapter 1 introduces the topic.

Chapter 2 represents the first project. By performing a systematic review of the literature, the measurement of new venture performance is assessed. For 15 years of literature, from 2007 to 2021, I portrait the way research measures performance in new ventures and display the change over the age of the new venture samples.

Chapter 3 contains the second study. I assess configurations of conditions which lead to performance in new ventures at the idea stage. The study is performed on a longitudinal sample of 181 new ventures from the Panel Study of Entrepreneurial Dynamics II (PSED II). Qualitative comparative analysis is performed of the outcomes of success and speed of getting an idea to the market.

TABLE 1: Overview of the dissertation studies

Research goal Advance research in the measurement and determinants of new venture performance		
Study	**Research Topic**	**Methodology**
Study 1 (Chapter 2)	Measurement of New Venture Performance	Systematic Literature Review
Study 2 (Chapter 3)	Configurations to Idea Stage New Venture Performance	Qualitative Comparative Analysis
Study 3 (Chapter 4)	Guideline to MAQCA	Combination of Qualitative Comparative Analysis and Meta-Analysis

Chapter 4 contains the third article of the dissertation. Therein, the novel method of assessing second level data is described. That is, the sequential use of meta-analysis and qualitative comparative analysis. By applying both methods, the advantages of meta-analysis can be elevated by assessing the more extreme findings for relationships between two constructs. In Chapter 5 a general conclusion of the dissertation is drawn and future research, as well as limitations of this dissertation are discussed. This concludes the dissertation.

2. Measuring New Venture Performance - A Systematic Literature Review with a Development Perspective[1]

2.1. Abstract

New venture performance is an important construct in entrepreneurship research. Reliable and valid research requires the identification of meaningful constructs and measures of new venture performance. Measurement of new venture performance is missing clarity and consensus in the literature. Additionally, the role of the development of a new venture is unclear. I conduct a systematic literature review of 255 articles measuring new venture performance. Building on existing literature, I assess the state of performance measurement in new venture research. I further align performance measurement with the development of new ventures. Scholars gain a better understanding about new venture performance measurement, with a novel perspective on venture age, allowing for informed decisions about their choice of new venture performance measure.

2.2. Introduction

The success of new ventures is one of the major drivers of business and economic growth (Acs and Armington, 2006; Schumpeter, 1934). Given the economic impact of new ventures it is important to measure their performance (Behn, 2003). Therefore, performance is often deemed as the ultimate dependent variable in management and entrepreneurship research (Richard et al., 2009). Conclusions from research can diverge, depending on the measurement of performance (Wibbens and Siggelkow, 2020). Therefore, the new venture performance measures employed in research must be well justified (Brush and Vanderwerf, 1992). To do so, researchers need to relate to a valid performance measurement classification. This is currently not possible. Researchers argue, that “there is no established consensus regarding suitable performance measures of new ventures” (Söderblom et al., 2015, p. 1505). This lack of guidance is acknowledged by many researchers (Combs et al., 2005; Kirby, 2005; Murphy et al., 1996; Reese et al., 2020; Richard et al., 2009). A widely accepted, valid measurement classification of organizational performance in management and entrepreneurship literature is missing (Carton and Hofer, 2006). For research on new ventures, choice of performance measurement is often driven by data availability (Henrekson and

[1] This project benefited from inputs from Artur Baldauf and Philipp Sieger, both University of Bern, Switzerland. A previous version of this paper was presented at the 2022 BCERC conference in Waco, USA.

Sanandaji, 2014), due to limited reporting in this context (Watson, 2007). This is unfortunate, as the specific characteristics of the study object have to be accounted for when measuring new venture performance (Barney, 2020; Zahra, 1996).

New ventures differ from established organizations in terms of resource endowment, size, age and performance (Barney, 1991; Henrekson and Sanandaji, 2020; Hult et al., 2008; Richard et al., 2009). In addition, the characteristics of new ventures change over time (Brockner et al., 2004; Hanks et al., 1993; Miller and Friesen, 1984). This effect is especially strong in the first years of existence (Coad, 2018).

Hence, we still miss guidance on choosing adequate performance measures in new venture research. Therefore, I intend to answer the research questions: *What measurements of new venture performance are used in entrepreneurship literature?* and *How does the use of performance measures change with new venture age?*

I tackle these issues by conducting a systematic literature review, following guidelines provided by Tranfield et al. (2003) and Kraus et al. (2020). This method is well-suited for the research purpose and enables providing theoretical advancement and insights for future research in the field (Alexander, 2020; Post et al., 2020).

To gain an overall understanding, the core concepts are defined as follows. New venture performance is a firm-level accomplishment in pursuing an opportunity, and may for example be expressed as survival or success (Shepherd et al., 2019). New ventures are independent ventures which are at an early stage of their lifecycle, with a maximum age of 15 years, given that this threshold allows for a comprehensive view on new ventures while being in line with previous research (Cockayne, 2019; Song et al., 2008).

These research findings should enhance the knowledge base in measuring new venture performance. This study provides an overview of measures used to assess new venture performance. Further the differences in performance measurement by age of the new venture are investigated.

The findings should facilitate the choice of new venture performance measures for researchers. Investors or policymakers can additionally benefit from my findings. A more attentive approach to choosing performance measures for research on new ventures is advised.

The article is structured as follows. First, the focal constructs. and research methodology are introduced. This is followed by the research results, which are thereafter discussed.

2.3. Definition of focal constructs

To be able to provide valuable insights to research, I first define the focal constructs, drawing from the literature and delineating the scope of this article. This study applies definitions of the constructs which allow for a broad overview and understanding.

New ventures

New venture is a commonly used term in entrepreneurship research. It often refers to any firm which is to be or has been created within a certain timespan. Research has been ambivalent about the length of this timespan, utilizing definitions with differing maximum ages of up to 15 years (Brush and Vanderwerf, 1992; Song et al., 2008). For this systematic literature review an approach is suitable that encompasses a broader age range, to get a better understanding of performance measurements along the development of a new venture. Other factors have also been considered for defining new ventures. For instance, lack of resources, high reactiveness, innovativeness, high risk exposure and not being able to sustain oneself may also indicate a new venture (Paternoster et al., 2014). In addition, incorporation often happens for reasons of liability or ease of funding (Brinckmann et al., 2011). In general new ventures may be described as: independent ventures which are at an early, critical stage of their lifecycle (Cockayne, 2019). Given that the aforementioned characteristics are linked to young firm age (Coad, 2018), I opt to follow previous research and define new ventures as ventures with a maximum age of 15 years (Song et al., 2008). The 15-year threshold is used to include a comprehensive scope of new ventures.

New venture performance

In the following, new venture performance is defined. There have been many attempts to conceptualize and measure the performance construct in business in general and in management and entrepreneurship specifically.

Shepherd et al. (2019) consider performance, in the entrepreneurship context, as a firm-level accomplishment in pursuing an opportunity. This definition of new venture performance is adopted for the present study. Knowing that performance measurement can happen at different levels (e.g., individual, team and firm level)

(Mayer-Haug et al., 2013), new venture performance is assessed at the firm level. The present definition is in line with other researchers. For example, Brownell et al. (2021) describe new venture performance as the success in development over the lifecycle of a new venture.

The complexity and dimensionality of performance has been subject to research for a long time. Venkatraman and Ramanujam (1986) have developed a model of performance measurement for businesses, arguing that there are three domains of performance: Financial Performance (e.g., sales growth or profitability), Business Performance (e.g., market share or new product introduction), and Organizational Effectiveness (Venkatraman and Ramanujam, 1986). They also differentiate among objective and subjective performance measurements, with information obtained from primary data or secondary sources (Venkatraman and Ramanujam, 1987). Cooper et al. (1994), with a focus on new ventures, classify performance of a venture along three categories: failure, marginal survival and growth.

Review of performance measurement classifications

In general, performance measures capture whether a desired state in pursuit of a specific target has been reached (Lebas, 1995; Shepherd et al., 2019). New venture performance measurement should be accurate in order to allow research to provide insights into the success of new ventures (Murphy et al., 1996). Performance measurement depends on the perspective that is chosen and the goals of stakeholders (Behn, 2003; Gilbert et al., 2006). The differences between established organizations and new ventures create the need for a distinct approach to measuring new venture performance. Measures have to be valid and reliable in order to provide an appropriate representation of reality and to be justified as measures of a construct (Rapp et al., 2020). New venture performance measures can exhibit diverging development along the lifecycle of a new venture (Robinson, 1999).

To grasp the existing dimensions of new venture performance, previous work which has classified dimensions of performance measurement is reviewed. The multidimensional approach to performance measurement has been discussed in organizational performance measurement. A better understanding of the dimensions will accuracy and relevance of management and entrepreneurship research (Hamann and Schiemann, 2021). The first investigated article, by Steers, was published in 1975. He assessed multiple multivariate models of organizational effectiveness. Venkatraman and Ramanujam (1986) proposed the dimensions of financial performance, business performance and organizational effectiveness. Hult et al. (2008) assess these dimensions in the context of international business research. Murphy et al. (1996) were amongst the first to assess performance measurement in the context of entrepreneurship. Combs et al. (2005) develop a conceptual model of organizational performance in various dimensions. Richard et al. (2009) review general organizational performance measurement. Carton and Hofer (2010) take a financial perspective on the dimensions of overall organizational performance measurement. Katsikeas et al. (2016) apply a performance measurement lens to the articles published in top tier marketing journals. Table 2 shows the dimensions highlighted by these articles and the number of performance measures they promote for each dimension.

The number of dimensions differs among the articles. This is a result of different approaches to conceptualize the dimensions. Venkatraman and Ramanujam (1986) and Hult et al. (2008) categorize performance measurement on only three dimensions. Another difference between the articles stems from the choice of grouping performance measures. While some aggregate the performance measures based on the underlying information, others choose to group based on other factors.

TABLE 2: Assessments of performance measurement, with dimensions and measures

Articles	Steers (1975)	Venkatraman & Ramanujam (1986) / Hult et al. (2008)	Murphy et al. (1996)	Combs et al. (2005)	Richard et al. (2009)	Carton & Hofer (2010)	Katsikeas et al. (2016)
Dimensions	Adaptability-Flexibility (-)	Financial Performance (-)	Efficiency (10 Measures)	Organizational: Accounting Returns (12 Measures)	Accounting (Obj./ Subj.) (20 Measures)	Profitability (6 Indicators)	Operational: Customer Based (14 Indicators)
	Productivity (-)	Business Performance (-)	Growth (12 Indicators)	Organizational: Stock Market (6 Indicators)	Financial Market (Obj./ Subj.) (9 Indicators)	Growth (4 Indicators)	Operational: Product Market (11 Indicators)
	Satisfaction (-)	Organizational Effectiveness (-)	Profit (14 Indicators)	Organizational: Growth (7 Indicators)	Tobin's Q Or Other Mixed Measure (17 Indicators)	Cash Flow (3 Indicators)	Organizational: Accounting (18 Indicators)
	Profitability (-)		Size (8 Measures)	Organizational: Hybrids (5 Measures)	Reputation Or Perception of Effectiveness (Subjective) (48 Indicators)	Liquidity (1 Measure)	Organizational: Financial Market (9 Measures)
	Resource Acquisition (-)		Liquidity (5 Measures)	Organizational: Survival (2 Measures)	Survival (1 Measure)	Survival (1 Measure)	Organizational: Company (4 Measures)
	Absence Of Strain (-)		Success/ Failure (8 Measures)	Organizational: Other (1 Measure)		Efficiency (1 Measure)	Miscellaneous (-)
	Control Over Environment (-)		Market Share (3 Measures)	Operational: Marketing (2 Measures)		Economic Value (2 Measures)	
	Development (-)		Leverage (4 Measures)	Operational: Outbound Logistics (3 Measures)		Cost Of Equity Capital (1 Measure)	
	Efficiency (-)		Other (3 Measures)	Operational: Technology Development (5 Measures)		Market (1 Measure)	
	Employee Retention (-)			Operational: Infrastructure (2 Measures)			
	Growth (-)			Operational: Hybrids (2 Measures)			
	Integration (-)			Operational: Human Resources (1 Measure)			
	Open Communications			Operational: Service Quality (1 Measure)			
	Survival (-)			Operational: Operations (7 Measures)			
	All Other Criteria (-)						
Total	15 Dimensions (No Specific Measures)	3 Dimensions (No Specific Measures)	3 Dimensions (67 Measures)	14 Dimensions (56 Measures)	5 Dimensions (95 Measures)	9 Dimensions (20 Measures)	6 Dimensions (56 Measures)
Referenced conceptual logic		Referred to Cameron & Whetten, (1983)	Referred to Venkatraman & Ramanujam, (1986)	Referred to Steers, (1975); Cameron & Whetten, (1981); Venkatraman & Ramanujam, (1986); Ray et al., (2004)	Stakeholder theory (Freeman, 1984); referred to Cameron & Whetten, (1983); Venkatraman & Ramanujam, (1986)	Referred to Peter (1979), Venkatraman & Ramanujam, (1986)	Referred to Rust et al., (2004); Keller and Lehmann, (2006); Petersen et al., (2009); Morgan, (2012)

Katsikeas et al. (2016), assign *Unit Sales* into the Dimension *Product Market,* whereas *Sales Revenue* is assigned into the *Accounting* dimension. Similarly, whilst current value of sales and growth of the latter are grouped into one dimension in some articles, (e.g. Richard et al. (2009) or Katsikeas et al. (2016)) others group these into diverging dimensions. For example Murphy et al. (1996) categorize *Change in Sales* into *Growth* dimension and *Sales Level* into the *Size* dimension. Carton and Hofer (2010) opt for a mixed approach where most growth rates are assigned the *Growth* dimension (e.g. *Growth Rate of Sales*), with the exception of *Growth Rate of Operating Cash Flow*, which is assigned to the *Cash Flow* dimension.

Overall, there are multiple classifications, which are rooted in their respective domains of research, and therefore differ from each other. These works are a starting point for the choice of new venture performance measurement. However, despite researchers efforts, little work has covered new venture performance measurement specifically, since the works of Brush and Vanderwerf (1992) as well as Murphy et al. (1996). Therefore, guidance for researchers on performance measurement in new ventures is scarce and the lack of convergence must be addressed to enable comparisons between studies (Zamanian and Myint, 2018).

New venture lifecycle

To appropriately measure new venture performance, it is crucial, to evaluate the lifecycle of a new venture (Lewis and Churchill, 1983), in order to account for differences in development (Zahra, 1996). Different lifecycle models have been conceptualized, that apply to new ventures (Levie and Lichtenstein, 2010). This review has a focus on early stages of the lifecycle, until a new venture matures into an established organization. Therefore, samples with a maximum mean age of 15 years are included, as most age related effects occur in the first years of a new ventures' existence (Coad, 2018). A new venture experiences the stages of existence, survival, success, take-off and ultimately resource maturity (Lewis and Churchill, 1983). In the first stage (existence) a new venture needs to assess, whether an opportunity exists and can be pursued. Then the venture moves to the next stage, where resources are collected, and first customers are attracted. Further, the venture scales up and it enters stages in which it can sustain itself, the stages of maturity and later either renewal and growth or a stage of decline (Brockner et al., 2004).

Risk taking declines over a new ventures' lifecycle, as uncertainties decrease (Chrisman et al., 1998). Firm size increases over time, until a firm experiences a decline in operations. Firm age, in general rises throughout the stages, however some firms can skip stages or return back to earlier stages over time (Miller and Friesen, 1984). It is important to highlight, that the lifecycle is not a deterministic concept, however. The stages are not following each other based on fixed age cutoffs, as analogies to human aging have been criticized (Coad, 2018). Rather, clusters of new ventures, exhibiting common characteristics may be formed (Hanks et al., 1993).

2.4. Research methodology

To address the research questions, the extant knowledge base in the domain of new venture performance measurement is assessed. Systematic literature reviews are of great value to synthesize a body of literature and capture the development of the research stream (Ohlsson, 1994). This systematic review of the literature, follows Tranfield et al. (2003) and Kraus et al. (2020). The systematic research process is reported in Figure 1, following the structure proposed by de Mol et al. (2015) and providing details on how the information base is derived and conclusions are drawn. First, the research objective is set, by outlining and defining the central concepts of new venture performance. The search terms are then used to perform the literature search, given the search boundaries and the cover period. Articles are excluded according to the exclusion criteria. To avoid bias from search terms, an independent search of literature is performed.

FIGURE 1: Research process, following de Mol et al. (2015)

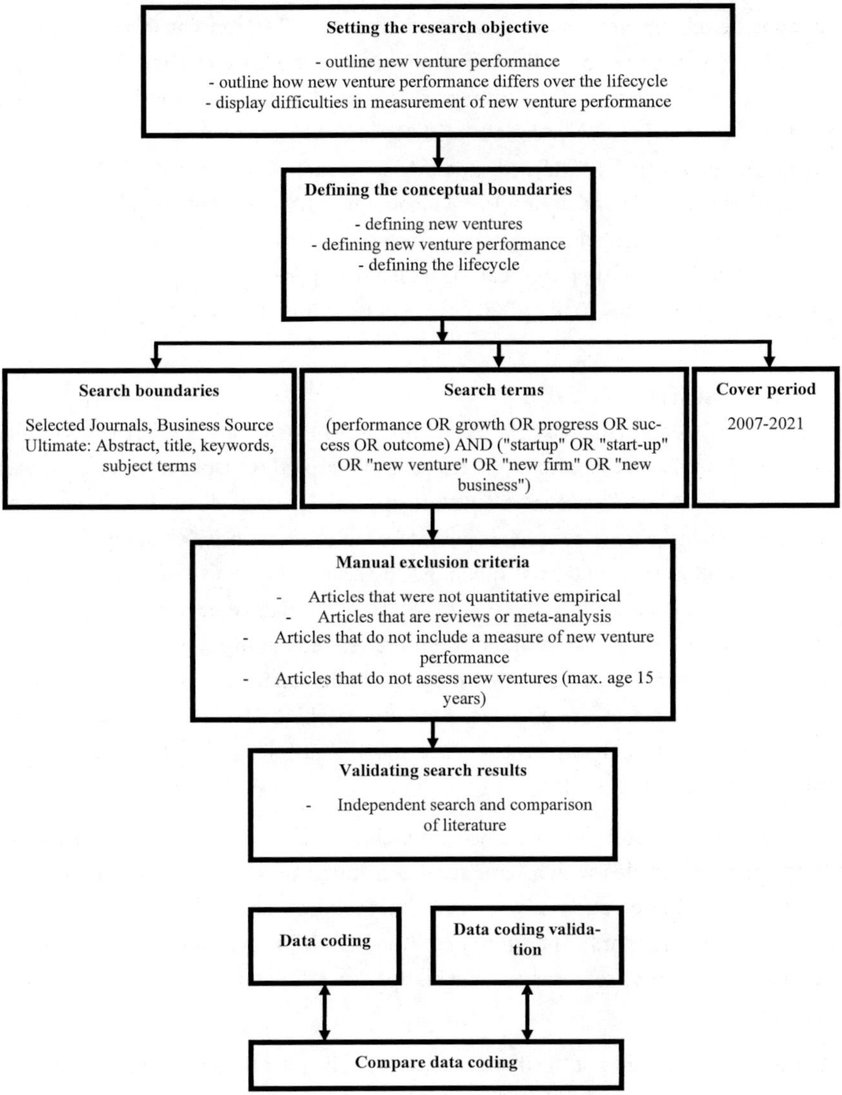

In identifying appropriate research to address the research questions, focus lies on the most renowned and influential journals in entrepreneurship research. Those are considered, that are ranked as top journals in the FT50 ranking (Ormans, 2016) and are highly recognized in Entrepreneurship (i.e., Research Policy (RP), Journal of Business Venturing (JBV), Entrepreneurship: Theory and Practice (ETP) and Strategic Entrepreneurship Journal (SEJ)) and Management (i.e. Academy of Management Journal (AMJ), Strategic Management Journal (SMJ), Journal of Management (JOM) and Journal of Management Studies (JMS)). This selection is done to assure high sample quality. A focus on less highly ranked, grey literature and inaccessible literature can decrease transparency and quality of the systematic review (Kraus et al., 2020). Research is limited to the 15-year period of 2007 to 2021.

Literature search

I used EBSCO and Business Source Ultimate to extract articles for the sample. The search terms in use are: (performance OR growth OR progress OR success OR outcome) AND ("startup" OR "start-up" OR "new venture" OR "new firm" OR "new business"). The search is performed in the categories abstract, title, keywords as well as subject terms. When linking search terms, use of "AND" as well as "OR" as Boolean operators is made. Articles which have been published before 2007 are excluded, as the Strategic Entrepreneurship Journal was first published in that year. Therefore, all research included in this analysis is based on the same timeframe and state-of-the-art in academic research, as research underlies change (Furrer et al., 2008). The search yielded the 184 articles published in the period from 2007 to the end of 2021.

However, to get a full view of articles which measure new venture performance, to account for articles which have not been found by the algorithm, avoiding a bias based on the selection of words used in the titles, abstracts, and keywords of the articles is important. Therefore, additionally all journals are evaluated article by article manually, to complete the sample of articles measuring new venture performance.

Any article which did not fulfil the criteria of inclusion is dropped. Firstly, articles based on their type are dropped. This excludes all articles which are editorials and articles that aggregate other articles (e.g., systematic literature reviews or meta-analysis), as well as case studies or book reviews. Secondly, all articles must focus on new ventures. If this is not the case, the article drops from the sample for not fitting the research scope. This is based on terminology and sample age of the articles. Articles with a sample of new ventures with a mean sample age of more than 15 years are therefore excluded. Thirdly, a measure of performance has to be used in the article. The measure of new venture performance must be a venture level measure, to justify inclusion. Articles which do not comply are excluded for lack of fit.

The final sample consists of 255 articles from 2007 until 2021. The distribution of the articles between the journals can be seen in Table 3. The journal in which the most articles are found is the Journal of Business Venturing, with 80 articles (31% of the sample) followed by Entrepreneurship: Theory and Practice (61 articles, 24% of the sample). The journals from which the least articles in my sample are derived are Journal of Management (7 articles, 3% of the sample) and Journal of Management Studies (3 articles, <1% of the sample). The publication years of the articles in my sample, by journal, show a constant stream of literature, assessing new venture performance over the years 2007 to 2021. Every year, apart from 2007, 2019 2020, and 2021, the number of articles published ranges between 10 and 20. The exceptions from this rule are 2007, where nine articles were published, and 2019 to 2021 with 28, 32 and 22 articles published respectively. The year with the most publications is 2020, with 32 publications (13% of sample). This shows that there is distributed literature over the different journals, assessing new venture performance.

TABLE 3: Distribution of publication by journals and years

Year of Publication	Total	JBV	ETP	SEJ	RP	SMJ	AMJ	JOM	JMS
2007	9 (4%)	2 (1%)	3 (1%)	- (-%)	3 (1%)	1 (<1%)	- (-%)	- (-%)	- (-%)
2008	11 (4%)	5 (2%)	3 (1%)	2 (1%)	- (-%)	- (-%)	1 (<1%)	- (-%)	- (-%)
2009	17 (7%)	3 (1%)	5 (2%)	2 (1%)	- (-%)	3 (1%)	2 (1%)	2 (1%)	- (-%)
2010	16 (6%)	5 (2%)	2 (1%)	2 (1%)	2 (1%)	4 (2%)	- (-%)	- (-%)	1 (<1%)
2011	10 (4%)	2 (1%)	4 (2%)	- (-%)	2 (1%)	1 (<1%)	- (-%)	- (-%)	1 (<1%)
2012	20 (8%)	8 (3%)	1 (0%)	3 (1%)	3 (1%)	3 (1%)	1 (<1%)	1 (<1%)	- (-%)
2013	17 (7%)	7 (3%)	5 (2%)	3 (1%)	- (-%)	- (-%)	1 (<1%)	1 (<1%)	- (-%)
2014	12 (5%)	4 (2%)	4 (2%)	1 (<1%)	1 (<1%)	2 (1%)	- (-%)	- (-%)	- (-%)
2015	15 (6%)	2 (1%)	7 (3%)	2 (1%)	3 (1%)	1 (<1%)	- (-%)	- (-%)	- (-%)
2016	17 (7%)	3 (1%)	4 (2%)	2 (1%)	4 (2%)	1 (<1%)	2 (1%)	1 (<1%)	- (-%)
2017	19 (7%)	6 (2%)	6 (2%)	2 (1%)	2 (1%)	2 (1%)	- (-%)	1 (<1%)	- (-%)
2018	10 (4%)	4 (2%)	3 (1%)	1 (<1%)	- (-%)	1 (<1%)	1 (<1%)	- (-%)	- (-%)
2019	28 (11%)	10 (4%)	4 (2%)	6 (2%)	4 (2%)	2 (1%)	1 (<1%)	- (-%)	1 (<1%)
2020	32 (13%)	9 (4%)	6 (2%)	8 (3%)	7 (3%)	1 (<1%)	1 (<1%)	- (-%)	- (-%)
2021	22 (9%)	10 (4%)	4 (2%)	5 (2%)	1 (<1%)	1 (<1%)	- (-%)	1 (<1%)	- (-%)
Total	255 (100%)	80 (31%)	61 (24%)	39 (15%)	32 (13%)	23 (9%)	10 (4%)	7 (3%)	3 (1%)

Legend:
AMJ: Academy of Management; Journal ETP: Entrepreneurship: Theory and Practice; JBV: Journal of Business Venturing; JMS: Journal of Management Studies; JOM: Journal of Management; RP: Research Policy; SEJ: Strategic Entrepreneurship Journal; SMJ: Strategic Management Journal

Data extraction

The 255 articles are evaluated, and the new venture performance measures used are extracted, as well as descriptive information, such as the sample mean age. The information on the operationalization of each measure of new venture performance in the analysis is extracted with respect to the definition of new venture performance above.

FIGURE 2: Histogram of mean sample age, abs. and rel. frequency (n=132)

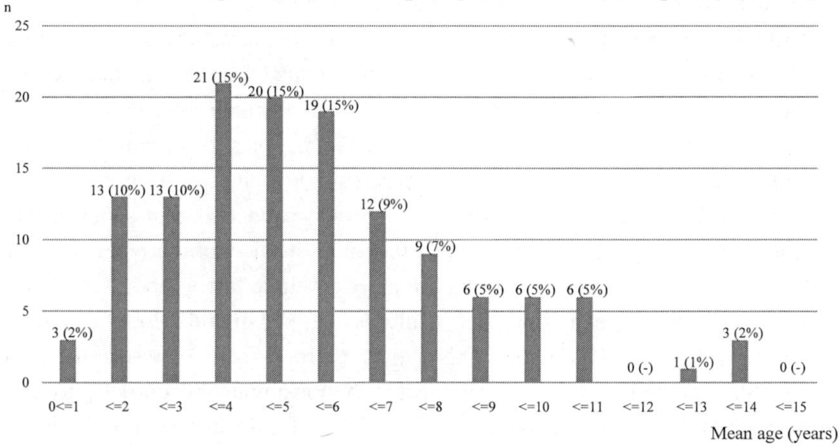

Figure 2 shows the distribution of the mean sample age for 132 new venture samples, in one-year increments. The inclusion of only a part of the sample, is a result of not all studies reporting mean sample age for the new ventures. Information on the sample age was extractable from 132 studies. The relative majority of the ventures have a mean sample age around three to six years, with only a small share having a mean sample age of over ten years. A similar distribution of sample age is found amongst the journals.

2.5. Research results

In the following, the results from systematically reviewing the literature on new venture performance measures are presented. Overall, the assessment of the 255 articles (100% of articles) revealed 489 performance measures (100% of measures), an average of 1.91 (Min: 1, Max: 6; Median: 2) performance measures used per article. Table 4 displays the descriptive statistics, with a distribution among the journals. In 122 (48%) of the articles one performance measure is used, and a maximum of six new venture performance measures is used by two articles.

Research Policy stands out from the other journals, as 22 articles (69%), use multiple performance measures, whereas the other journals with more than 10 articles, half use single new venture performance measures and the other half multiple. 77 articles (30%) base their research on primary data, 161 (63%) use secondary data and 17 articles (7%) a mix of both or other options. This is similar over all journals. Most new venture performance measures (435 measures, 89%) are (quasi-) objective, with 54 (11%) of the measures being subjective measures. Cross-sectional data for performance measures have been collected in 117 articles (47%) and 134 articles (53%) have focused on longitudinal data, with observations of at least two points in time. Research has been conducted mostly in the western world. Most research refers to the United States, accounting for 105 samples, or 42%. Germany (15 samples, 6%) and China (14 samples, 6%), and the United Kingdom (13 samples, 5%) are the next largest single countries, from where samples are drawn. Several other European countries are locations of samples, like Sweden, Italy, or Denmark. Contrarily, other areas of the world are not often assessed. New ventures from Australia are assessed three times (about 1% of the samples). The articles examining new ventures in mixed or undisclosed countries, account for 18%, or 49 articles. This shows a strong focus of research on the United States and Europe. In terms of the distribution among the journals, the SEJ, JOM and AMJ have a higher-than-average share of US-samples. Entrepreneurship: Theory and Practice and Research Policy on the other hand, display a lower share of US-samples. Articles in these two journals utilize mixed samples more often.

TABLE 4: Descriptive statistics by journal, absolute and relative frequencies

Descriptive statistics	Total	JBV	ETP	SEJ	RP	SMJ	AMJ	JOM	JMS
Number of articles	255 (100%)	80 (31%)	61 (24%)	39 (15%)	32 (13%)	23 (9%)	10 (4%)	7 (3%)	3 (1%)
Performance measures	489 (100%)	148 (30%)	117 (24%)	76 (15%)	78 (16%)	38 (8%)	16 (3%)	11 (2%)	5 (1%)
Articles with single measure	122 (48%)	41 (53%)	30 (50%)	20 (50%)	10 (31%)	12 (55%)	4 (40%)	4 (57%)	1 (33%)
Articles with multiple measures	133(52%)	39 (47%)	31 (50%)	19 (50%)	22 (69%)	11 (45%)	6 (60%)	3 (43%)	2 (67%)
Information sources									
Primary	77 (30%)	26 (33%)	21 (34%)	11 (28%)	8 (25%)	5 (22%)	3 (30%)	2 (29%)	1 (33%)
Secondary	161 (63%)	49 (61%)	38 (62%)	27 (69%)	23 (72%)	14 (61%)	6 (60%)	3 (43%)	1 (33%)
Mixed/Other	17 (7%)	5 (6%)	2 (3%)	1 (3%)	1 (3%)	4 (17%)	1 (10%)	2 (29%)	1 (33%)
Subjective / Objective measures									
(Quasi-) / Objective	435 (89%)	131 (87%)	94 (80%)	73 (96%)	74 (95%)	36 (94%)	13 (81%)	10 (91%)	4 (80%)
Subjective	54 (11%)	17 (13%)	23 (20%)	3 (4%)	4 (5%)	2 (6%)	3 (19%)	1 (9%)	1 (20%)
Cross-sectional / Longitudinal data									
Cross-sectional	121 (47%)	28 (33%)	42 (70%)	14 (39%)	12 (38%)	11 (45%)	8 (80%)	5 (71%)	1 (33%)
Longitudinal	134 (53%)	52 (67%)	19 (30%)	25 (61%)	20 (62%)	12 (55%)	2 (20%)	2 (29%)	2 (67%)
Sample location									
USA	105 (42%)	37 (15%)	20 (8%)	20 (8%)	9 (4%)	10 (4%)	5 (2%)	4 (2%)	-
Mixed / Undisclosed	49 (18%)	10 (3%)	19 (8%)	6 (2%)	7 (3%)	4 (1%)	2 (1%)	1 (<1%)	-
Germany	15 (6%)	2 (1%)	5 (2%)	3 (1%)	2 (1%)	2 (1%)	1 (<1%)	-	-
China	14 (6%)	5 (2%)	3 (1%)	1 (<1%)	2 (1%)	1 (<1%)	-	2 (1%)	-
UK	13 (5%)	4 (2%)	3 (1%)	1 (<1%)	3 (1%)	1 (<1%)	-	-	1 (<1%)
Sweden	10 (4%)	4 (2%)	2 (1%)	2 (1%)	1 (<1%)	-	1 (<1%)	-	-
Canada	6 (2%)	3 (1%)	2 (1%)	-	1 (<1%)	-	-	-	-
Italy	6 (2%)	1 (<1%)	-	3 (1%)	1 (<1%)	-	-	-	1 (<1%)
Denmark	4 (2%)	3 (1%)	-	1 (<1%)	-	-	-	-	-
Netherlands	3 (1%)	2 (1%)	-	-	-	-	1 (<1%)	-	-
Australia	3 (1%)	1 (<1%)	2 (1%)	-	-	-	-	-	-
Belgium	3 (1%)	1 (<1%)	1 (<1%)	-	-	-	-	-	1 (<1%)
Finland	3 (1%)	2 (1%)	-	-	1 (<1%)	-	-	-	-
Other (n < 3)	21 (8%)	5 (2%)	4 (2%)	2 (1%)	5 (2%)	5 (2%)	-	-	-
Total	255 (100%)	80 (31%)	61 (24%)	39 (15%)	32 (13%)	23 (9%)	10 (4%)	7 (3%)	3 (1%)

New venture performance measures

In the following a description of the new venture performance measures is provided: First referring to the raw findings and present the performance measures extracted from the articles. Then they are assigned to specific performance dimensions. In Table 5, the most frequent measures of new venture performance are display, i.e., those which are found at least five times, to focus on the most common new venture performance measures. This distribution provides a concise overview of the prevalence of different metrics in the analyzed studies. The most frequently used measure of new venture performance is sales growth, used 37 times (8% of all performance measures). The second most common new venture performance measure is a binary measure of survival, assessing whether the new venture has survived as an independent venture (32 times, 7%). Further common new venture performance measures are the absolute volume of sales (23 times, 5%), Return on Assets (16 times, 3%), a new venture reaching a crowdfunding target (15 times, 3%), the total value of funds received (14 times, 3%). Absolute employment count, internal multi-item rating, and satisfaction with new venture performance each represent 2% (10 occurrences) of the uses. The review reveals that new venture performance measures with the same operationalization are often named differently. For example, relative sales growth was called "Sales Growth Rate", "Change in Revenues" or "Revenue Growth" in different studies.

TABLE 5: Frequency of most common measures

Measure	Titled as:	In article (ID):	Frequency
Relative sales growth	Sales Growth Rate; Relative Growth in Sales; Sales Growth; Revenue Growth; Annual Growth; New Venture Performance; Growth; Revenue Change; Turnover Growth; Change in Revenues; Firm Sales Growth	14; 22; 31; 33; 56; 65; 68; 74; 82; 82; 86; 88; 91; 106; 108; 111; 114; 115; 116; 145; 148; 153; 157; 165; 174; 179; 181; 200; 205; 206; 207; 210; 212; 214; 218; 222; 254	37 (8%)
Firm survival (binary)	Venture Survival; Exit; Survival; Failure; Startup Failure; Firm Closure; Operating; Business Survival; Firm Performance; New Venture Survival; Business Survival; Firm Failure	8; 9; 18; 22; 41; 42; 51; 55; 59; 61; 62; 78; 94; 101; 106; 114; 122; 123; 126; 143; 149; 153; 158; 160; 177; 217; 220; 221; 230; 241; 242; 253	32 (7%)
Sales (absolute amount)	Sales; Size; Total Sales; Firm Sales; Start-Up Size; Total Sales; Sales; Log Turnover; Entrepreneur Performance; Turnover; Firm Size; Revenue	10; 22; 22; 37; 62; 80; 111; 114; 144; 161; 177; 192; 197; 202; 203; 208; 215; 218; 225; 227; 247; 248; 251; 254	23 (5%)
Return on assets	RoA; Profitability; Return on Assets Ratio (RoA); Operating Return on Assets; Return on Assets; Pretax RoA; Operational Profit	3; 54; 61; 63; 65; 72; 90; 124; 176; 192; 197; 218; 224; 243; 245; 251	16 (3%)
Crowdfunding goal achieved (binary)	Crowdfunding Performance; Success; Crowdfunding Success; Successfully Funded; Successfully Financed; Fundraising Success; Funding Goal Reached; Funded	43; 46; 47; 48; 52; 96; 119; 125; 132; 134; 135; 168; 184; 185; 187; 252; 255	15 (3%)
Total value of funding received	Investor Funding Amount; Total Funding Amount; Equity Funding Change; Private Financing; Funds Raised; Equity Invested; Cumulative Investment	37; 45; 46; 95; 102; 117; 144; 164; 165; 192; 195; 226; 229; 248;	14 (3%)
Absolute employment growth	Growth; Employment Growth Rate; Change in Employee Numbers	16; 18; 31; 41; 56; 86; 145; 165; 178; 210; 254	11 (2%)
Received VC funding (binary)	VC Funding; CVC Investment; Subsequent Funding from VCs; Deal CVC; VC Financing; VC Backing	28; 42; 95; 97; 107; 139; 162; 163; 169; 192; 249;	10 (2%)
Internal multi item rating compared to competitors	New Venture Performance; Innovation Performance; Competitiveness During Firm Growth Stage; Perceived Performance; Subjective New Venture Performance; Subjective Performance	77; 92; 93; 109; 118; 131; 136; 182; 205; 228	10 (2%)
Total yearly employment count	Size: Employees (n); Employment; Number of Employees, Log (Firm Size); Employment Size	62; 76; 78; 80; 156; 177; 194; 230; 248; 254	10 (2%)
Internal multi item satisfaction with new venture performance	Entrepreneurial Forecast Performance; Performance Above or Below Firms' Social Aspirations; Subjective Firm Performance; Perceived Performance; Subjective Performance; Market Performance	9; 18; 21; 138; 183; 188; 196; 211; 244	9 (2%)
Total amount of funding pledged by crowdfunding backers	Funding Amount; Fundraising Performance; Funds Raised; Money Pledged	38; 47; 146; 184; 233; 252; 253; 255	8 (2%)
Absolute profit	Entrepreneurial Earnings; Profit; Earnings from Entrepreneurship; Income; Operating Income; Financial Performance; Profit; Net Income	13; 50; 57; 58; 94; 161; 177; 232; 251	8 (2%)

TABLE 5: continued

Measure	Titled as:	In article (ID):	Frequency
Duration of survival from the starting date of the firm	Survival Duration; Organizational Mortality; Firm Closure; Survival; Duration of a Firm; Years of Operation; Longevity	13; 23; 78; 102; 153; 161; 173; 208	8 (2%)
Profitability status	Time Spent in Excess of Overdraft; Achieved Early-Stage Profitability; Business Financial Success; Venture Viability; Profitability; Profit Status; Performance-To-Plan	16; 73; 76; 110; 123; 165; 209	7 (2%)
Received any type of funding from professional investors (binary)	Subsequent Professional Funding; External Investment; Access to Capital; Investments; Capital Received	78; 94; 146; 157; 160; 235	6 (1%)
Tobin's Q	IPO Valuation, Tobin's Q, MV to BV, Book-to-Market Value	63; 190; 194; 197; 239; 241;	6 (1%)
Cumulative number of IP granted to the focal firm up to t	Patents Granted; Copyrights; Trademarks; Patent Stock	128; 128; 128; 154; 159; 194	6 (1%)
Number of crowdfunding backers who pledge money	Number Of Backers; Number of Investors	47; 96; 168; 184; 233; 252	6 (1%)
Relative employment growth	Growth Rate of Employees	14; 74; 80; 211; 213	5 (1%)
Exit success	Growth; Successful Exit; Liquidity Event; Investment Success	2; 95; 98; 164; 236	5 (1%)
Categorical outcome (IPO, Acquired, Private, and Failure)	Exit Status	39; 72; 102; 103; 112	5 (1%)
Applied for intellectual property protection (binary)	Patents; Patent Filed; Degree of Innovation	69; 81; 94; 155; 157	5 (1%)
Number of applications for intellectual property	Number of Patent Filings; Patents; Rate of Innovation	2; 81; 98; 154; 175	5 (1%)
Sales total / employment total	Sales-per-Employee; Revenues per Lawyer; Generated Slack	11; 18; 32; 32; 192	5 (1%)
Time to funding	Time-to-funding	138; 187; 188; 189; 253	5 (1%)
IPO underpricing:	IPO underpricing, Initial returns	179; 202; 206; 249; 253	5 (1%)

Having extracted the 489 new venture performance measures, they are aligned to the dimensions indicated in Table 2, for each classification individually. Based on the operationalization, they get assigned to the dimensions of performance measures developed in the articles described in Table 2. The result of this procedure is displayed in Table 6 below. The new venture performance measures are considered to fit the dimensions of performance measures when they are equal or conceptually very closely linked (e.g.: Return on Assets (RoA) and Return on Equity (RoE)) to the new venture performance measures listed. If a precise classification is impossible, they are assigned to the *Miscellaneous/ All other* in case such a dimension is present, if not, to the dimension *Not assignable*. Table 6 shows, that a considerable number of performance measures are assigned into the *Not assignable* dimension or to the *Miscellaneous/All other* dimensions. For example, the classification of Carton and Hofer (2010) does not encompass 369 (75%) out of the 489 new venture performance measures. Only performance measure classifications referring to high levels of abstraction, like Venkatraman and Ramanujam (1986) and Hult et al. (2008), or which provide an unspecified dimension (e.g., "All other measures" in Steers (1975)) offer opportunities to assign all performance measures. The multitude of classifications provides different sets of dimensions, which results in differences in the number of new venture performance measures which could be assigned.

In the classification of Steers (1975) for example, the dimensions, to which I can assign the most new venture performance measures, are "Resource Acquisition", "Growth" and "Profitability". "Growth" and "Accounting Returns" are dimensions to which most performance measures are assigned in the classification of Combs et al. (2005). However, 195 new venture performance measures (40%) do not fit a dimension in that classification. This highlights a gap of knowledge in terms of dimensions of new venture performance and which new venture performance measures are contained in them.

TABLE 6: Existing classifications and dimensions, assigned performance measures

Steers (1975)	**n**	**Venkatraman & Ramanujam (1986) / Hult et al. (2008)**	**n**	**Murphy (1996)**	**n**	**Combs et al. (2005)**	**n**	**Richard et al. (2009)**	**n**	**Carton & Hofer (2010)**	**n**	**Katsikeas et al. (2016)**	**n**
Adaptability-Flexibility	1	Financial	223	Efficiency	35	Organizational: Accounting Returns	53	Accounting (Objective/ Subjective)	160	Profitability	37	Customer Based	1
Productivity	3	Business	167	Growth	75	Organizational: Stock Market	28	Financial Market (Objective/ Subjective)	21	Growth	72	Product Market	17
Satisfaction	24	Organizational Effectiveness	99	Profit	45	Organizational: Growth	120	Reputation or Perception of Effectiveness	-	Cash Flow	1	Accounting	131
Profitability	51			Size	141	Organizational: Hybrids	-	Tobin's Q or Other Mixed Measure	9	Liquidity	2	Financial Market	15
Resource Acquisition	126			Liquidity	8	Organizational: Survival	40	Survival	40	Survival	2	Company	68
Absence of Strain	10			Success / Failure	62	Organizational: Other	2			Efficiency	-	Miscellaneous	257
Control over Environment	3			Market Share	-	Operational: Marketing	1			Economic Value	-		
Development	38			Leverage	1	Operational: Outbound Logistics	5			Cost of Equity Capital	-		
Efficiency	7			Other	3	Operational: Technology Development	15			Market	6		
Employee Retention	11					Operational: Operations	29						
Growth	80					Operational: Hybrids	1						
Integration	1					Operational: Human Resources	-						
Open Communications	-					Operational: Service Quality	-						
Survival	40												
All Other Criteria	94												
Assignable **Not Assignable** **Total**	489 0 489	**Assignable** **Not Assignable** **Total**	489 0 489	**Assignable** **Not Assignable** **Total**	370 119 489	**Assignable** **Not Assignable** **Total**	294 195 489	**Assignable** **Not Assignable** **Total**	230 259 489	**Assignable** **Not Assignable** **Total**	120 369 489	**Assignable** **Not Assignable** **Total**	489 0 489

Therefore, dimensions of new venture performance are conceptualized, by grouping the performance measures by operationalization, based on the classifications from existing literature. Doing so, especially adds to the group of dimensions proposed by Richard et al. (2009). This is to arrive at a group of dimensions which encompasses all new venture performance measures, which I find in the literature.

In Table 7, the dimensions of new venture performance measures are described. These are *Accounting, Financial market, Sales performance,* and *Mixed financial performance, Employment, Exit, Funding, Gestation, Innovation, Opportunity, Resources (nonfinancial)* and *Subjective New Venture Performance*. The dimension *Other* is conceptualized, for new venture performance measures which cannot be assigned to any specific dimensions.

Accounting-based performance measures refer to ratios (e.g., Return on Assets (RoA), Return on Sales (RoS)), profits (e.g., growth in profit, absolute profit), costs (e.g., salary mass) and assets (asset value, asset growth). New venture performance measures of *Employment* either display total employment or change in employment over a certain period, in absolute or relative terms. Measures of *Exit* performance disclose categorically or binary, whether exit activities have successfully taken place, denoting the liquidation of an equity position in the new venture, potentially by initial public offering (IPO) or acquisition. *Financial market* performance measures assess the value of an IPO, post-IPO performance (e.g., cumulative abnormal returns) or underpricing or IPO premium. Measures of new venture *Funding* performance assess mostly the amount of funding that has been achieved, or funding success binarily, whilst often focusing on a certain type of funding source (e.g., venture capital or crowdfunding). *Gestation* activities assess the progress through tasks in managing a new venture. These are assessed, either by the binary completion of a list of activities or single activities, or the progress happening.

TABLE 7: Description of new venture performance dimensions

Dimension	Description
Accounting-based Performance	This dimension contains measures of new venture performance, which refer to accounting standards like GAAP. Example: Return on Assets
Employment Performance	Employment performance relates to the workforce of a new venture. Example: Growth in Employment
Exit as Performance	Measures in this dimension refer to a change in ownership of a new venture documented through IPO, merger, or acquisition. Example: IPO Success
Financial market-based Performance	Measures of new venture performance which fall into this dimension are assessments linked to the stock market. Example: IPO valuation
Funding as Performance	The measures in this dimension refer to financing (funding) activities of the new ventures, concerned with the inflow of external financial capital into the new venture. Example: Amount of Funding Received
Gestation as Performance	Gestation measures refer to input performance in terms of activities performed by a new venture. Example: Number of activities performed, e.g. from list of Katz and Gartner (1988) or Davidsson and Honig (2003).
Innovation as Performance	Measures in this dimension contain innovativeness and innovation output in a new venture. Example: Innovativeness of a new venture
Mixed financial Performance	This dimension contains measures which are a combination of different financial dimensions of performance. Example: Tobin's Q
Opportunity as Performance	Measures in this dimension assess the opportunity a new venture is pursuing. Example: Quality of business idea
Other	This dimension contains measures new venture performance that are not captured by the predefined dimensions.
Resources (Non-financial)	Nonfinancial resources contain the accumulation of resources within the firm that is not financial capital, rather, either intellectual property or social capital. Example: Number of patents
Sales-based Performance	Measures within this dimension related to the sales or market share of a new venture. The crucial importance of sales leads to it being a distinct dimension from accounting measures (Richard et al., 2009). Example: Relative sales growth
Subjective New Venture Performance	Subjective New Venture Performance contains multi-item measures assessing a new ventures' performance. Example: Rating of sales, growth, and innovation performance, in comparison with competitors
Survival-based Performance	This dimension contains measures, which indicate whether a new venture stays in business. Example: Binary: Firm survived

Innovation performance is assessed by rating scales of innovativeness or novelty of a new ventures offering. In the dimension of *Mixed financial performance*, the performance measures employed are Tobin's q, Altman's Z, or the Sharpe ratio. The base of competitiveness and ability to perform well is the *Opportunity*, which a new venture pursues. New venture performance in these terms is assessed by rating opportunity quality, quantity, and feasibility. *Other* performance measures are used in three studies, where the total factor productivity is assessed. *Resources (nonfinancial)* comprises the intellectual and social capital that is available to a new venture, like patents. Performance in terms of *Sales* is mostly assessed by absolute amounts of sales or growth in sales. *Subjective New Venture Performance* is mostly a multi-item construct where the founders assess the performance of their new venture and how they perform compared to competitors. *Survival* is either measured as a dummy or as a time-continuous performance measure of a new venture staying in the market.

In Table 8, the specific new venture performance measures which I have assigned to the performance dimensions defined in Table 7 are shown. The assignments have been based on the operationalizations of the new venture performance measures and matching them to the descriptions from Table 7. Those performance measures are displayed, which are found at least three (3) times, to focus on new venture performance measures, which have been used in multiple pieces of research. For the dimension *Opportunity* the new venture performance measure which has been used twice is shown, as this is the most common performance measure in that dimension.

The 489 new venture performance measures which are found in the assessed literature can be summed and related to 168 different operationalizations of measures of new venture performance. The multitude of performance measures in use, reflecting the diverse approaches used by researchers to assess new venture performance, is visible from Table 8.

The most commonly used measures of new venture performance refer to the *Funding* dimension (107 measures (22%)). *Sales performance* accounts for the second most frequently considered performance measures (89 measures, 18%). *Accounting* is the third most common dimension with 71 measures (15%). *Financial market* and *Survival* are also common measures of new venture performance, which are also found in established categorizations. Two performance measures fit two dimensions. The first one is a measure of initial revenue, which was coded into the dimension *Sales performance* as well as the dimension *Gestation*. The second performance measure is called growth firm, classifying a firm which grows at least 20% in terms of employment OR sales, and is assigned to those two dimensions respectively.

TABLE 8: New venture performance measures by dimension, ID, and frequency

Accounting: n=71 (100%)		
Performance measure	**In article (ID):**	**Frequency**
Return on assets	3; 54; 61; 63; 65; 72; 90; 124; 176; 192; 197; 218; 224; 243; 245; 251	16 (22%)
Absolute profit	13; 50; 57; 68; 94; 161; 177; 232; 251	9 (12%)
Profitability status	16; 73; 76; 110; 123; 165; 209	7 (10%)
Return on sales	27; 149; 153; 211	4 (6%)
Industry adjusted return on assets	71; 240; 241	3 (4%)
Asset value	124; 150; 176	3 (4%)
Employment: n=37 (100%)		
Performance measure	**In article (ID):**	**Frequency**
Absolute employment growth	16; 18; 31; 41; 56; 86; 145; 165; 178; 210; 254	11 (29%)
Total yearly employment count	62; 76; 78; 80; 150; 177; 194; 230; 248; 254	10 (24%)
Relative employment growth	14; 74; 85; 214; 216	5 (15%)
Average annual employment growth (two-year period)	115; 174; 181; 206	4 (12%)
Total yearly employment count in fulltime equivalents	97; 159; 222; 238	4 (12%)
Exit: n=16 (100%)		
Performance measure	**In article (ID):**	**Frequency**
Total yearly employment count	2; 95; 98; 164; 236	5 (31%)
Categorical outcome (IPO, Acquired, Private, and Failure)	39; 72; 102; 103; 112	5 (31%)
Financial market: n=21 (100%)		
Performance measure	**In article (ID):**	**Frequency**
IPO Premium: IPO offer price minus pre-IPO book value per share as a fraction of the offer price	129; 231; 232; 245	4 (22%)
IPO underpricing: First-day closing price minus the offer price, divided by the offer price.	176; 199; 203; 249; 253	5 (17%)
IPO value: Total value of the capital raised by IPO less the underwriters' fees	192; 194; 202	3 (17%)
Funding: n=107 (100%)		
Performance measure	**In article (ID):**	**Frequency**
Binary: Crowdfunding goal achieved	43; 46; 47; 48; 52; 96; 119; 125; 132; 134; 135; 168; 184; 185; 187; 252; 255	17 (15%)
Total value of funding received	37; 45; 46; 95; 102; 117; 144; 164; 165; 192; 195; 226; 229; 248; 252	15 (13%)
Binary: received VC funding	28; 44; 95; 97; 107; 139; 162; 163; 169; 192; 249	11 (10%)
Binary: received any type of funding from professional investors	78; 94; 146; 157; 160; 235	6 (6%)
Total amount of funding pledged by crowdfunding backers	38; 47; 146; 184; 233; 253; 255	7 (5%)
Number of crowdfunding backers who pledge money	47; 96; 168; 184; 233; 252	6 (5%)
Pre-money valuation: price per share in the financing round times the number of shares outstanding prior to the round.	2; 75; 100; 229	4 (4%)
Change in value between two rounds of funding	75; 172; 190; 219	4 (4%)
Total amount of VC financing received	137; 154; 173; 190	4 (4%)
Time to funding	135; 184; 185; 186; 253	5 (4%)
Post money valuation: equity value plus amount of funds invested	20; 29; 171	3 (3%)
Crowdfunding pledged divided by funding goal	119; 120; 168	3 (3%)
Gestation: n=24 (100%)		
Performance measure	**In article (ID):**	**Frequency**
Number of completed activities from a set of activities	19; 90; 121	3 (13%)

TABLE 8 continued

Performance measure	In article (ID):	Frequency
Innovation: n=15 (100%)		
Performance measure	**In article (ID):**	**Fre-quency**
Binary: introduced product innovation	144; 156; 167	3 (20%)
Mixed financial performance: n=9 (100%)		
Performance measure	**In article (ID):**	**Fre-quency**
Tobin's Q	63; 190; 194; 197; 239; 241	6 (67%)
Opportunity: n=7 (100%)		
Performance measure	**In article (ID):**	**Fre-quency**
Idea originality scale of 1 (common, mundane, or boring business idea) to 4 (rare, unusual, ingenious, imaginative, or surprising business idea) by two expert raters agreeing on rating	1, 234	2 (28%)
Other: n=3 (100%)		
Performance measure	**In article (ID):**	**Fre-quency**
Firm's total factor productivity	153; 180; 250	3 (100%)
Resources (nonfinancial): n=29 (100%)		
Performance measure	**In article (ID):**	**Fre-quency**
Cumulative number of patents/IP granted to the focal firm up to t	128; 128; 128; 154; 159; 194	6 (21%)
Binary: applied for intellectual property protection	69; 81; 94; 155; 157	5 (17%)
Number of applications for intellectual property	2; 81; 98; 154; 175	5 (17%)
Sales performance: n=89 (100%)		
Performance measure	**In article (ID):**	**Fre-quency**
Relative sales growth	14; 22; 31; 33; 56; 65; 68; 74; 82; 82; 86; 88; 91; 106; 108; 111; 114; 115; 116; 145; 148; 153; 157; 165; 174; 179; 181; 200; 205; 206; 207; 210; 212; 214; 218; 222; 254	37 (43%)
Sales (absolute [currency] amount)	10; 22; 22; 37; 62; 80; 111; 114; 143; 161; 177; 192; 197; 202; 203; 208; 215; 218; 225; 227; 247; 248; 251; 254	24 (24%)
Sales total / employment total	11; 18; 32; 32; 192	5 (6%)
Average annual sales growth rate	28; 34; 89	3 (4%)
Subjective New Venture Performance: n=23 (100%)		
Performance measure	**In article (ID):**	**Fre-quency**
Internal multi-item rating compared to competitors	77; 92; 93; 109; 118; 131; 136; 182; 205; 228	10 (43%)
Internal multi-item satisfaction with new venture performance	9; 18; 21; 138; 183; 188; 196; 211; 244	9 (39%)
Internal multi-item rating	26; 36; 67; 225	4 (17%)
Survival: n=40 (100%)		
Performance measure	**In article (ID):**	**Fre-quency**
Binary: Firm survived	8; 9; 18; 22; 41; 42; 53; 55; 59; 61; 62; 78; 94; 101; 106; 114; 122; 123; 126; 143; 149; 153; 158; 160; 177; 217; 220; 221; 230; 241; 242; 253	32 (79%)
Duration of survival from the starting date of the firm	13; 23; 78; 102; 153; 161; 173; 208	8 (21%)

Employment is another important dimension of new venture performance, which has been added in this research and contains new venture performance measures referring to the number of employees, or growth in employees, also reflecting the importance of new ventures for the economic development (Schumpeter, 1934). Other important dimensions are *Gestation* (24 measures, 5%) of the new venture, the *Resources (nonfinancial)* a new venture has at hand (29 measures, 6%) and the *Innovation* (15 measures, 3%), which a new venture produces.

Having assessed the literature in terms of the performance measures used in new venture research, the question concerning the usage of performance measures in the new venture's lifecycle is addressed. As new ventures display diverging characteristics, changing with as they develop, performance measurement has to adapt (Barney, 2020; Brockner et al., 2004; Zahra, 1996). To get an understanding of how researchers adapt their choice of new venture performance measurement, the mean sample age from the studies, which assess new ventures and their performance is investigated. Age is used as a proxy for the lifecycle, as there is no data available on the lifecycle stages of the samples. The distribution of sample age can be observed in Figure 2, above.

New venture performance and the lifecycle

Table 9 refers to dimensions of new venture performance. To get an impression of the sample age within the dimensions, the mean sample age per dimension is assessed. In Table 9, the dimensions of new venture performance are organized in ascending order, concerning the mean sample age per dimension. There are two measures of new venture performance, which fit two categories, therefore the total frequency of the 489 new venture performance measures results in 491 new venture performance measures in Table 9. Dimensions, which contain more traditional performance measures are generally used on new venture samples with higher mean sample age. This highlights, that the use of performance measures in new ventures may be associated with new venture age.

TABLE 9: Dimensions of new venture performance measurement

Dimensions of new venture performance measures	Frequency	Mean sample age
Opportunity	7 (1%)	2.6
Gestation	24 (5%)	3.6
Resources (Nonfinancial)	29 (6%)	3.9
Innovation	15 (3%)	4.3
Subjective new venture performance	23 (5%)	4.4
Survival	40 (8%)	4.6
Funding	107 (22%)	4.8
Employment	37 (8%)	4.9
Sales performance	89 (18%)	4.9
Exit	16 (3%)	5.4
Accounting	71 (14%)	5.6
Financial market	21 (4%)	6.5
Mixed financial performance	9 (2%)	6.7
Other	3 (1%)	8.6
Total	**491 (100%)**	**5.2**

New venture performance measures which refer to the *Opportunity* dimension are often used on firms at a young age. The performance measures which are used on the oldest samples are relating to a firm's factor productivity (*Other*).

Based on this observed issue an interest arises to learn more about the links between the lifecycle stages (represented by age) of a new venture and the specific measures used to assess the new venture performance in certain stages. Therefore, Figure 3 is developed, which displays the dimensions of measures of new venture performance and the sample age. Sample age is displayed in clusters of one year, for zero to ten years. For instance, that means, all samples with a mean sample age between zero and one years are grouped into the first cluster. The exception is the cluster of sample ages over ten years, given the low number of observations and reduced speed of development (Coad, 2018).

FIGURE 3: Sample age (x) by dimensions of new venture performance (n=295)

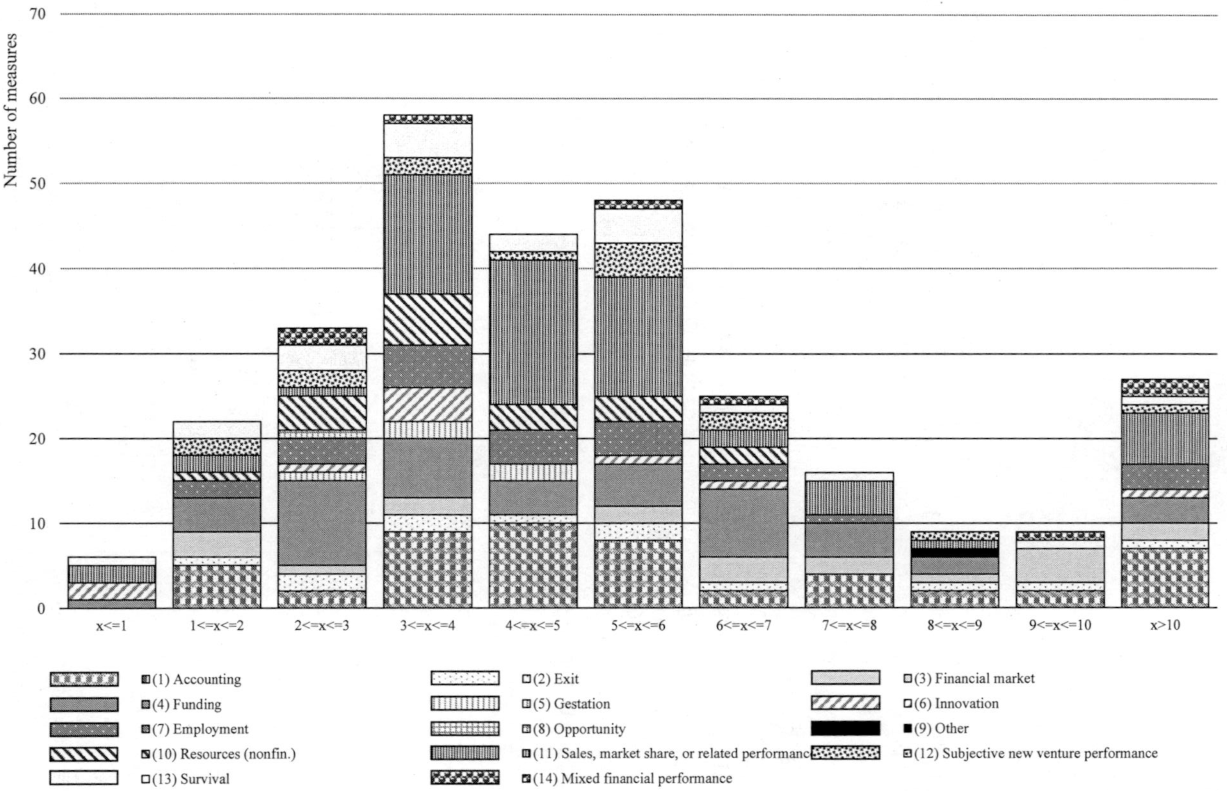

In the very early stages of the lifecycle, at young venture age, measures of *Innovation* performance (2 measures, 33%), *Funding* and *Sales performance* (2 measures, 33%) and *Survival* are used in the literature for performance measurement. *Opportunity* and *Gestation* performance measures are used in the earlier years, as well. *Sales performance* measures are highly common over the development of new ventures. In samples reporting an average age of about six years, measures of *Financial market, Mixed financial performance* and *Exit* become more prominent. Measures of *Funding* performance (up to 30% of measures for ages until three years old) are relevant from early age, with decreasing importance at the later stages. Subjective estimates of new venture performance are consistently used, on a less frequent level of up to 11%. *Accounting* measures are relevant at all ages but become more prominent with age, with 15% to more than 20% of the measures used at certain ages.

Considering the new venture performance measures over the lifecycle, it is recognized that some performance measures are used to assess the new venture performance in different stages of their development, like *Mixed financial performance*. However, performance measures of *Gestation*, and *Resources (nonfinancial)* are used for earlier new venture assessment. Subjective assessments of new venture performance are used for a similar period at slightly later ages. *Survival, funding, and Sales performance* measures are used from early age on. *Employment* is used for a shorter time frame, with similar mean age. *Accounting, Exit, Financial and Mixed financial performance* are used for new ventures which have already reached high age.

2.6. Discussion

In this study, the measures of new venture performance are investigated over 15 years of research. Systematically assessing 255 articles, 489 instances of new venture performance measures are found, representing 168 measures of new venture performance. Based on extant research, they are assigned into 14 dimensions of new venture performance measures and it is found that the application of these performance measures differs by new venture age. A further important point is the terminology, used by researchers. Interestingly though, similar or equal operationalizations are used, researchers use a variety of construct names. These inconsistencies in terminology cause problems for the comparability of research and hamper the possibility to uncover all relevant research articles in systematic searches.

Previous research is confirmed, in finding no consensus in the definition and conceptualization of performance for new ventures (Reese et al., 2020; Richard et al., 2009; Söderblom et al., 2015). This is apparent from the multitude of performance measurement frameworks found (see Table 2), as well as the many measures of new venture performance which fit the diverse frameworks. None is comprehensive enough to support researchers in the choice and assignment of new venture performance measures. This may be caused by the lack of focus on new ventures and their development over time. This study strives to provide guidance for researchers, overcoming this difficulty. It is proposed to pay attention to the choice of new venture performance measures. Using Figure 3 in combination with Table 7 and Table 8, researchers can assess their performance measurement in new ventures. Depending on the age of the target sample, researchers may adapt their choice of new venture performance measure. Additionally, this choice should be aligned with the general research setting.

In general, new venture performance measurement needs to be considered over the lifecycle. At first, new venture performance is centered on the assessment of an idea and whether the new venture can find a market for its product (Brockner et al., 2004). Measures of opportunity, innovation, and gestation performance could be suitable for assessing a new ventures performance during these stages. They may be especially suitable, when the performance in early tasks in starting a new venture is assessed. Then the venture moves to collecting resources and attracting customers (Brockner et al., 2004). Here measures of funding performance and in terms of nonfinancial resources, including employment, can be fitting to assess a new ventures performance in these stages. Measures of *Sales performance* are then also becoming more feasible and provide more insights into new venture performance, when the new ventures more commonly exhibit revenues. Then the venture scales up and it enters stages in which it can sustain itself (Brockner et al., 2004). Now, new venture performance measures can be based on the broadened availability of information, like from accounting standards and the new ventures history. Exit performance measures are also becoming more relevant, as early-stage shareholders might seek to adapt ownership distribution. Survival is crucial to the ongoing performance of new ventures throughout the growth, but especially up until the first decade of existence, as only 10 % survive for that long (Timmons and Spinelli, 2009).

The importance of the focus on the differences between new ventures and established organizations declines with venture age, as the most important age-related changes happen in the first five to seven years (Coad, 2018). Research proposes measuring new venture performance on a multitude of dimensions (Baum and Silverman, 2004).

Researchers should be further encouraged to exactly specify what criteria were used in sample selection to delineate new ventures. Only 132 (57%) out of 255 articles provide information on the mean sample age. A greater lack of information on sample age coincides with certain dimensions of performance measures. 86% of articles which use an *Opportunity* performance measure do not disclose mean sample age. Further examples are *Gestation* (80%), *Funding* (52%) and *Survival* (49%). This may be a result of lacking information for very young new ventures, which cannot provide clear information in this regard.

Furthermore, a large amount of research does not specifically define new ventures in their studies when assessing their performance. This should also be common practice in research.

Limitations and future research agenda

This systematic literature review has some limitations, which are starting points for future research. Information on the age of the sample of new venture is often not provided in the studies in the sample. This is especially true for studies focusing on new ventures in earlier stages. The limited availability of data on new venture age posts a challenge in comparing research. Future research may therefore go into more detail on the measurement of new venture performance at very young age.

The focus in age and stage in the lifecycle of a new venture, had to rely on reported data in prior research. Therefore, a precise determination of lifecycle stages is impossible. In addition, the number of observations in some dimensions are low, indicating a need for research to increase the generalizability of my findings by assessing these in more detail.

Performance can be influenced by random events (Denrell, 2004; Powell, 2003) and comparisons between performances of firms are most valid when the homogeneity of the assessed group is high (e.g., firms in the same strategic group) (Davis and Pett, 2002). Therefore, more research should tackle the differences in performance, its antecedents, and lagged outcomes.

Future research should furthermore assess the relationships between measures of new venture performance and stages of development, to achieve a better understanding of the suitability of measures of new venture performance at certain stages. How properties other than age of the new venture affect new venture performance over the lifecycle is a further starting point for future research. Given the lack of data at very early points in time of the development of a new venture, research at these points in time should be especially pursued.

This article concludes with three calls to action for research:

Firstly, researchers need to be precise about their study subjects. This includes definitions of new ventures applied as well as providing descriptive information about the development of the new ventures in terms of age and stage.

Secondly, researchers are encouraged to justify their use of performance measures. Measuring performance needs to encompass the characteristics of the study subject. This requires aligning the definition of new ventures with the performance measurement.

Thirdly, performance measurement needs to be adapted with the age and development of the new ventures. The changes which a new venture experiences over time, call for adaptation of performance measurement. This study shall assist researchers by highlighting the multitude of new venture performance measures and how they are used over the lifecycle.

Implications for research

The present study on the measurement of new venture performance provides some implications for researchers. Clear terminology in terms of performance measurement is important for researchers to be able to provide comparable and valuable research. Researchers shall be very explicit and clear about the terms which they use to describe the performance measures, which they use. This is currently not the case and diverse names are used for performance measures of equal operationalization. Another implication is, that researchers should make use of the multitude of new venture performance measures, and not use single performance measures. This is especially important, due to the development, that new ventures experience. There may not be correlation between different new venture performance measures along the life cycle (Robinson, 1999). In order to grasp the development over a new venture's lifecycle, employing multiple new venture performance measures can be valuable to research. The choice of new venture performance measures needs to be well justified (Murphy et al., 1996). Balancing between the dimensions of new venture performance measures, is therefore to be considered, as the dimensions allow for diverging insights. Theory shall provide an understanding of the relationships between dimensions of performance in new ventures (Richard et al., 2009). It should further be considered that performance may not be achieved equally across all dimensions, but rather can interfere with each other (Murphy et al., 1996). The use of multiple new venture performance measures can help researchers in to get to more fine-grained findings and insights into which dimensions of performance support each other and which hamper each other in new ventures (Katsikeas et al., 2016). The development of the new ventures over the lifecycle is a key characteristic of new ventures, where changes happen more drastically (Coad, 2018). The assumption that risk in new ventures declines (Chrisman et al., 1998) may not be equally linked to all dimensions of new venture performance. Therefore, researchers need to select measures of new venture performance, which are suitable over the entire period of observation. Failing to acknowledge the changes along the lifecycle can decrease the insights that researchers can offer.

Implications for practitioners

This work holds several implications for practitioners. It is important that practitioners, like managers and entrepreneurs, select a multitude of new venture performance measures, in relation to their importance, given their objectives. The choice of new venture performance measures may differ, based on the intentions, which practitioners hold towards the new venture. Therefore, entrepreneurs can develop a system of performance measures to effectively and efficiently manage their new venture and track competitors and understand their performance with time (Katsikeas et al., 2016). Selecting suitable performance measures, given the development and aims for a specific new venture is crucial for success. Especially the interlinking nature of dimensions of new venture performance should be considered (Katsikeas et al., 2016; Murphy et al., 1996). Another implication is, that entrepreneurs become aware of performance measures, which their competition may use to adapt their strategy for a competitive advantage. Being in possession of such knowledge is a valuable asset when competing for example for customers or funding. Stakeholders and shareholders may also refer to the measures of new venture performance displayed in this study, in order to align their interests with those of the new venture and track common goal progress. In addition, the non-financial new venture performance measures can provide insights that may be lacking from the increasingly used financial indicators (Katsikeas et al., 2016). The changes in usage of new venture performance measures over time and the related development of new ventures is another important implication for practitioners. This study is further useful to governmental entities, which can adapt their efforts in supporting new ventures by assessing their supporting activities with an improved choice of performance measures for the new ventures.

2.7. Conclusion

Referring to issues of performance measurement for new ventures, two research questions were answered: *What measurements of new venture performance are used in entrepreneurship literature?* and *How does the use of performance measures change with new venture age?*

Researchers use a large variety of performance measures. Many of these performance measures do not fit existing classifications of performance measures. This shows that researchers adapt performance measurement to the new venture context. The heterogeneity in usage of performance measures exists also over the new venture's lifecycle. So, this study contributes to research clarity and selection of appropriate performance measures for new ventures (Reese et al., 2020; Söderblom et al., 2015). By displaying the potential performance measures, this study assists researchers in choosing suitable new venture performance measures. The display over the new venture age provides further guidance for researchers and practitioners. Stakeholders are enabled to support new ventures based on an increased understanding of performance measurement by optimizing their resource allocation and support.

3. From Idea to Market: Configurations for Idea Stage Success and Speed of New Ventures[2]

3.1. Abstract

Getting an idea to the market is a crucial step in the development of a new venture. Research is inconclusive about what combinations of factors drive a new venture from an idea to the market. This study addresses the issue by employing qualitative comparative analysis (QCA) to a longitudinal sample of 181 idea stage new ventures in the United States. It assesses which combinations of conditions in new ventures lead to an idea reaching the market (quickly). The elements of the Timmons (1999) model of the entrepreneurial process are considered. The findings show multiple successful configurations, especially highlighting the role of industry experience in combination with an attractive opportunity for new venture performance. The results hold several novel implications for researchers and practitioners.

3.2. Introduction

Researchers have attributed much time and effort into understanding new ventures and their performance. Conceptual models of phenomena relating to new venture performance have been developed, such as the Timmons (1999) model of the entrepreneurial process. Empirical research has been conducted on the factors which drive the success of new ventures (Albert and DeTienne, 2016; Chrisman et al., 1998; Lichtenstein and Brush, 2001; Song et al., 2011; Xie et al., 2020). Additionally, meta-analyses have been conducted, to aggregate knowledge on influential factors on new venture performance (Brinckmann et al., 2010; Jin et al., 2017; Mayer-Haug et al., 2013; Rosenbusch et al., 2013; Song et al., 2008; Unger et al., 2011).

Getting an idea to the market is essential for new ventures (Song et al., 2011). Therefore, research has also had a specific focus on the factors influencing new venture performance at the idea stage. In such, effects of resources (Brush et al., 2008; Cooper et al., 1994; van Praag et al., 2005), team characteristics (Almer-Jarz et al., 2008; Brinckmann et al., 2011; Chandler et al., 2005; Jin et al., 2017; Steffens et al., 2012; Thiess et al., 2016), or (strategic) decisions (Bamford et al., 2000; Khan et al., 2019), have been researched.

[2] This project was conducted with the inputs from Artur Baldauf, University of Bern, Switzerland. A version of this paper was presented at the 2023 AOM conference in Boston, USA.

It is known that, in general, initial conditions affect new venture performance (Bamford et al., 2000). However, for new venture performance, many interconnected aspects need to be considered (Almer-Jarz et al., 2008; Debrulle et al., 2023; Du and Kim, 2021; Santarelli and Tran, 2013). This is because factors in new venture performance do not work in isolation, but rather interact with one another (Linder et al., 2020; Razmdoost et al., 2020). Nonetheless, knowledge is limited on how different configurations of conditions contribute to performance (Gruber et al., 2010). Understanding which configurations of starting conditions are linked to success is crucial to the development of research on new ventures and their performance (Linder et al., 2020). Hence, the existing insights concerning new venture performance need to be complemented by a configurational view, which is currently lacking (Douglas et al., 2020; Du and Kim, 2021).

Following this call to action, it is explored how the elements of the Timmons (1999) model of the entrepreneurial process are related from a configurational perspective. Having such configurational insights is valuable for research as well as practice. This is because it adds a level of insights we are currently lacking. Configurational analysis can disclose multiple pathways to an outcome, accounting for the complexity that is present in new ventures (Douglas et al., 2020; Du and Kim, 2021; Mello, 2021). Insights from this research will elaborate on the role of resources, team, opportunity and the business plan, and their interlinkage. This advances research on the drivers of new venture performance in the idea stage. Entrepreneurs and other practitioners can benefit, as they gain information on which setup of a new venture is promising. Supporting activities further profit from such research, as they can provide more targeted support, when they learn from research findings.

To add to the literature, the conditions under which new ventures are operating at the idea stage are assessed. Based on the Timmons (1999) model of the entrepreneurial process, resources, team, opportunity, and the business plan are conceptualized as influential elements in the entrepreneurial process. This model is referred to, to investigate two outcomes for new ventures getting an idea to the market. First, it is assessed why new ventures experience success or failure in reaching the market. Second, for those who are successful, the configurations which explain differences in the speed at which they reach the market are assessed. A configurational view is advised, given the interconnected nature of the elements in the Timmons (1999) model, as well as the fact that there are interdependencies between these elements (Dahlqvist et al., 2000; De Carolis et al., 2009; Emami et al., 2023; Santarelli and Tran, 2013). Configurations enable the study of complex relationship amongst inputs, without oversimplifying the phenomenon of interest (Dess et al., 1993). For such a configurational issue, qualitative comparative analysis is a suitable tool (Douglas et al., 2020), allowing for novel insights (Fiss, 2007). Interactions between multiple potential influential elements may be studied better that way (Harms et al., 2009). The aim is to extract the configurations of the idea stage conditions which are linked to the outcomes. Therefore, the research issue is approached by answering the following research question:

What configurations of idea stage new venture conditions are linked to a new venture reaching the market [fast]?

The study is organized as follows. First, the importance of the research question is supported by providing conceptual background to the entrepreneurial process. It is displayed how the elements of the Timmons (1999) model should be linked to the success of a new venture. The research method and the data to which it is applied are described, followed by the presentation and discussion of the findings of the analysis, including their implications, concluding with future research avenues.

3.3. Conceptual foundations

The Timmons (1999) model of the entrepreneurial process is comprised of three main elements: Resources, opportunity, and team. These elements are interlinked via the business plan. If these elements fit together, higher new venture performance will be generated (Timmons, 1999). Resources, team and opportunity have been subject to prior investigation on initial sales in a new venture (Bamford et al., 2000; Brush et al., 2008; Gruber, 2007; Gruber et al., 2010; Santarelli and Tran, 2013). Interconnections between the elements are present, as founders base their actions on the entrepreneurial opportunity, given their situation in terms of resources and team (Garnsey, 1998; Garnsey et al., 2006). In the following, the role of the elements of Timmons (1999) model in extant research is briefly discussed.

Resources

Resources in the Timmons (1999) model are defined as the inputs into a new venture. They may be considered in terms of financial resources, assets and people (Spinelli and Adams, 2012). The resources form the basis of a new venture (Bhide, 2000) and they have been found to be a decisive factor in new venture performance (Albert and DeTienne, 2016; Lichtenstein and Brush, 2001; Ruiz-

Jiménez et al., 2021; Song et al., 2008; Song et al., 2011), specifically in achieving first product success (Brush et al., 2008; Zhao et al., 2015). Other conceptual logics, like the resource-based view (Barney, 1991; Penrose, 1959; Wernerfelt, 1984) or resource-dependence-theory (Pfeffer and Salancik, 2003), also argue for the importance of resources for firm performance. Resources are linked to new venture performance, as they can help to succeed in the challenges a new venture faces (Brüderl et al., 1992), especially in terms of the problems arising from firms being young and small (Aldrich and Auster, 1986).
The study focusses on a new ventures' people, or network of support (*social capital*) as an important resource in new ventures (Davidsson and Honig, 2003; Linder et al., 2020; Westlund and Bolton, 2003). This logic seems to be supported, as entrepreneurs should think about their financial resources last (Spinelli and Adams, 2012). Focusing on people also refers to the external help which a new venture receives. Networks can help overcome scarcity in other resources (Herrmann et al., 2020; Stuart et al., 1999; Uzzi, 1996), and, as such, enhance performance (Baron and Markman, 2000; Linder et al., 2020). The value of social capital to new ventures is also based on the knowledge that is being introduced to the new venture by external helpers (West and Noel, 2009). Social capital is especially linked with success in going through the entrepreneurial process and achieving first sales (Davidsson and Honig, 2003). Based on these arguments, social capital represents the element resources from the Timmons (1999) model in this study.

Team

A new ventures' team is defined as the individuals who establish a business in which they have equity stake (Kamm et al., 1990). The team is an essential element of the new venture (Spinelli and Adams, 2012; Timmons, 1999). Crucial characteristics of the team are the relevant experience, motivation and risk tolerance (Spinelli and Adams, 2012). The new venture team is responsible for the decision making and operations of the new venture (Klotz et al., 2014). New venture teams are commonly characterized by the team size, experience and education (Almer-Jarz et al., 2008). This study focusses on the relevant experience that the team possesses, given its importance in extant research (Furlan, 2019; Song et al., 2008; Wise and Valliere, 2014). *Industry experience* has been most commonly measured by assessing the amount of time spent in a specific industry (Boeker and Wiltbank, 2005). As it has been found to be a significant factor in enhancing new venture performance in meta-analysis (Song et al., 2008), it is utilized in this study for the team element.

Opportunity

An entrepreneurial opportunity is defined as the option of introducing new goods or services and receiving financial gains from doing so (Shane and Venkataraman, 2000). An opportunity is characterized by market demands, structure, size and margins. The presence of these makes an opportunity stand out (Spinelli and Adams, 2012). The evaluation of the opportunity is central to entrepreneurship (Wood and McKelvie, 2015). Given the dimensions of the opportunity, a focus is on the value that entrepreneurs expect from the opportunity. The expected value of the opportunity encompasses the effects of the opportunity in which a new venture is set. The evaluation of an opportunity is a future-oriented process (Haynie et al., 2009). Following Campbell (1992), a new venture opportunity is pursued when the expected net present benefits are positive, considering opportunity cost of wage labor. In such, the probability weighed expected income of a new venture has to be taken into account, as it affects new venture creation (Campbell, 1992). This is also affected by the overall situation of a new venture (Garnsey, 1998; Garnsey et al., 2006). More attractive opportunities have been found to positively influence the emergence of new ventures (Dimov, 2010). As the expectations towards the opportunity play a major role in moving forward in the entrepreneurial process (Davidsson, 2015; Edelman and Yli–Renko, 2010; Emami et al., 2023; Shepherd et al., 2007), the expected future value of the opportunity is an important element of Timmons (1999) model.

Business plan

The business plan interconnects the three elements described above. A business plan is defined as a document comprising the work of the entrepreneurs in gathering information and specifying how to act on this information, given an opportunity in a new venture (Castrogiovanni, 1996; Delmar and Shane, 2003). The business plan documents a new ventures set-up, is used to communicate to stakeholders of all kind, and provides a roadmap to be held accountable to (Spinelli and Adams, 2012). Having a business plan has been found to be an influential factor for new venture performance (Gruber, 2007; Hopp and Greene, 2018; Lange et al., 2007). It can assist with decision making and reduction of uncertainty (Delmar and Shane, 2003). Therefore, business plans enable new venture creation and improve performance (Brinckmann et al., 2010; Greene and Hopp, 2017;

Mayer-Haug et al., 2013). Business planning benefits new ventures, independent of the formal level of the business plan (Zhang et al., 2013), as it has been found to increase likelihood of emergence more than twofold (Liao and Gartner, 2006). Therefore, the presence or absence of a business plan in the new venture is considered in this study.

Different combinations of the elements are expected to provide divergent configurations to the two outcomes concerning new venture performance: success and speed. The value of the business plan depends on the specific characteristics of the new venture (Gruber, 2007), here in terms of resources, team and opportunity. The exploitation of an opportunity is affected by the level of knowledge (team) (Emami et al., 2023). Further, industry experience (team) and social capital (resources) are found to be interlinked phenomena (Santarelli and Tran, 2013). The presence of these interactions leads to a configurational research question. In the following the methodology with which the research question shall be answered is referred to and information on the research sample is provided.

3.4. Research methodology

Given the research questions, next the research method, qualitative comparative analysis, and the sample on which this analysis is performed are described.

Research methodology

Qualitative comparative analysis (QCA) (Ragin, 1987) is used to answer the research question. QCA, is a configurational method, which seems to be appropriate to apply, given the underlying logic of interactions between the elements in Timmons (1999) model of the entrepreneurial process. It is further aligned with the need for configurational understanding of new venture performance drivers (Douglas et al., 2020; Gruber et al., 2010). This need arises from the interconnectedness of the elements, as described in the research mentioned above (Emami et al., 2023; Gruber, 2007; Santarelli and Tran, 2013). Other methodological approaches do not fully grasp the patterns in combinations of the elements, and the pathways in which they are linked to the outcome (Fiss, 2013; Linder et al., 2020). This is especially true, given the present study of the elements of the Timmons (1999) model.

QCA, as a method, is gaining importance in social sciences and allows to find patterns, that are not discovered by other methods (Douglas et al., 2020; Duşa, 2019). It allows finding multiple combinations of conditions leading to the same outcome (equifinality). In QCA terminology conditions are the influencing factors that are assessed, which in the case of this study refer to the elements of the Timmons (1999) model of the entrepreneurial process. This causal complexity is central to QCA (Mello, 2021).

Equifinality is important to the research framework, to find the multitude of configurations to high or low success and detect which measure of new venture performance is suitable under what conditions. The procedures follow Mello (2021) and Duşa (2019).

There are different types of QCA, with the crisp-set QCA (csQCA) and fuzzy-set QCA (fsQCA) being the most prominent ones. csQCA is a variant of QCA considering only two options for membership in a certain set, either fully in or fully out. fsQCA, on the other hand, is a type of QCA, where partial set membership is possible (Duşa, 2019). For example, a firm which is 100% family-owned may be considered fully inside the set of family firms, while a firm with 60% of shares owned by the founding family may be considered partially inside this set, whereas a firm with 100% of shares listed on the stock market would be considered fully out of this set. Based on the measurement properties of the conditions, I employ QCA, with crisp set calibrations in this study.

A configurational perspective expects that conjunctural causation is present, meaning that an effect from one condition will be in place under the presence of a (set of) other conditions (Schneider and Wagemann, 2012). This poses a difference from other methods of analysis (e.g., regression), where the same effect is assumed to be present for a condition on the outcome over all considered cases (Mello, 2021). That means that configurational methods allow researchers to find diverging results for a condition on the outcome, given a change in the combination of the other conditions assessed.

Research sample

To answer the research question, the database of the Panel Study of Entrepreneurial Dynamics II (PSED II) (Curtin and Reynolds, 2018) is referred to. This longitudinal, six-wave, assessment of new ventures in the United States is suitable for my purposes, as it contains data for my outcomes and conditions of interest. The data therein was collected after screening interviews by telephone to identify a representative sample of nascent entrepreneurs for the United States. The selected individuals were trying to start a new business and had engaged in some start-up activities over the past 12 months, without having reached operating status. All respondents expected to be shareholders in the new venture (Reynolds & Curtin,

2011). The full sample consists of 1214 respondents, viewed as nascent entrepreneurs. Some exemplary pages from the survey are provided in Appendix C.
From October 2005 to March 2006 data was collected from these 1214 nascent entrepreneurs in a first wave. This procedure was repeated annually until 2010 when the sixth wave of the survey was completed. This sample is representative of new ventures in the United States (Reynolds and Curtin, 2007). The design of the survey also allows for tracking new ventures in their development, in either direction. This is valuable as it is not only considering surviving firms, which avoids the survivorship bias.

TABLE 10: Distribution of answers to question AD6 (selection criterion)

Response option (AD6)	**N=1214 (100%)**
1. Completed and ready for sale or delivery	n= 406 (33%)
2. Prototype/procedure tested with customers	n= 181 (15%)
3. Model/procedure is being developed	n= 115 (9%)
4. Still in the idea stage; no work done	*n= 295 (24%)*
NA/ not independent	n=217 (18%)

3.5. Analysis and results

For analysis, independent new ventures with their product in the idea stage at the first wave of observation are targeted. Therefore, only new ventures for which it was indicated, that the product or service was still at the idea stage are assessed (Question AD6 = 4). Question AD6 is: *Is the product or service that this new business will sell completely developed and ready for sale or delivery, has it been tested with customers as a prototype or procedure, is it being developed as a model or procedure, or is the product or service still in the idea stage?* This was true for 295 new ventures, as shown in Table 10. Of all respondents, 56 do not provide an answer to this question, which are coded as *NA* or do not classify as an independent venture (161 cases). 406 new ventures (33%) were ready for sale or delivery and 181 (15%) were testing with customers and 115 worked on a model (9%). Further observations which had missing data are listwise deleted (Question AA10 must be = 1). Observations that end up in a state different from idea stage or ready for sale in the later waves are dropped. The final sample size in the study is 181 new ventures. The sample is fitting to the research purposes, as it holds information on all constructs involved. This is supported by the fact that it has been frequently used in the context of new venture creation (Honig and Hopp, 2019; Linder et al., 2020; Reynolds, 2011). Table 11 displays descriptives on the entrepreneurs.

TABLE 11: Descriptives on the entrepreneurs at wave A (n=284)

Age (years)	**Median**	**Mean**	**SD**	**Minimum**	**Maximum**
	40	42	13	18	81
Sex	**Male**			**Female**	
	179 (63%)			105 (37%)	
Education	**Education category**			**Absolute and relative frequencies**	
	Up to eighth grade			1 (<1%)	
	Some high school			24 (8%)	
	High school degree			79 (28%)	
	Technical or vocational degree			15 (5%)	
	Some college			62 (22%)	
	Community college degree			15 (5%)	
	Bachelor's degree			61 (21%)	
	Some graduate training			3 (1%)	
	Master's degree			14 (5%)	
	Law, MD, PHD, EDD, degree			8 (3%)	
	Don't know			2 (1%)	

The sample consists of a total of 284 founders for the 181 new ventures. 179 (63%) are male founders and 105 (37%) are female founders. The mean age is 42 years, at Wave A. Age spans between 18 and 81 years. Mean age is 42 years, the standard deviation is 13 years. The relative majority of 79 entrepreneurs (28%) holds a high school degree. 62 people (22%) have attended some college, 61 (21%) hold a bachelor's degree, while 14 (5%) hold a master's degree and 8 obtained a PhD or MD or equal (3%). Occupations, displayed in Table 12, by master occupation code groups, are distributed as follows between the entrepreneurs. The most common group of occupations, "Other", consists of students, homemakers and un- or self-employed people, accounting for 34 entrepreneurs, or 12%.

TABLE 12: Occupation of the entrepreneurs, by category at wave A (n=284)

Occupation category	Absolute and relative frequencies
Other	34 (12%)
Construction Trades	25 (9%)
Office and Administrative Support Occupations	25 (9%)
Sales Occupations	23 (8%)
Management Occupations	21 (7%)
Transportation and Material Moving Occupations	19 (7%)
Production Occupations	18 (6%)
Education, Training, and Library Occupations	12 (4%)
Financial Specialists	12 (4%)
Healthcare Practitioners and Technical Occupations	11 (4%)
Personal Care and Service Occupations	10 (4%)
Business Operations Specialists	9 (3%)
Food Preparation and Serving Occupations	9 (3%)
Architecture and Engineering Occupations	8 (3%)
Installation, Maintenance, and Repair Workers	7 (2%)
Life, Physical, and Social Science Occupations	7 (2%)
Arts, Design, Entertainment, Sports, and Media Occupations	6 (2%)
Military Specific Occupations	6 (2%)
Protective Service Occupations	5 (2%)
Building and Grounds Cleaning and Maintenance Occupations	4 (1%)
Computer and Mathematical Occupations	3 (1%)
Healthcare Support Occupations	3 (1%)
Community and Social Services Occupations	2 (1%)
Extraction Workers	2 (1%)
Legal Occupations	2 (1%)
Farming, Fishing, and Forestry Occupations	1 (<1%)

25 entrepreneurs (9%) are working in occupations of each of the two groups "Office and administrative support occupations" and "Construction trades". Further common occupations are "management occupations", for 21 entrepreneurs (7%), "transportation and material moving occupations", for 19 entrepreneurs (7%), and "production occupations", for 18 entrepreneurs (6%). In Table 13, I display descriptive information on the new ventures legal form and number of founders, while Table 14 displays the industry frequencies.

TABLE 13: Descriptive statistics on the new ventures (n=181)

Legal form	Absolute and relative frequencies
Not yet determined	83 (46%)
Sole proprietorship	64 (35%)
Limited liability corporation or LLC	10 (6%)
General partnership	8 (4%)
Limited partnership	7 (4%)
Sub chapter S corporation	4 (2%)
Don't know	3 (2%)
General corporation	2 (1%)
Number of founders	**Absolute and relative frequencies**
1 founder	105 (58%)
2 founders	55 (30%)
3 founders	12 (7%)
4 founders	7 (4%)
5 founders	2 (1%)

At Wave A, 46% of new ventures (83 instances) have not yet determined a legal form for their business. 35% (64 instances) run the new venture as a sole proprietorship. 10 new ventures (6%) are registered as LLCs. Ownership is concentrated in one person in 105 new ventures (58%), two owners make up 30% of new ventures (55 instances), three owners are present in 12 cases (7%), four in seven cases (4%) and five in two cases (1%). The most common industry, by NAICS industry code categories is "construction" with 18% (32 new ventures), followed by "retail trade" with 13% (23 new ventures), and "professional, scientific, and technical services" as well as "other services (except public administration)", both with 21 new ventures (12%).

TABLE 14: Distribution of the new ventures' industries (n=181)

NAICS Industry	Absolute and relative frequencies
Construction	32 (18%)
Retail Trade	23 (13%)
Other Services (Except Public Administration)	21 (12%)
Professional, Scientific, and Technical Services	21 (12%)
Administrative and Support and Waste Management and Remediation Services	12 (7%)
Manufacturing	12 (7%)
Accommodation and Food Services	11 (6%)
Transportation and Warehousing	9 (5%)
Real Estate and Rental and Leasing	8 (4%)
Agriculture	6 (3%)
Wholesale Trade	6 (3%)
Health Care and Social Assistance	5 (3%)
Arts, Entertainment, and Recreation	4 (2%)
Finance and Insurance	4 (2%)
Information	4 (2%)
Educational Services	3 (2%)

Measures

Two outcome measures of new venture performance are assessed. The first one is a binary measure of success in terms of getting the product to the market (*Success vs. Failure)*. The second one is the speed with which new ventures make it to the market (*Speed*).

Success: product ready for market

The first outcome observed is, whether the new ventures were able to get from the idea stage (Question AD6=4) to the market at any later stage of observation (iD6=1), with i from B to F depicting the waves of observation.

This performance of getting the product to the market is called *Success* (coded as "1"). Therefore, the outcome is calculated as:

$$Success = For\ all\ Waves\ (i)\ from\ A\ to\ F\text{: min } (iD6)$$

The outcome is then assessed as a binary variable, where 68 new ventures (27%) reach the market. 113 new ventures (73%) did not reach the market over the six waves of observation. This is shown in Figure 4.

FIGURE 4: Distribution of success (n=181)

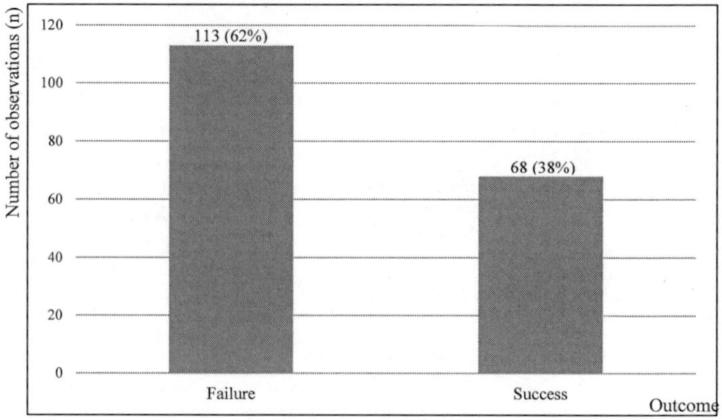

Speed: time to get the product to market

To obtain the second outcome of interest, how fast new ventures reach the market is assessed. This is operationalized by the number of waves it takes a new venture to first reach the market with their product. For example, a new venture which is in the idea stage in wave A and reaches the market in wave B, receives a score of "5", while one that reaches the market in wave F gets a score of "1" assigned. This is equivalent to the total time of data collection, six years, minus the number of years it took a new venture to get from idea to market.

In Figure 5, it is shown that 37 new ventures (54%) reach the market at the second wave of observation (Note: idea stage in the first wave). 18 new ventures (26%) get their idea to market after two waves, five new ventures (7%) after three waves and eight new ventures (12%) reach the market at the last wave of observation.

FIGURE 5: Distribution of speed to market (n=68)

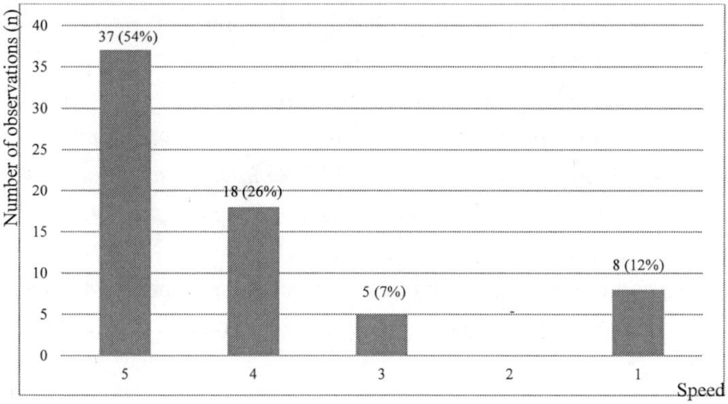

Conditions

In the following, the operationalization of the conditions are described, with reference to the Timmons (1999) model (Note: In the Timmons (1999) model, the "conditions" are the elements). All conditions are observed at wave A of the data collection. This allows us to assess the conditions a new venture possesses at the idea stage. The descriptive statistics can be found in Table 15, below. One condition per element of Timmons (1999) model is used, and a robustness check is performed where social capital as the condition for resources is substituted with financial capital.

Resources

This study operationalizes resources with the amount of social capital in a new venture. Following existing literature (Linder et al., 2020; Westlund and Bolton, 2003), the number of people who did support the new venture, without being employees or having ownership is utilized. Hence, the numbers provided in questions AG13 and AG18 of PSED II are added up.

These are: *How many other people, who will not have an ownership share, have provided significant support, advice, or guidance on a regular basis to this (new) business? + How many other people, who will not have an ownership share, have made a distinctive contribution to the founding of this new business, such as planning, development, financial resources, materials, training, or business services?* Considering "social capital", the maximum number of helpers is 13, with a minimum of zero helpers. The median is 1.00 while the mean is 1.32 with a standard deviation of 2.23.

Team

The team from the Timmons (1999) model is represented by a firm level measure of experience. The relevant industry experience that the team possesses is focused on, given its importance in extant research (Furlan, 2019; Song et al., 2008; Wise and Valliere, 2014). This is utilized over experience in terms of the number of start-ups founded, as it has been proven to be an influential factor for new venture success, whereas start-up experience is not a significant predictor (Song et al., 2008). *Industry experience* is mostly measured by assessing the amount of time spent in a specific industry (Boeker and Wiltbank, 2005).

Industry experience is therefore operationalized, by summing the responses for the co-owners to the questions AH11_1 to AH11_5 (*How many years of work experience have you / [has co-owner] had in the industry where this (new) business will compete?).* The answers are given in years of experience per owner and summed, as common in research (Boeker and Wiltbank, 2005). The median is seven years of experience, with data ranging from 0 to 76 years. The mean equals to 10.69 years with a standard deviation of 13 years.

Opportunity

The element opportunity is represented by the expectations towards the future monetary gains from the exploitation of the entrepreneurial opportunity in question. This condition encompasses the expected value of the opportunity. Therefore, it is operationalized using the data from question AT3 (*What annual revenue is expected when the business is in its fifth year of operation?*) in PSED II. This provides metric data in US-Dollars. The minimum value is $400, the maximum $7,500,000, with a median of $100,000 and a mean of $526,499 and a standard deviation of $1,138,618.

Business plan

The last considered element from the Timmons (1999) model is the business plan. In assessing whether a new venture has a business plan, question AD1 in the PSED II dataset is considered (*Have you already begun preparation of a business plan for this new business, will you prepare one in the future, or is a business plan not relevant for this new business?*). The data is used in a binary way, meaning a value of 1 for every new venture that has a business plan and 0 for every other new venture. 114 (63%) of new ventures do not have a business plan at Wave A. In Table 15, the descriptive statistics for the two outcomes and all conditions are displayed, as described above.

TABLE 15: Descriptive statistics for outcomes and conditions of new ventures (n=181)

Set	Median	Mean	SD	Minimum	Maximum	Abs. and rel. frequencies	
						"0"	"1"
Outcome of interest							
Success (binary)	-	-	-	0	1	113 (62%)	68 (38%)
Speed (subset with n=68)	5.00	4.12	2.15	1.00	5.00	-	-
Causal conditions							
Social capital	1.00	1.32	2.23	0.00	13.00	-	-
Industry experience	7.00	10.69	13.00	0.00	76.00	-	-
Expected value	100,000	526,499	1,183,618	400	7,500,000	-	-
Business plan	-	-	-	0	1	114 (63%)	67 (37%)
Financial capital (Robustness)	2,000	25,574	108,162	0.00	1,300,000	-	-

In Table 16, the correlations of the "conditions" (as metrics) are shown. For this table, all outcomes and conditions with metric data are considered. Overall, the correlations are found to be low. The highest, and statistically significant correlations are between social capital and the expected value of the opportunity, with 0.26 at the 0.1% level of significance, and a correlation of 0.25 between industry experience and financial capital (0.1% significance level). The third and last significant correlation is between industry experience and the expected value of the opportunity, with 0.15, at the 5%-significance-level. All correlations below 0.15 are not significant.

TABLE 16: Correlation table for metric conditions

	1.	2.	3.	4.
1. Social capital	1.00			
2. Industry experience	0.08	1.00		
3. Expected value of opportunity	0.26***	0.15*	1.00	
4. Financial capital (Robustness)	0.00	0.25***	0.01	1.00
*n = 181; *p < .05, **p < .01., ***p < 0.001; all values are rounded to two decimals.*				

Having provided descriptive statistics on the "conditions" and "outcomes" QCA is applied. The procedure of QCA is performed in three steps (Mello, 2021)

- Calibration of the data
- Construction of the truth table
- Logical minimization of the truth table

Calibration of sets

For qualitative comparative analysis (QCA), the outcome and conditions of interest need to be calibrated (Ragin, 2008). This is the process of assigning a set membership score to each case. There are two ways of assigning these scores. Either a score can be assigned using a crisp set or a fuzzy set. The choice of calibration method depends on the data quality of the raw data. Crisp sets can be calculated for any level of data quality. Fuzzy sets can only be calculated from data which is on an interval or ratio level of measurement (Duşa, 2019). Given these boundaries, crisp sets are used in this study (Rohlfing, 2020). Problems arise from having data equal to the cross-over point. This is the point of maximum ambiguity between being part of the set and not being part of it. It results in maximum ambiguity values of 0.50, which cannot be assigned to the truth table (Ragin, 2008). To solve this problem, the recommended procedure of applying a constant of 0.001 to the threshold to avoid computational problems is followed (Fiss, 2011). The calibration of the outcomes and conditions can be observed in Table 17. *Success* is calibrated as a crisp set, with 0.50 as the cross-over point. Therefore, full membership is present for those new ventures, which get the idea to the market, and full non-membership is present for those who do not reach the market. The second outcome, *Speed,* is calibrated by with a cross-over point of 4.5. This is done to represent the difference between the new ventures, which reach the market within one wave of data collection, and those new ventures that take time to get there. This conceptually important difference is represented by the threshold. The business plan is a crisp set with a crossover point which separates the cases into absence and presence of the condition. Given that the data is binary, the middle between the values is utilized to calibrate the set (0.50). For financial capital, social capital, expected value, and industry experience and are calibrated using the 75%-quantile as the crossover-point (0.50), to distinguish between high levels and not-high levels of presence in the conditions (Mello, 2021).

TABLE 17: Calibration of outcome and conditions[3]

Set	Cross-over point (0.50)
Outcome of interest	
Success	0.50
Speed	4.50
Causal conditions	
Social capital	2.00
Expected value	300,000
Industry experience	15.00
Business plan	0.50
Financial capital	10,000

Construction of the truth table

The truth table encompasses all possible combinations of conditions. Each row in the truth table represents one specific combination of conditions. In total, the number of rows in the truth table is equal to 2^k where k equals the number of conditions. Therefore, in the case of this study, with four conditions, the number of truth table rows is 16 (Mello, 2021). This is shown in Table 18.

[3] To avoid ambiguous values, a technical adaptive value of 0.001 is applied (Fiss (2011)).

TABLE 18: Truth table for outcome *Success*

Row number	Social capital	Industry experien ce	Opportu - nity	Business plan	Outcome Success	n	Consiste ncy	PRI
1	0	0	0	0	0	54	0.35	0.35
2	0	0	0	1	0	26	0.35	0.35
3	0	0	1	0	0	10	0.20	0.20
4	0	0	1	1	0	9	0.11	0.11
5	0	1	0	0	0	9	0.44	0.44
6	0	1	0	1	0	7	0.14	0.14
7	0	1	1	0	0	7	0.29	0.29
8	0	1	1	1	1	2	1.00	1.00
9	1	0	0	0	0	20	0.30	0.30
10	1	0	0	1	0	10	0.50	0.50
11	1	0	1	0	0	5	0.60	0.60
12	1	0	1	1	0	5	0.60	0.60
13	1	1	0	0	0	7	0.57	0.57
14	1	1	0	1	0	6	0.50	0.50
15	1	1	1	0	1	2	1.00	1.00
16	1	1	1	1	1	2	1.00	1.00

Cases are assigned to the truth table in the row in which they hold the highest membership score (Ragin, 1987). The membership score represents the extent to which the cases fit a set. That means that for each condition, the membership in the set is assessed for a case. This corresponds to the configuration of memberships and non-memberships for all conditions in question, which is present in the specific case. For example, a case that is inside a set for condition 1, outside the set for condition 2 and inside the set for condition 3, it would get assigned to the truth table row C1:”in”, C2:”out”, C3:”in”.

Logical minimization of the truth table

Then analysis of necessity is performed. Afterwards the sufficient configurations leading to the outcome are derived from the truth table.

To gain a thorough understanding of the factors which drive a new venture to get an idea successfully and fast to the market, run two subsequent analyses are run. The first analysis is run on the outcome *Success*, that means whether a new venture gets the idea to the market. The second analysis is run on the outcome *Speed*, which measures, for the subset of successful new ventures, how quick a new venture gets an idea to the market.

In both cases, the analysis is performed for the outcome as well as the non-outcome, to get a deeper understanding on the conditions driving a new venture (Linder et al., 2020). The non-outcome in Boolean logic is the part of a set which is not covered by the outcome.

Logical minimization of the truth table for success

In the following, the conditions and configurations of conditions which are linked to a new venture getting an idea to the market are analyzed. One condition per element of the Timmons (1999) model of the entrepreneurial process is used. The analysis is performed with the software RStudio[4] using the Consistency Cubes algorithm on about 45 cases per condition, which is far above the minimum threshold of 4-5 cases per condition (Mello, 2021). For the construction of the truth table, an inclusion score of 0.75 and a minimum n per row of the truth table of 2 are used, to be included as the outcome. The threshold of 0.75 is the minimum threshold of consistency for accepting a configuration as sufficient for the outcome (Schneider and Wagemann, 2012). Increasing the frequency cutoff to a number greater than 1 is suggested with larger n (Duşa, 2019), whilst still including at least 80% of cases, (Fiss, 2013; Greckhamer et al., 2013; Rutten, 2022) which is true for n=2 in the analysis for success. This contains all 16 possible combinations of values for the conditions. For example, row one exhibits all conditions absent, while row 16 exhibits all conditions present. The outcome column shows whether at least 75% of cases exhibit the outcome. This is true for rows eight, 15 and 16. Whether the threshold is met can be seen in the consistency column. The 75%-threshold is commonly applied (Linder et al., 2020; Mello, 2021).

Necessity

The first step in the analysis of the truth table in QCA is analyzing the necessity of the conditions for the outcome. Necessity of a condition means that the condition is always present when the outcome arises (Mello, 2021). For a condition to be necessary, the consistency of necessity for that condition has to be higher than the threshold of 0.90 (Duşa, 2019; Mello, 2021). When analyzing the conditions, no single necessary condition is found for either the outcome "Success", or the non-outcome "Failure".

Sufficiency

Next, the truth table is analyzed for sufficient conditions (Table 18). By minimizing the truth table, configurations, that lead to the outcome, are found. A sufficient

[4] Calculations are performed using the packages QCA (Duşa (2019)) and SetMethods (Oana and Schneider (2018))

condition means that, when the condition, or combination of conditions is present, the outcome happens.

Configurations of conditions for reaching the market and not reaching the market are assessed, using the parsimonious solution, as it is assumed to be more generalizable (Duşa, 2019; Mello, 2021) and has been found to deliver more robust results (Baumgartner and Thiem, 2020). The configurations which lead to success are displayed in Figure 6. The notation relates to Fiss (2011), where a black circle ● indicates the presence of a condition, a circle with an "x" ⊗ indicates the absence of a condition and blank spaces indicate non-relevance of the condition for the specific configuration. For exemplary purposes, a case where all conditions were present would be described as follows. It possesses high levels of social capital, the expected value of the opportunity is high, high industry experience is present, as well as a business plan. Therefore, this case would be displayed with black circles for all conditions in Figure 6. Such a case might be considered having ideal starting conditions, according to the Timmons (1999) model.

FIGURE 6: Configurations for outcome *Success*

	Solution (pars.)	
Configuration	Success 1	Success 2
Resources	●	
Team	●	●
Opportunity	●	●
Business plan		●
n	4	4
Consistency	1.00	1.00
Raw Coverage	0.06	0.06
Unique Coverage	0.03	0.03
Overall Solution Consistency	1.00	
Overall Solution Coverage	0.09	

For the outcome *Success*, two configurations which explain the outcome are found. Both configurations exhibit good consistency and are comprised of four cases, with a coverage of 0.06 each. Consistency represents the share of the outcome, within a certain configuration of conditions. So, for a consistency of 1.00, all cases with the configuration show the outcome, if the consistency were 0.50, half the cases would show the outcome. Coverage is the share of cases of the total sample, that is characterized by the displayed configuration of conditions (Duşa,

2019). For consistency a value of at least 0.75 is considered to warrant researchers attention. For coverage a specific minimum level that should be achieved cannot be determined, as it depends on the research context, and lower levels should be expected for exploratory research, and research in multivariate contexts. Furthermore, a tendency exists for a counterplay of high levels of consistency and coverage (Duşa, 2019; Greckhamer et al., 2013; Mello, 2021). If coverage levels are (close to) "1.00" this may represent a choice of conditions that lacks explanatory power (Mello, 2021). The first configuration ("Success 1") is characterized by high levels of social capital, industry experience and opportunity. The second configuration ("Success 2") is characterized by high levels of industry experience and opportunity and the presence of a business plan. Consistency of the solution is 1.00, with a coverage of 0.09, sufficient values for this context that are in line with other research on new venture performance (Linder et al., 2020). Both configurations represent four cases.

FIGURE 7: Configurations for non-outcome Not Success

	Solution (pars.)	
Configuration	Fail 1	Fail 2
Resources	⊗	⊗
Team	⊗	●
Opportunity	●	⊗
Business plan		●
n	19	7
Consistency	0.84	0.86
Raw Coverage	0.14	0.05
Unique Coverage	0.14	0.05
Overall Solution Consistency	0.85	
Overall Solution Coverage	0.20	

For the non-outcome (i.e., new venture not getting an idea to the market), a model that provides a coverage of 0.20 and consistency of 0.85 for the overall solution is found, which are sufficient levels (Linder et al., 2020). This is displayed in Figure 7.

Configuration one ("Fail 1") and Configuration two ("Fail 2") are characterized by absence of social capital. In case of Configuration one ("Fail 1"), high industry experience is absent, and an attractive opportunity is present. For Configuration two ("Fail 2") industry experience and a business plan are present, while an attractive opportunity is absent. “Fail 1” represents 19 cases and “Fail 2” seven cases. Consistency for both is about 0.85. Configuration one has a coverage of 0.14, configuration two of 0.05. These values prospect insightful results.

Logical minimization of the truth table for speed

More detail is assessed by performing analysis on the speed of successful new ventures, making use of the longitudinal structure of the data collection and focus on the new ventures which are successful in getting an idea to the market. For those, the configurations which lead to a new venture being more or less quick to the market are analyzed. This means, analyzing the configurations which are found to be linked with the speed of a new venture getting an idea to market. For the analysis of this outcome (*Speed*), the number of observations drops to 68, resulting in 17 cases per condition, which still meets the threshold of four to five cases per condition. Given the lower number cases, the frequency cutoff is kept at 1 and the inclusion threshold at the recommended 0.75 (Schneider and Wagemann, 2012).

Necessity

Again, the first step in analysis of conditions in QCA is analyzing the necessity of the conditions for the outcome. If a condition is always present, when the outcome arises, it will be considered necessary (Mello, 2021). For a condition to be necessary, the consistency of necessity for that condition has to be higher than the threshold of 0.9 (Duşa, 2019; Mello, 2021). No single condition is found necessary for either the outcome *Speed*, or the non-outcome.

Sufficiency

In the analysis of sufficiency, the truth table is minimized using the “QCA” (Duşa, 2019) and “SetMethods” (Oana and Schneider, 2018) packages in RStudio. The parsimonious solution is reported.

For the outcome *Speed*, a model that is characterized by two configurations is found, which provides an overall solution consistency of 0.86 and an overall solution coverage of 0.16.

FIGURE 8: Configurations for outcome Speed

	Solution (pars.)	
Configuration	Speed 1	Speed 2
Resources	●	⊗
Team	●	⊗
Opportunity		●
Business plan	⊗	●
n	6	1
Consistency	0.83	1.00
Raw Coverage	0.14	0.03
Unique Coverage	0.14	0.03
Overall Solution Consistency	0.86	
Overall Solution Coverage	0.16	

The solution contains two configurations. The configurations are displayed in Figure 8. Configuration one ("Speed 1") to the outcome, high speed in reaching the market, is characterized by the presence of social capital, industry experience and no business plan. The second configuration ("Speed 2") displays absence of social capital and industry experience with presence of an attractive opportunity and a business plan.

In Figure 9, the results for the non-outcome of *Speed* (i.e., a new venture takes longer to get an idea to the market) are displayed. Three configurations describe the model. Overall solution coverage is 0.16, with an overall consistency of the solution of 1.00. Configuration one ("Slow 1") is a configuration, where all four conditions are present. The second configuration ("Slow 2") is characterized by absence of social capital, and the absence of an attractive opportunity, with the presence of industry experience and a business plan. Configuration Three ("Slow 3") contains two absent conditions, in social capital and a business plan. Industry experience and an attractive opportunity are present.

FIGURE 9: Configurations for non-outcome Not Speed

	Solution (pars.)		
Configuration	Slow 1	Slow 2	Slow 3
Resources	●	⊗	⊗
Team	●	●	●
Opportunity	●	⊗	●
Business plan	●	●	⊗
n	2	1	2
Consistency	1.00	1.00	1.00
Raw Coverage	0.07	0.03	0.07
Unique Coverage	0.07	0.03	0.07
Overall Solution Consistency	1.00		
Overall Solution Coverage	0.16		

Robustness of results

The amount of *financial capital* is a second type of resource for a new venture, that has been identified as a significant driver of success in new ventures (Song et al., 2008).

It refers to the funds at a new ventures' disposal. It can be used to facilitate progress as it can be employed to substitute other missing resources (Linder et al., 2020; Wiklund and Shepherd, 2005). The amount of financial capital prior to first sale positively affects survival and growth of new ventures (Cooper et al., 1994). Funding the early stage and testing ideas is further enabled by financial capital (Garkavenko et al., 2022). It also determines the leeway that a new venture has in terms of speed and effort that can be employed towards pursuing the opportunity (Coad et al., 2013; Cosh et al., 2009; Linder et al., 2020) and it lowers external dependencies, which are given with social capital (Colombo and Grilli, 2005). Given this importance, a robustness analysis is performed, with financial capital as the operationalization of resources.

Financial capital is operationalized as the funding provided by the owners. It is calculated as the sum of owner equity and loan funding. Data is gathered from questions AQ12x and AQ13 in the PSED II. As already shown in Table 15, the median funding amount is \$2,000, with a mean of \$25,574 and a standard deviation of \$108,162. The maximum amount is \$1,300,000 and the minimum is \$0.

This supports the findings, especially those on success and failure, as solutions which are identical to "Success 2" and a specific case of "Fail 1" are found. This is also in line with research describing financial capital as important to success

(Coad et al., 2013; Cooper et al., 1994; Song et al., 2008). For speed the results are more ambiguous, hinting towards a diverging role of social and financial capital for getting an idea to market and the speed at which it gets to the market.

3.6. Discussion and implications

In the following, the results of the analysis are discussed. For the configurations to success, displayed in Figure 6, it is found, that in both configurations industry experience and the expected value of the opportunity are required for success. In addition, one configuration requires resources, in terms of social capital, while the other requires a business plan. This solution with two configurations adds insights to several streams of literature in management and entrepreneurship.

Overall, the findings support the Timmons (1999) model of the entrepreneurial process in its configurational nature. The fact that a configuration ("Success 1") for success is found, that is characterized by resources (social capital), team (industry experience) and opportunity (expected value of the opportunity) shows that those key elements in combination can lead to success. The configurational nature of new venture performance drivers is further supported by the lack of necessary conditions, that are sole explanatory elements for successful new ventures. It confirms the need to match resources to attractive opportunities in new ventures. New ventures must decide on whether to pursue an opportunity (Garnsey, 1998). It is found that this is done successfully when an opportunity is attractive and high industry experience is present in the team ("Success 1", "Success 2"). These two conditions need to be present, either in combination with high social capital or a business plan. Then new ventures successfully get their idea to market. These results add to findings in the literature of the positive effects of industry experience on new venture performance (Cooper et al., 1994; Dahlqvist et al., 2000). This study further specifies the role of industry experience to only be effective in combination with an attractive opportunity and one of either social capital or a business plan. This interaction also adds to the work on rationality in entrepreneurship (Miller, 2007). Experienced entrepreneurs seem to be able to assess the quality of an opportunity well, enhancing their chances of success. This confirms the role of the opportunity for entrepreneurial success (Campbell, 1992; Davidsson, 2015; Dimov, 2010; Emami et al., 2023; Shepherd et al., 2007). Industry experience may therefore be linked with better estimates of opportunity value (Shepherd et al., 2007).

The configuration for not reaching the market consists of two configurations, displayed in Figure 7. Configuration one ("Fail 1") characterizes new ventures which pursue an attractive opportunity, while they lack industry experience as well as social capital. Configuration two ("Fail 2") describes new ventures, which have a business plan and industry experience, while they lack an attractive opportunity as well as social capital. The first configuration ("Fail 1") shows the importance of the entrepreneurs' characteristics for new venture performance. Despite an attractive opportunity, the lack of social capital and industry experience is linked to the new ventures not reaching the market. This confirms the findings from extant research about the important role of these two factors for new venture performance (Baron and Markman, 2000; Dahlqvist et al., 2000; Davidsson and Honig, 2003; Furlan, 2019; Song et al., 2008). This may characterize a situation of overly optimistic entrepreneurs, that see an attractive opportunity, but then find out that they lack the industry experience and social capital to get the idea to market. The second configuration ("Fail 2") for new ventures which do not make it to the market is characterized as follows. Entrepreneurs with high industry experience and a business plan tackle an unattractive opportunity with low social capital. These new ventures fail to get to the market, which confirms previous findings on the importance of the joint presence of social capital and industry experience (Santarelli and Tran, 2013). In short, an experienced team with a plan will still fail when they lack resources in terms of social capital and if the opportunity is not attractive. This is in line with Garnsey (1998), in terms of the necessity to have resources that are aligned with the opportunity.

For the analysis of the successful subgroup of new ventures, two configurations leading to high speed and three to low speed are found. Configuration one ("Speed 1"), that quickly leads to the market, is described as having high social capital and industry experience but lacking a business plan. While this may seem contradictory to the value of the business plan (Brinckmann et al., 2010; Hopp and Greene, 2018; Mayer-Haug et al., 2013), it rather confirms the value of knowledge network and its interplay with business planning (Zhang et al., 2013). These new ventures can quickly enter the market without having to put effort into business planning, as they possess the necessary industry experience and social capital to do so. This confirms that the value of a business plan depends on the environment (Gruber, 2007). Configuration two ("Speed 2") does confirm the value of business planning. Here, given an attractive opportunity, a new venture with a business plan gets an idea quickly to the market, despite a low social capital and industry experience. This confirms research on the increased likelihood of emergence

through business planning (Liao and Gartner, 2006). As Configuration two consists of a single case, this situation seems to be rather rare.
For the new ventures which reach the market, but do so only after some time, a solution with three configurations is found. The first configuration ("Slow 1") exhibits the presence of high levels in all four conditions. This result highlights the value of the elements of Timmons (1999) model for new venture performance. However, while cases of "Slow 1" experiences success, they do so only after some time. Therefore, the combination of presence of high levels in all conditions can be seen as a recipe for success, without guaranteeing speed in this success. Rather, new ventures which are aware of their strong setup, may show higher levels of persistence in overcoming obstacles on the configuration to the market. This adds to findings on opportunity expectations as a decisive factor in getting to the market (Townsend et al., 2010). This finding also supports the value of university entrepreneurship programs in helping entrepreneurs identify their potential as entrepreneurs, as they can help clear their vision (Eesley and Lee, 2021). The second configuration ("Slow 2") is a single case, where high industry experience and a business plan lead to slow success on a less attractive opportunity with little social capital. This special case is also present in configuration "Fail 2", where it is the only case to reach the market. This can be conducted from the consistency of the solution (0.86, with n=7). This finding is valuable, as it provides two insights. The first is, that the elements of the Timmons (1999) model are not perfect predictors of new venture performance. The second is that entrepreneurs can overcome challenging times in their new ventures and still get their idea to market if they persist. The third configuration ("Slow 3") describes new ventures which possess high industry experience and have an attractive opportunity but lack social capital and a business plan. This configuration hints towards the value of business planning and social capital. While still reaching the market, doing so without having a plan and network to rely on, it takes time. This is, because the business plan assists in decision making and reduces uncertainty (Delmar and Shane, 2003), while social capital is beneficial to overcome early problems (Davidsson and Honig, 2003; Stuart et al., 1999).
Overall, it is found that new ventures need a combination of an attractive opportunity and high industry experience to successfully get their idea to the market. If one of the two is missing, the idea will not see the market.

Implications for research

The present study holds several implications for research. This study adds to the underlying concepts of this study in the Timmons (1999) model. The complex nature of new venture performance and configurational aspect of the model are confirmed, as no single necessary conditions for any outcome is found. The fact that the cases with ideal set of elements are successful, underlines the theoretical value of the Timmons (1999) model of the entrepreneurial process in explaining the relationship between the elements and new venture performance. It is further found, that for success, a high industry experience (team) and an attractive opportunity need to be present simultaneously. If one of the two is missing, failure to get an idea to market occurs. This answers calls from literature to better understand the multiple pathways in which conditions in new ventures interact, and encourage scholars to continue to do so (Douglas et al., 2020; Gruber et al., 2010). The study confirms the importance of social capital and financial capital as resources for new venture performance (Colombo and Grilli, 2005; Cooper et al., 1994; Davidsson and Honig, 2003; Garkavenko et al., 2022; Linder et al., 2020; Wiklund and Shepherd, 2005). However, it is clarified, that the presence of financial capital is not found as a relevant factor to success, whilst a lack of it can be associated with cases of failure to get an idea to market. Therefore, this may become more relevant in later stages of the development of a new venture (Garnsey, 1998; Garnsey et al., 2006). An additional implication for elements affecting new venture performance is that the most common way to failure ("Fail 1") is the combination of an attractive opportunity with an unexperienced team and a lack of social capital. The findings holds several implications. Firstly, contrary to some earlier research findings (Arentz et al., 2013) social capital and industry experience often do not seem to be necessary to spot an attractive opportunity, questioning the theoretical link between them. Secondly, while an attractive opportunity generally enhances the emerge of new ventures (Dimov, 2010), successfully acting on the opportunity calls for a combination with resources and experience ("Success 1", "Success 2", "Fail 1"). This further supports the configurational nature of new venture performance drivers and implies the need for configurational aspects in entrepreneurship theories (Douglas et al., 2020). That is true for both social capital as well as financial capital as indicators for resources, underlining their value (Baron and Markman, 2000; Brush et al., 2008; Davidsson and Honig, 2003; Linder et al., 2020; Stuart et al., 1999). Further, business planning is less valuable in situations where the new venture is in possession of high social

capital and industry experience ("Success 1", "Speed 1"), where (quick) idea-to-market performance is reached. This may be grounded in the fact that entrepreneurs in such a strong starting position do not need a formal business plan, but rather know what to do. That is in line with findings, that a business plan helps to reduce uncertainty (Delmar and Shane, 2003). These strong new ventures may not experience such uncertainty in the first place, so that the value of the business plan depends on the configuration of the new venture (Gruber, 2007).
If a new venture is strong, as in "Slow 1", it will be more likely to persist through obstacles on the way to the market. This implies that these situations of strength should be strived for, supporting Timmons (1999) model, in terms of entrepreneurial persistence.

Implications for practice
The results hold implications for practitioners. These may be the entrepreneurs themselves, or supporting institutions, like investors, universities, or government bodies. For entrepreneurs, trying to get their idea to the market, my findings mean, that they should be aware of the setup of their new venture in terms of the elements of the Timmons (1999) model. Specifically, they should assess the value of their opportunity and the amount of industry experience they amass within the new venture, as the presence of these two elements is found to be essential for success ("Speed 1", "Speed 2"). Failure will especially occur, when the lack of one of the two aforementioned factors is coupled with a lack in social capital ("Fail 1", "Fail 2"). For investors, the findings highlight the importance of a fit between an attractive opportunity and the necessary industry experience. New ventures with this configuration should be preferably considered as investment targets. In addition, a business plan may not be valuable for investors, in a situation, where high social capital and industry experience are present, for the purpose of getting the idea to market, as this usually happens quickly in such configurations ("Speed 1"). New ventures which lack this configuration, may be precisely supported by providing experienced supporters, in terms of social capital or as an addition to the new venture team. This can help them in adapting, which is essential to success (Song et al., 2010). Governmental institutions, accelerators and university support agencies can also focus on these lacking factors to provide new ventures with promising starting conditions to get their idea to market. This may help overcome some current struggles in the support activities (Chowdhury and Audretsch, 2023). The research results show that there is much value to be found in these supporting

activities. (Fichter and Tiemann, 2018; Hallen et al., 2023; Schimperna et al., 2021).

3.7. Future research and limitations

As with any piece of research, this study is not without limitations, which can be taken as starting points for future research. The data, whilst being representative for the US (Curtin and Reynolds, 2018), is limited to the context of one country. Future research could test the findings in different cultural backgrounds and across countries or continents. Based on the results for the configurations leading from an idea to market, this study encourages researchers to overcome the limitations of the data and venture out to test other conditions which fit with the Timmons (1999) model. This might highlight decisive factors about the configurations which lead to a new venture getting an idea to the market. Furthermore, multivariate time series (Tsay, 2013) may prove valuable in assessing the details of speed to market analysis. In addition, the chosen approach does not account for the capability of the new ventures to learn throughout their development. This may be a crucial factor for their performance, given the benefits of organizational learning in established organizations (Jiménez-Jiménez and Sanz-Valle, 2011).

The consistent configurations only link to a part of the cases in the sample. To some extent, this is inherent in the QCA method. It may however, hint towards other explanatory factors for new venture performance, which are not addressed in this study, and can be assessed in future studies, for example market growth rate, patent protection or supply chain integration, which have previously been identified as relevant factors (Song et al., 2008).

Furthermore, researchers may assess, how actors in the entrepreneurial ecosystem can specifically enhance a new ventures odds to success, by going into depth on the elements of the Timmons (1999) model. There could specifically be more research into which configurations of support are the most beneficial, when provided, for example by universities. However, the Timmons (1999) model may be criticized for an overemphasis of the founders' control. The success of a new venture also depends on external conditions that may not be influenced (Shepherd et al., 2000). Additionally, the characteristics of a market are not fully accounted for in the model, despite playing a pivotal role (Chandler and Hanks, 1994; Parry and Song, 2010). Another factor that Timmons (1999) does not account for is the strategy a new venture pursues, which has been conceptualized in other models (Baum et al., 2001; Chrisman et al., 1998). That can affect the success new ventures with equal configurations in Timmons (1999) elements experience. This study assessed, which configurations of conditions lead to new ventures reaching the market and doing so quickly, however, not whether the new ventures which reach the market with their product experience success on the market. Future research might take this as a starting point for adapting the outcome, to evaluate whether the conditions from the Timmons (1999) model are suitable to explain success on the market.

3.8. Conclusion

The present study aims to explore the configurations of conditions which lead to a new venture reaching the market. To assess this, QCA was performed on the binary outcome of reaching the market, as well as the speed at which a new venture reaches the market. Referring to a sample of 181 idea stage new ventures from the United States, configurations which lead to a new venture (not) reaching the market are found. The success of a new venture is dependent on the presence of an attractive opportunity in conjunction with industry experience. Failure to get an idea to market happens when resources are missing and one of either industry experience or attractive opportunity are not given. The findings support the Timmons (1999) model of entrepreneurial process in its configurational nature, highlighting the value of all elements. This should benefit researchers to understand the complexity of new venture creation as well as the difficulty, for research and practice to single out one driving force of new venture performance.

4. MAQCA: Combining Meta-Analysis and Qualitative Comparative Analysis to Establish Configurations of Patterns in Research Findings [5]

4.1. Abstract

This article provides guidelines for meta-analysts to combine their meta-analytical logic with a configurational logic. We suggest that, after conducting a meta-analysis (MA), subsequently performing qualitative comparative analysis (QCA) has the potential to add another important perspective on meta-analytical results. Specifically, MAQCA[6], enables researchers to display patterns of study conditions (e.g., firm age, firm size, operationalization of constructs) of their meta-analytical synthesis, which are associated with the strength of the relationship in question. As such, meta-analysts' findings are enriched by an understanding of the impact of study conditions. This adds value to implications and future research recommendations of meta-analysts. To illustrate, how this multi-method research may be performed, we conduct MAQCA with data on absorptive capacity and firm performance. We elaborate on the additional insights we gain as we combine the two methods and specify boundaries for and implications from applying MAQCA.

4.2. Introduction into the knowledge aggregation challenge

To consolidate, organize, and synthesize prior research findings, scholars apply a wide range of qualitative and quantitative methods (Kunisch et al., 2018). Meta-analyses are among the most widely used methods to aggregate prior knowledge (Bergh et al., 2016), other than literature reviews (Aguinis et al., 2023; Hoon, 2013). While meta-analyses have their advantages, they also share several limitations that impact researchers' ability to generalize from aggregated findings. This study suggests, that researchers are able to overcome the limitations of the existing aggregation methods: (i) limited scope of aggregation, (ii) limited empirical explanation, (iii) limited theoretical and contextual integration (Borenstein et al., 2009; Flor et al., 2018; Lane and Lubatkin, 1998; Marabelli and Newell, 2014) by combining meta-analysis and QCA.

---

[5] This study is part of a research project in collaboration with Esther Moosauer, University of Bern, Switzerland; Tatiana R. Stettler, Kent State University, USA; Simone A. Schweiger, University of Bern, Switzerland; and Artur Baldauf, University of Bern, Switzerland.

[6] We propose this term, as the combination of the terms meta-analysis (MA) and qualitative comparative analysis (QCA).

The first limitation – *limited (or narrow) scope of aggregation* – stems from the fact that aggregation methods rely on the underlying data quality and therefore, have been considered separately. The divide between qualitative and quantitative findings also imposes constraints onto the type of questions that an aggregation study may pose. Meta-analytic studies usually focus on the strength and directionality of the (main) effect between two constructs and help to answer the question: Is there an effect? And if so, how strong is the effect and which factors affect its strength and directionality? (Maldonado et al., 2018; Song et al., 2018; Yao et al., 2020; Zou et al., 2018). Meta-analytic studies capture the *effects* of that concept's operationalization (i.e., construct) onto other concepts and their operationalizations (Borenstein et al., 2009; Cooper et al., 2009; Cooper, 2015; Davis et al., 2014; Snyder, 2019). Therefore, they provide insights into the average strength of a relationship over multiple pieces of research. However, this does not fully account for the differences in findings.

The second limitation – *limited empirical explanation* – manifests itself in aggregations of quantitative data and in a predominant focus therein on the main effects analyses describing the *presence* of a particular effect (Marabelli and Newell, 2014; Volberda et al., 2010). As other covariance-based methods, meta-analyses in organizational studies help to explain the main effects of a particular predictor on the outcome of interest (Borenstein et al., 2009). Thereby, researchers assume the relationship to be linear and symmetrical (i.e., affected by reverse causality): for example, if higher "x" leads to higher "y", a lower "x" is expected to lead to lower "y". With this logic, considering the impact of an *absence* of an effect is not possible. Neglecting this so-called causal ambiguity[7], researchers miss explanations and non-linear relationships (Duşa, 2019; Mello, 2021).

The third limitation in scientific knowledge aggregation arises from the tendency for *limited theoretical and contextual integration.* Organizational phenomena are fundamentally complex, dynamic, and systemic, which means, interdependencies between these phenomena are difficult (if ever possible) to untangle. Traditional knowledge aggregation methods neglect the possibility that multiple distinct combinations of causal conditions may *co-occur* and thereby be *equally* associated with a presence of an outcome (i.e., equifinality). In empirical terms, this

[7] Causal ambiguity refers to a scenario in which researchers possess limited or inadequate understanding regarding the essence or orientation of causal connections amidst concepts (Meuer and Rupietta (2017a)).

challenge is known as the endogeneity problem, whereby the major scholarly concern is tied to omitted variable bias, simultaneity bias and sample selection bias (Doty and Glick, 1998). While there are several estimation methods to address endogeneity concerns – for example, Heckman two-stage model, fixed or random effects and other (Sharma et al., 2009), they rely on the fundamental belief that complex interdependencies between constructs can be controlled for and biases therefrom can be estimated. Yet without a direct comparison of the possible alternative solutions and embracing of the potentially conflicting theoretical explanations, the findings obtained from traditional aggregation approaches remain fragmented.

Our research serves as a guideline for overcoming these limitations of meta-analyses. We propose that meta-analytical study findings can greatly be enriched by subsequently performing QCA. This sequential mixed method approach reveals patterns of study conditions (e.g., firm age, firm size, operationalization of constructs) of their meta-analytical synthesis that can serve as a sensitivity analysis to the meta-analytical findings. It allows for deeper insights into the underlying reasons for diverging findings in studies on the same relationship between constructs.

In the following, we present an overview of mixed methods, meta-analysis and QCA, followed by the introduction of MAQCA and a description of its benefits to enhance the value of meta-analytical research. Thereafter, we describe the MAQCA process in detail. Finally, we conclude with the illustration of MAQCA in an exemplary, simplified case. We ultimately discuss benefits and limitations of the method.

4.3. Introduction into mixed methods, meta-analysis, and QCA

The proliferation of mixed-method methodologies[8] has continued to advance the way scholars aggregate scientific knowledge (Molina-Azorin, 2012). While some methods allow to assess competitive models (e.g., MASEM by Bergh et al. (2016)) and others provide opportunities to capture complexity and multidimensionality of results (e.g., Meuer and Rupietta's (2017b) integration of QCA and conventional statistical analyses), a combination of both methods offers extended benefits that cannot be captured with a single method.

[8] Mixed methods research systematically combines multiple research approaches (Meuer and Rupietta (2017a).

To increase the impact and value of research methods and address its limitations, researchers keep developing mixed method approaches (Hesse-Biber and Johnson, 2015). The main goal of such integration is usability in tackling specific problems in research. With different degrees of integration of the underlying methods (Teddlie and Tashakkori, 2012), mixed method approaches address weaknesses of one method with strengths of another (Meuer and Rupietta, 2017a, 2017b); Johnson et al., 2007; Molina-Azorin, 2012; Jick, 1979). Given their characteristics – breadth and width of consideration – mixed methods bear the potential for multidimensional insights (Teddlie and Tashakkori, 2012).

There are several design alternatives for integrating research methods: the parallel design, the sequential design, and the conversion design (Creswell, 2014). While the former design weaves two types of data together, the sequential design orders them chronologically, and the conversion design transforms qualitative data into quantitative data. Some questions lend themselves into a parallel design – where qualitative and quantitative information deliver different information on the same research question – others are better addressed sequentially (one method adds a level of explanation to the findings from the other, e.g., Kallmuenzer et al. (2019)). Further options are conversion, the multilevel design across different levels of analysis, and the fully integrated design, where integration happens across all stages of the study (Tashakkori and Teddlie, 2010; Teddlie and Tashakkori, 2012).

In Table 19, we display an overview of mixed methods, which are based on meta-analytic data. Common options are meta-analytic structural equation modeling (MASEM) (Bergh et al., 2016), meta-analytic regression (MARA) (Lipsey and Wilson, 2001) or meta-synthesis (Hoon, 2013). These methods may be used to work on a vary of applications, like establishing the robustness of findings against a controls and moderators (MARA) (Lipsey and Wilson, 2001). Each of these methods has different research emphasis, and underlying logic, which makes them suitable to specific research questions. Meta-syntheses are used to assess qualitative research, MARA is a quantitative technique, applied to assess the influence of moderators on effect sizes. MARA, in comparison to MASEM is less complex, with a focus on the role of moderators, where MASEM is employed to test comprehensive theoretical models.

In this study, we combine meta-analysis and QCA relying on a sequential mixed method for knowledge integration. We describe MAQCA as a mixed method which has value in finding the conditions under which research outcomes occur. Such a configurational perspective is seldomly used in management and entrepreneurship research (Douglas et al., 2020). Meta-analyses test the direction and strength of a relationship based on a quantitative synthesis of a research field (Bergh et al., 2016; Borenstein et al., 2009; Geyskens et al., 2009). Traditionally, meta-analyses compute a weighted mean effect size for the relationship of interest and the variance among the investigated primary studies (Aguinis et al., 2011; Borenstein et al., 2009). Specifically, when there are conflicting findings in extant research, i.e., when there is evidence, that coefficient effects between constructs differ between studies, the method has proven to be valuable in providing more clarity in fragmented research fields by identifying the overall direction of a relationship. Meta-analyses have already been combined with other methods such as structural equation modeling (e.g., Bergh et al. (2016)).

A meta-analysis integrates primary research and is a quantitative synthesis of a specific research field (Borenstein et al., 2009; Geyskens et al., 2009; Hunter and Schmidt, 1990). Meta-analyses account for research quality (e.g., reliability and validity) and sample size of the primary studies to produce an estimate of the direction and strength of the relationship of interest (Hunter and Schmidt, 2004; Schmidt and Hunter, 1999; Song et al., 2008). For an accurate aggregation, the meta-analytic procedure has to be followed. It is pivotal to perform transparent analyses that account for possible measurement and contextual biases. The study selection as well as the coding procedure are central (Song et al., 2008; Villiger et al., 2022).

TABLE 19: Overview of combined meta-studies / meta-analytic synthesis methods

Synthesis method	Meta regression (MARA) / subgroup analysis	Meta-analytic structural equation modeling (MASEM)	Meta-synthesis	Meta-analytic qualitative comparative analysis (MAQCA)
Meta-studies represent an analysis of the analysis – "grounded in the understanding of knowledge building as an evolutionary sequence" (Glass, 1977)				
Research emphasis	Examining the relationship between independent variables and effect sizes as outcome variables (Lipsey & Wilson, 2001)	Comparing theories or models that contain diverging implications for the data (Harrison et al., 2006)	Extracting and analyzing qualitative research from different databases	*Boundary conditions of diverging research findings*
Logic Primary benefit	Reduction of constructs as effect size is seen as dependent variable	Synthesis through the reduction of complexity	Synthesis through the reduction of complexity	*Synthesis, Causal complexity, equifinality,*
Exemplar mechanisms to be tested	Moderation (with or without control variables)	Mediation	Relationships between constructs	*Relationships between constructs and circumstances under which they occur*
Exemplary questions to be tested	Relationship between effect size and moderating variables	(Competitive) theory testing	Theory building	*Research question 1: What is the relationship between AC and INN? (MA)* *Research question 2: Which configurations of boundary conditions lead to differences in the relationship between AC and INN? (QCA)*
Exemplar outputs	Impact on the main effects from X on Y by the other factors (Z)	Path models detailing necessary conditions (Z) for the relationship (X-Y) to occur	"Contributions beyond those achieved in the original studies"	*Typologies detailing co-occurrence of X, Y, Z*
Primary data types (Input data)	Quantitative	Quantitative	Qualitative, inductive	*Quantitative and qualitative*
Primary data sources	Empirical studies (*published and unpublished)*	Empirical studies (*published and unpublished)*	Qualitative case studies (*published only*)	*Empirical studies (published and unpublished)*
Key benefits	Establishing the robustness of findings against a broad spectrum of control variables and methodological moderators (Lipsey & Wilson, 2001)	Testing variables of models that are not included in each primary study	Systematic synthesis of the literature can be helpful for guiding practice and asking future research questions	*Clarification of boundary conditions under which a phenomenon occurs*
Key limitations – i.e., Boundaries in application	The input (i.e., primary-level studies) can be "a mass of reports—good, bad, and indifferent" (Eysenck, 1978, p. 517).	Unable to provide "higher-level assessments, such as comparing competing models that might have multiple permutations of predictors, mediators, and outcomes" (Bergh 2016: 1): not as useful when lacking competing hypotheses or models, not feasible with limited prior studies; no immunity to construct validity threats; excessive use of missing data substitution or imputation technique; difficulties testing moderation, within most SEM packages (Bergh 2016: 3)	Sample selection may reduce the range of interpretations of a phenomenon	*Limitation from original data may not allow to work on full MA sample in QCA part; number of conditions to be tested is limited by sample size*
Further details and execution guidelines	Aggregation and interpretation	Bergh et al. (2016, SMJ) Aggregation and interpretation	Hoon (2013, ORM) – synthesis as aggregation, interpretation, or as translation	*Current study Aggregation, interpretation, or as translation*
Exemplary studies in management & entrepreneurship	Kirca et al. (2005)	Nardi et al. (2020)	Rouhani et al. (2017)	-

However, research findings are often not perfectly comparable (Borenstein et al., 2009). A meta-analysis cannot fully account for differences in the design or methodology of studies (Bergh et al., 2016). Differences in the setting of a study, the operationalization of measurements and boundaries of constructs are prominent. Researchers need to account for these differences, when combining and comparing results in a meta-analytic synthesis. Potential boundary conditions (or moderators) of the relationship between constructs can be identified by creating subgroups and investigating differences between those groups (Borenstein and Higgins, 2013; Hunter and Schmidt, 2004). This approach, however, has limitations, when studying certain research questions. When moderators need to be studied in more detail because researchers want to know which combinations of boundary conditions lead to the same result, the use of QCA can provide additional insights. QCA's combination with other methodological approaches has been vetted and the resulting mixed-method approach has been deemed beneficial for research questions of high complexity (e.g., Jackson and Ni (2013)) (Meuer and Rupietta, 2017a). The taxonomy of conditions that are commonly linked to certain outcomes is the key benefit from this method because it adds depth and detail to the research findings and allows scholars to provide more nuanced explanations of multiple possible configurations to the outcome of interest.

Qualitative comparative analysis (QCA) has been introduced into the social sciences by Charles Ragin (1987), who refers to the works of Leibniz, Cantor, and Boole (1854). QCA allows finding patterns, which other methods do not discover (Douglas et al., 2020). It operates on the basis of sets (Duşa, 2019) of which such as constructs or variables could be part of. An element may, for example, be a construct or a variable. There are distinct types of QCA. Crisp-set QCA (csQCA) and fuzzy-set QCA (fsQCA) are the most common ones. csQCA is a variant of QCA with two options for membership in a set, either fully in or fully out. fsQCA, on the other hand, is a type of QCA, where partial set membership is possible (Duşa, 2019). Typically, scholars employ fsQCA, with crisp set calibrations, when the level of data categorization does not allow to pursue fsQCA (e.g., binary categories like 'door is locked' vs 'door is *not* locked')[9]. Here no intermediate value can be found.

[9] Fuzzy set membership scores allow for any value between zero and one.

QCA produces configurations of conditions under which an outcome is present or absent (Schneider and Wagemann, 2012). In this process, QCA can find multiple combinations of causal conditions[10] which lead to the same outcome (Mello, 2021). This feature of QCA is known as 'equifinality' and refers to a central point of distinction in the QCA outcome compared to regression methods. Moreover, equifinality is tied to causal complexity[11] which implies that there may be (and most likely are) different explanations for the presence of an outcome and the non-outcome (Mello, 2021). The non-outcome hereby is any instance that does not fall into the set of the outcome. For example, if the presence of an outcome tall person is defined as a height of more than two meters, any person with a height under two meters would be experiencing a non-outcome. By finding configurations of causal conditions which are associated with either the presence or the absence of an outcome, equifinality allows to detect relevant combinations of those conditions.

Additionally, QCA has the potential to uncover intricate connections that can benefit research by more accurately capturing the mechanisms underlying the studied relationships (Douglas et al., 2020; Linder et al., 2020; Mello, 2021). The underlying Boolean logic is fundamentally different to "correlational statistics" as it is based on "presence" (1) or "absence" (0) of a condition. As a case-based method, any case is either considered inside the set where the condition is present, or outside (Duşa, 2019; Mello, 2021). In addition, it employs, so called, logical operators (AND, OR, NOT), which are used to describe operations (Whitesitt, 2012). Logical operators link different sets. Together, this can be used to describe configurations which consist of multiple sets. For example, a case may have a configuration where it is inside the set "blue color" AND outside the set "round". This would describe any objects which are blue and not round. From a configurational perspective, it is expected that the presence of one condition will only have an effect under the influence of another (set of) conditions (Schneider and Wagemann, 2012). Considering these characteristics of QCA, it can contribute to extended insights, when applied in meta-analysis. This sets it apart from other analytical techniques, which assume that the same effect will be present for a

[10] A causal condition is a factor which is included in QCA, as it is deemed potentially necessary or sufficient for the outcome Mello (2021).

[11] Causal complexity is a situation where a specific outcome arises from multiple different combinations of causal conditions (Ragin and Fiss (2008) The use of the notion of causality differs in QCA from traditional methods.

condition across all cases examined (Mello, 2021). Therefore, configurational methods enable researchers to identify diverse outcomes for a particular condition based on changes in the combination of other assessed conditions.

4.4. Introduction and benefits of MAQCA

In this article, we suggest a sequential mixed method approach combining meta-analysis (MA) and qualitative comparative analysis (QCA). The value of such approaches has been highlighted in other scientific contexts, like medicine (Moore et al., 2018; Thomas et al., 2014). With this article, we aim to encourage management and entrepreneurship researchers to consider combining these methods in their research endeavors. Specifically, we display the application of MA, followed by QCA. The combination of the MA and QCA sheds new light on meta-analytical data and provides important contributions to existing meta-analytical knowledge aggregation methods. Meta-analysts can use this approach to extend the value of their research. They can do so with data they can extract from the literature used in the meta-analysis. Data on the measurement of the core constructs or the sample context could be utilized in QCA to explore reasons to diverging research findings.

The contributions of this article are threefold. First, by combining correlational/covariance results from meta-analysis with Boolean logic (Whitesitt, 2012) in terms of QCA, researchers generate insights that otherwise would remain hidden. Indeed, statistical methods that are based on correlations between variables are sometimes ill-suited in the analysis of causal pathways (Douglas et al., 2020; Meuer and Rupietta, 2017a).

Second, the proposed methodology is particularly suited for the analysis of the complex and interdependent boundary conditions. These represent a critical element in theory development, referring to the ''who, where, when'' aspects of a theory and thereby describe the scope of generalizability of a theory (Busse et al., 2017). In a traditional meta-analysis, contextual and measurement factors are tested separately to establish the extent to which the results obtained, hold under varying conditions (Hansen et al., 2022). However, it may be that "apples and oranges" are mixed in meta-analyses, when research is not performed on common grounds (Borenstein et al., 2009). An example is, when comparing studies on the effect of CEO age on organizational performance for a sample firms which diverge in age and size (Borenstein et al., 2009). Therefore, it is important to evaluate, under which conditions the theory or research findings are considered. One can assess the boundary conditions affecting a relationship between constructs. This is facilitated by applying QCA to a meta-analysis.

Third, MAQCA allows to understand conflicting research findings and deduce plausible causes for the observed results. As an outcome in this case may be the strength of the relationship between two constructs, where differences can possibly be attributed to researched conditions. This relates to the benefit of QCA enabling researchers to consider equifinality which entails that multiple combinations of conditions can lead to a certain outcome (Mello, 2021). Researchers can thereby assess the differences in presence and absence of an outcome in the solution paths. MAQCA allows them to research scenarios where studies may find equal results, which come to live under different conditional configurations. Researchers can provide additional value to their research findings by discussing these equifinal configurations.

4.5. The MAQCA process

The MAQCA process can be characterized by five steps in which specific tasks need to be performed. These steps and tasks are described below. An overview of the process is provided in Table 20. This overview of the steps and tasks provides guidance on how to perform MAQCA. After the explanation of our sequential mixed method approach, we illustrate the MAQCA process on data which are available to the authors from previous research endeavors (Hahn-Notter, 2021; Marttila et al., 2017) on the relationship between absorptive capacity (AC) and innovation (INN).

Step I: Research question and methodology

At the beginning of a MAQCA study, as in any other research, researchers have to determine the research problem they want to address. They also have to select and justify their methodology. In the case of MAQCA, this means that the research question needs to be of meta-analytic and configurational nature (Moore et al., 2018).

Task #1 - Definition of research question

The first step to a MAQCA study is the definition of a research question. Researchers need to select a problem whose investigation promises value to the research community (Alvesson and Sandberg, 2011; Barley, 2006; Davis, 1971).

TABLE 20: Steps and tasks to perform MAQCA

Steps	Tasks	Description / Specification	Source
(I) Research Question and Methodology	#1 - Definition of Research Question	Definition of research question and assessing fit of MAQCA method	(Alvesson and Sandberg, 2011; Barley, 2006; Davis, 1971)
(II) Study Identification and Preparation	#2 – Literature Search	Relevant studies are identified according to the research question formulated.	(Aguinis et al., 2011; Borenstein et al., 2009; Cooper et al., 2009; Cooper, 2015; Davis et al., 2014; Lipsey and Wilson, 2001; Stock, 1994)
	#3 – Data Collection	Data have to be collected in a comprehensive search process by searching databases for published and unpublished studies. Also, the inclusion criteria have to be defined.	
	#4 – Coding	A coding protocol is established describing the information to be obtained from the studies. The independent coders exchange their approach and adjust the protocol, if necessary.	
(III) Meta-Analytic Procedure	#5– Data Correction	The data must be corrected for statistical artifacts such as measurement and sampling errors.	(Borenstein et al., 2006; Borenstein et al., 2009; Hunter and Schmidt, 1990, 2004)
	#6 – Computation of the Main Effect Size	The effect size for each study is computed. Data in individual studies can differ.	
(IV) QCA Procedure	#7 – Description and Calibration of Outcome and Conditions	Conditions and the outcome need to be described. Then the data must be calibrated for QCA use.	(Duşa, 2019; Mello, 2021; Oana and Schneider, 2018, 2021; Schneider and Wagemann, 2012)
	#8 – Analysis of Necessary and Sufficient Conditions	QCA analysis of necessity and sufficiency of the included conditions	
	#9 - Assessment of Configurations	Researchers need to assess the configurations which lead to the (non-)outcome	
(V) Reporting, Development and Extension	#10 – Discussion of Results and Limitations	MAQCA-Results are reported and discussed and Implications on theory and methods are discussed	(Edwards, 2010; Shepherd and Suddaby, 2017)
	#11 – Future Research Opportunities	Research implications on future research are discussed	

The constructs which shall be assessed have to be defined and put into relation with each other. This should be based on existing literature, which needs to be reviewed and critically evaluated. MAQCA requires the presence of studies on which a meta-analysis can be based and need to contain information required to apply MA and QCA. Therefore, the minimum ratio of cases to conditions (4-5 cases/condition) must be respected (Borenstein et al., 2009; Mello, 2021). Conditions are the elements which are assessed in QCA, as they are deemed to be possibly influential (Mello, 2021).

Step II: Study identification and preparation

Task #2 – Literature search

Findings from existing literature is the base for any MAQCA study. Therefore, this task is essential to the quality of the study. Identifying pertinent studies related to the research problem is crucial in providing research evidence that addresses the formulated research question. A comprehensive search process for published and unpublished studies has to be performed. The inclusion of unpublished studies can prevent publication bias. The inclusion and exclusion criteria are defined, i.e., which studies are excluded and included in the sample (Cooper, 2015). These may be related to article language, publication period among others. The search process must be reported in detail (Borenstein et al., 2009; Kraus et al., 2020).

Task #3 – Data collection

After the set of articles to be included in the MAQCA study has been identified, the relevant information must be extracted from them. This means for MAQCA, extracting descriptive information (e.g., sample size), bivariate correlations and information on the outcome and conditions for QCA. Usually, conditions in the QCA part are boundary conditions of the studied relationship. This means, they assess the operationalization of constructs and research descriptives (e.g., high-tech context). Not all studies may provide information on all conditions in the QCA part. Researchers may choose to include only articles which deliver full information on all aspects or to consider also articles which lack information on some QCA conditions. This choice results in either equal or different sample sizes for the meta-analysis and the QCA. One option is having full overlap between the MA and the QCA sample. This results, when only studies with full information on all necessary variables and conditions are included. The second option maximizes the number of studies which can be evaluated in the MA part. This happens when the exclusion of studies for missing data happens in two steps. The sample of studies drops in size for the QCA part then, as studies which lack information, necessary for the QCA part, are only excluded then.

Task #4 – Coding

Some data cannot be utilized directly from the articles in MAQCA, (e.g., nominal data, like the countries from which the samples are drawn). To allow researchers to work with this information, it has to be coded. To ensure coding reliability and accuracy, a coding protocol is developed outlining the information to be extracted from the studies. Each study is coded at least twice and from independent coders. The coding protocol is adjusted throughout the coding process. To ensure consistency, the independent coders should exchange their approach and adjust it if necessary (Lipsey and Wilson, 2001; Stock, 1994).

Step III: Meta-analytic procedure

The next step in carrying out MAQCA is performing the meta-analysis.

Task #5– Data correction

Data that has been extracted from the primary studies may need to be corrected before conducting the meta-analysis, usually done with software, like the Comprehensive Meta-Analysis software (Borenstein et al., 2006). The procedure requires correcting the data for statistical artifacts, such as measurement and sampling error. To correct for measurement error in the studies using perceived measures for the independent and dependent variable, the formula by Hunter and Schmidt (2004) may be used. When studies do not report Cronbach alpha or use single-item measures, the missing information may be substituted with the mean reliability of the particular construct across all studies (Geyskens et al., 1998). To account for sampling error, the effect sizes are weighted by the sample sizes from primary studies. This corrects the individual effect by giving more accurate studies more weight (Geyskens et al., 2009).

Task #6 – Computation of the main effect size

To perform the meta-analytic calculations researchers can utilize the Comprehensive Meta-Analysis software (Borenstein et al., 2006). For calculation, a choice for random or fixed effects is to be made. The random effects model rather than the fixed effects model may be preferable in order to generate more precise outcomes (Hunter and Schmidt, 2004; Schmidt and Hunter, 1999). When reporting the results, researchers should be transparent in reporting all results, including the underlying total sample size (Borenstein et al., 2009; Hunter and Schmidt, 2004).

Step IV: QCA procedure

The next step in the MAQCA process is conducting the QCA part of MAQCA. Herein the general rules of QCA should be followed (Duşa, 2019; Mello, 2021; Ragin, 1987, 2008). Multiple options allow performing QCA via software. RStudio (Posit team, 2022) using the packages from Duşa (2019) and Oana and Schneider (2018) is an option which gives the researcher good control whilst having guidance (Duşa, 2019; Mello, 2021). Other common options are fs/QCA and Tosmana, which, however, are less advanced. By using QCA, researchers are able to process data from various sources and types, including both qualitative and quantitative data. Via the process of calibration, data like the "correlational data" from meta-analysis can be assessed in QCA processes.

Task #7 – Description and calibration of outcome and conditions

To understand the differences in the correlation between the constructs that are assessed in the meta-analysis, QCA is employed. Therefore, researchers need to explain the conditions which they investigate. The conditions and the outcome must be described to then calibrate them. Calibration is the process of transforming raw data into data that can be used in QCA. Therefore, the target set has to be conceptualized and named, and the calibration thresholds have to be selected, depending on the method of calibration (Mello, 2021). Here researchers shall follow the established practices (Duşa, 2019; Mello, 2021). The level of measurement poses a restriction as to which specific set membership can be calculated (Mello, 2021).

Task #8 – Analysis of necessary and sufficient conditions

Then the analysis of necessity and sufficiency of the (configurations of) conditions is performed. Therefore, the truth table is constructed, which is rooted in the combinations of conditions, which are observed. All possible combinations of conditions are included in the truth table (Mello, 2021). In MAQCA, typically, researchers would set the data from the correlation tables as the outcome in the truth table. All assessed cases are allocated to the truth table rows. From that, researchers arrive at the necessary and sufficient conditions. These are best found using the CCubes algorithm, as it is computationally more efficient than the older QMC or eQMC algorithms (Duşa, 2019). Researchers need to report details on the configuration of their assessment.

Task #9 - Assessment of configurations

After having found the necessary and sufficient configurations of conditions, researchers need to assess them. This entails describing the configurations of conditions which either lead to the outcome or the non-outcome. The number of configurations may vary. In case of multiple ambiguous models, a common selection criterion of the models is the product of coverage and consistency, where the maximum is selected.

Step V: Discussion, development and extension

The next step in performing MAQCA is reporting and discussing results, and developing insights from these, and offering future research directions.

Task #10 – Discussion of results and limitations

Then the results of the MAQCA analysis have to be discussed. For instance, the reasons why studies find diverging correlations and how this contributes to literature and the advancement of research need to be provided. This means, that MAQCA studies should report on their meta-analytic findings, but also on the results from the QCA part, where configurations to diversity in underlying research findings is discussed. Further, limitations of the study need to be debated. Especially potential shortcomings in methodological perspective have to be highlighted.

Task #11 – Future research opportunities

Ultimately researchers shall discuss, how future research may be performed to resolve issues that were present in the study or that have been uncovered in the study. These configurations shall call for new research that is inspired from the study in theoretical or methodological ways.

After having described the MAQCA process, we illustrate this process through an example. We display the use of MAQCA on the exemplary relationship between absorptive capacity and innovation.

4.6. MAQCA illustration via the absorptive capacity-innovation relationship

Throughout this example, we provide guidance on how to stepwise perform MAQCA. Given, that the goal of this illustration is to display the application of the MAQCA process, we do not go into detail on the facets of the constructs "absorptive capacity" (AC) and "innovation" (INN). We focus on the methodological instead of the theoretical insights. Referring to the steps indicated in Table 20, we present an example of the application of QCA to meta-analytic data[12]. We define

[12] As mentioned, this relationship was chosen, given the existing dataset and the multitude of meta-analysis that find diverging results, see also Hahn-Notter (2021) and Marttila et al. (2017).

AC as a firm's ability to identify, assimilate and exploit knowledge from the environment, as introduced by Cohen and Levinthal (1989) . Innovation is defined as accomplishments in the creation and success of processes, products and services of a firm (Lane et al., 2006).

Step I: Research question and methodology

The first step in performing MAQCA studies is the introduction into the researched subject and the review of the literature on the topic, introduce the constructs, which are going to be assessed, as well as the motivation of the research question and the justification of MAQCA as the utilized method.

Review of AC and INN

AC is an extensively studied concept in management and entrepreneurship research (Zou et al., 2018). It entails a firm's capability to acquire, assimilate, and exploit knowledge (Cohen and Levinthal, 1989, 1990). Moreover, AC embraces a complex set of organizational processes of how firms accumulate, reconfigure, and apply knowledge to commercial ends (Cohen and Levinthal, 1990; Lane et al., 2006; Zahra and George, 2002). Research findings indicate that AC promotes innovation (INN) as, for instance, creating and utilizing knowledge exposes firms to new ideas and motivates them to amend existing processes and structures (Volberda et al., 2010; Zhou and Li, 2012). Extant research reports a positive relationship between AC and INN (Jiménez-Jiménez and Sanz-Valle, 2011; Leal-Rodríguez et al., 2014; Tsai, 2001). This has also been confirmed in meta-analyses investigating this relationship (Song et al., 2018; Zou et al., 2018). While the positive impact of AC on INN seems to be conceptually uncontroversial (e.g., Cohen and Levinthal, 1990; Volberda et al., 2010), some empirical findings also reveal contradicting, weak (Kapoor et al., 2015; van de Vrande et al., 2011) or even negative effects of AC on INN (Belderbos et al., 2015; Jain, 2013; Phelps, 2010). Most, but not all studies report that firms' capability to absorb externally available knowledge yields positive innovation effects (Kostopoulos et al., 2011). Discrepancies in empirical findings may arise due to misperception of a universality of the construct's impact on innovation and originate from a lack of a common understanding of the boundary conditions of these concepts. Drawing on the vast literature on the AC-INN relationship, we use MAQCA to investigate the interdependencies between important factors that yield different levels of innovation. Our results provide theoretical and methodological implications for entrepreneurship scholars and draw attention to contexts in which firms either benefit or not benefit from absorbing more knowledge. This sheds light on the conditions under which combined, jointly affect certain outcomes for the AC-INN relationship.

Definition of research question

The first step in performing a study is defining the research question. Two groups of conditions may explain why some studies observe that high levels of AC do not necessarily result in high INN performance levels. On one side, these conditions may pertain to sampling aspects in terms of firm context: firms with certain characteristics (size, industry) may be less capable to commercialize knowledge and create innovation from invention. Due to liability of smallness (Aldrich and Auster, 1986; Freeman et al., 1983) and inherent resource limitations, small and medium-sized firms (SMEs) may face more challenges in monetizing knowledge. Likewise, high-tech firms operating in knowledge intensive competitive environment may convert knowledge into innovation over longer periods of time.

On the other side, the research context may also impact the magnitude and direction in this relationship, where certain ways of measuring knowledge absorption may be less conducive to superior innovation. For example, objective measures of AC like research and development (R&D) intensity may not accurately capture the process of knowledge absorption (such as R&D expenses) and thereby fail to assess the depth and breadth of knowledge acquisition and application (Ali et al., 2016; Lewin et al., 2011). Indeed, while many scholars rely on objective measures of absorption, some have followed Zahra and George (2002) and captured perceived AC by asking managers about the processes instilled to accumulate, reconfigure, and apply knowledge. A meta-analysis by Zou et al. (2018) highlights that according to managerial perceptions, AC is strongly related to INN ($r = 0.48$ to $r = 0.64$, $p < 0.001$ for various measures). Yet, this effect virtually vanishes when AC is measured objectively over time ($r = 0.04$, $p < 0.05$ for panel studies of impacts of AC's archival proxies on innovation).

We summarize prior empirical findings on AC–INN relationship and test the effects of three groups of factors that may alter its strength: what (construct level), when (temporal level), and where (contextual level).

A lack of a common understanding of the boundary conditions – what AC and INN is (and what it is not) and how each can (and cannot) be measured – motivated us to clarify underlying misperceptions about the universality of AC's positive impact on INN.

Boundary conditions refer to the ''who, where, when'' aspects of a theory (Whetten, 1989) and detail the boundaries in time, space, and the researcher's values (Bacharach, 1989; Busse et al., 2017). In this study, we investigate the following four boundary conditions in AC–INN relationship: (i) process nature of AC, and (ii) temporality, (iii) type, and (iv) context of innovation. Although most scholars agree on a process-oriented conceptualization of absorptive capacity (AC), various subjective and objective measures have been used to operationalize what it is, yielding different effects on INN (e.g., Zou et al., 2018). The AC–INN relationship is frequently investigated in a cross-sectional rather than sequential manner, even though knowledge absorption takes time and therefore, when performance effects are captured may bias the results. Scholars may disregard differences in the effect between quantity and quality of INN performance measures, thereby disregarding where the positive effects of AC surface in organizations (Maldonado et al., 2018; Zou et al., 2018). ACs impact has been studied across many different firm contexts, with potentially diverging findings depending on size or industry (Zou et al., 2018).

Prior aggregations of research findings on the AC-INN relationship investigate various dimensions of AC and their impact on (technological) innovation among other mediators and outcome variables. They find that the mean effect size of AC on INN is significant and positive (Song et al., 2018). By examining more than one AC dimension, prior meta-analyses can compare the overall directions and strengths of their investigated dimensions on innovation performance. To gain insights into differences among primary studies, subgroup meta-analyses have been performed (Maldonado et al., 2018; Song et al., 2018). With a subgroup meta-analysis, questions like "To what extent does the mean effect size of the investigated relationship change when including moderators?" can be answered. However, such subgroup analysis focusses on one boundary condition and its effect on the investigated relationship, it does not show an "interaction" between boundary conditions. In our study, we first seek a confirmation of the positive and significant relationship between AC and INN. We then assess the necessary and sufficient combinations of boundary conditions that are required for a strong positive, weak positive, and negative relationship between AC and INN.

We address the two research questions:

- *Is the relationship between AC and INN positive and significant?* and
- *Which configurations of boundary conditions lead to differences in the relationship between AC and INN?*

We utilize MAQCA to assess these two related research questions. Assuming that the AC-INN relationship is not universal in nature but is observable and present under specific conditions only, we intend to disentangle the fragmentation in the current literature. Specifically, we consider conditions that may make a difference in this relationship: the operationalization of both concepts, the time lag of ACs impact on INN as well as sampling aspects such as firm size and industry. With this study, we aim (a) to establish boundary conditions in the AC-INN relationship (Busse et al., 2017), and (b) to inform researchers about the impact of operationalizations of AC and INN on their study results. This is why we combine meta-analysis and QCA to MAQCA, with the intent to achieve more fine-grained insights.

To answer our research questions, we utilize a novel combination of meta-analytical methods and qualitative comparative analysis (MAQCA) to analyze the findings in empirical studies capturing the AC-INN relationship (Fiss, 2007; Ragin, 1987). Combining the configurational perspective with meta-analytical data enables us to identify the role of research design and firm context–with their different configurations–leading to specific outcome levels of the AC-INN relationship.

Step II: Study identification and preparation

At step two we perform literature search, data collection, and coding. To apply MAQCA, the relevant studies need to be identified, data has to be collected in a comprehensive way, and a coding protocol has to be established (Borenstein et al., 2009). We use an existing dataset that was available to the researchers (Hahn-Notter, 2021; Marttila et al., 2017). Despite this, we describe the data collection process in the following, for sake of completeness of illustration.

Literature search

Researchers need to identify relevant studies to the formulated problem. The comprehensive literature search included several online databases (Business Source Ultimate/EBSCO, Google Scholar, JSTOR, EconLit, Elsevier Science Direct) for published studies as well as the PROQUEST database for unpublished studies.

The inclusion of unpublished studies can prevent publication bias. The creators of the dataset also went through the reference list of existing meta-analyses on AC (Song et al., 2018; Maldonado et al., 2018; Zou et al., 2018). They used the term "absorptive capacity" and searched for empirical articles addressing the relationship between AC and INN and providing correlations at the firm or business unit level. The inclusion criteria are defined, i.e., which studies are excluded and included in the sample for the meta-analysis (Cooper, 2015). Included studies reported correlations between AC (e.g., R&D intensity, multidimensional dynamic capability) and INN outcomes (e.g., patents, new products, share of new products of the total sales) at the firm or business unit level. We excluded articles that were not in English. When the information in primary studies was too vague or not sufficient, e.g., the number of firms was not reported in the sample, we excluded these articles from our analysis. In some cases, the AC measurement was unclassifiable and could not be aligned with our established AC categories. Our finale sample is 145 empirical studies based on the chosen inclusion and exclusion criteria.

Data collection

Given the sample of literature collected, researchers need to extract the data from the articles, which is relevant to their research question. Data is systematically collected from the uncovered studies. This entails especially data from the correlation tables, as well as sample size and data on the conditions that are to be assessed. In this case that means measurement of AC and INN, temporality of INN, firm size and industry.

Coding

To ensure coding reliability and accuracy, a coding protocol is developed outlining the information to be extracted from the studies. A coding protocol is a document which provides guidelines for all coders on how to evaluate information from the literature and contains information on the information to be extracted, the levels of data quality and how to value certain occurrences of information in comparison over all literature (Lipsey and Wilson, 2001) Each study is coded at least twice and from independent coders. The coding protocol is adjusted throughout the coding process. To ensure consistency, the independent coders should exchange their approach and adjust it if necessary (Lipsey and Wilson, 2001; Stock, 1994). We coded each study based on a detailed coding protocol at least twice and categorized its research design and firm context. For research design, we distinguished between objective versus subjective measurement of AC, quantitative versus qualitative measurement of innovation, and lagged versus cross-sectional examination of the AC-INN relationship. For firm context, we coded firm size (large firms versus non-large firms) and industry (high-tech versus non-high-tech).

Step III: Meta-analytic procedure

Meta-analysis is used to integrate quantitative results across previously conducted studies and estimate the mean effect size between two variables (Hunter and Schmidt, 2004). It enables researchers to investigate the combined effect sizes and individual moderators of the studied relationship.

Data correction

The procedure requires correcting the data for statistical artifacts, such as measurement and sampling error. To correct for measurement error in the studies using perceived measures for the independent and dependent variable, we use the formula by Hunter and Schmidt (2004).

When studies did not report Cronbach alpha, which is a measure for the internal consistency of a scale (Cronbach, 1951), or used single-item measures, we substituted the missing information with the mean reliability of the particular construct across all studies (Geyskens et al., 1998). To account for sampling error, the effect sizes were weighted by the sample sizes from primary studies. This corrects the individual effect by giving more accurate studies more weight (Geyskens et al., 2009).

Computation of the main effect sizes

For our meta-analytic calculations, we used the Comprehensive Meta-Analysis software (Borenstein et al., 2006). We selected the random effects model rather than the fixed effects model in order to generate more precise outcomes, when effect sizes are not homogeneous (Hunter and Schmidt, 2004; Schmidt and Hunter, 1999). The results of our bivariate analysis of the relationship between AC and INN is shown in Table 21. This meta-analysis provides results with effect sizes from 145 independent studies representing 798,650 firms or business units from the existing dataset (Hahn-Notter, 2021). The boundaries of the 95% confidence interval (CI) are $\rho = 0.31$ and $\rho = 0.36$. In total, the weighted overall effect between AC and INN is positive ($\rho = 0.33$) and significant ($p < 0.01$). That means, that we can assume the "true" effect of AC on INN to be significantly positive and within the 95%-confidence interval of 0.31 to 0.36.

TABLE 21: Meta-analytic results of the AC-INN relationship

				95% CI		Test of null	
	k	N	ρ	Lower	Upper	Z-value	*p*-value
AC → INN	**145**	**798'650**	**0.33**	**0.31**	**0.36**	**22.72****	**< 0.01**

Notes : k = number of effect sizes; N = number of total observations; ρ = weighted mean correlations corrected for sampling and measurement error; CI 95% = 95 percent confidence interval for corrected r AC = absorptive capacity; INN = innovation performance

† $p < 0.1$
* $p < 0.05$
** $p < 0.01$

Step IV: QCA procedure

QCA allows to analyze how different explanatory attributes jointly contribute to a specific outcome (Fiss, 2011). The main benefit of this approach is the combination of qualitative and quantitative analytic features. Specifically, QCA handles high levels of causal complexity and analyzes patterns based on assessment of set memberships between causal conditions and the outcome of interest to produce configurations of high consistency and sufficiency. Two central premises underlie this set-theoretic approach: (a) cases are constituted by combinations of theoretically relevant attributes (i.e., research design and firm context); (b) the relationships between these attributes and outcomes of interest (e.g., negative or absent AC-INN relationship) can be viewed as subset relations and set membership (Fiss, 2007; Ragin, 2008). Each theoretically relevant attribute is considered to be a domain in which a case could have membership.

Reaching the same outcome (e.g., in our case "high correlation between AC and INN") through multiple configurations (equifinality) is a central characteristic of QCA (Mello, 2021). This causal complexity is reached by the combinations of conditions, which are linked to outcome or non-outcome. Those two themselves may be reflected by differing configurations of conditions. Equifinality provides value to MAQCA, as the discovery of the relationship between the outcome and the boundary conditions is the focus. In the procedures for QCA, we follow Mello (2021) and Duşa (2019).

Crisp-set QCA (csQCA) and fuzzy-set QCA (fsQCA) are the most common analytic approaches in QCA. csQCA is a style of QCA which considers membership in a certain set to be either fully in or fully out. FsQCA, allows for partial set membership (Duşa, 2019). We employ QCA, with crisp set calibrations, for all conditions and a fuzzy set calibration for the outcome. This is done because of the underlying data structure.

QCA can add value to research based on the ability to uncover complex relationships. This is based on the assumption that conjunctural causation is present. The configurational perspective expects, that a specific set of conditions is present, when an effect from one condition on the outcome is observed (Schneider and Wagemann, 2012). Adopting this perspective is a difference to other methods of analysis, which assume a constant effect of a condition on an outcome over all considered cases (Mello, 2021). The change in conditions between cases affects the relationship between a condition and the outcome. This can be uncovered using configurational methods, like QCA. When utilizing QCA for analysis, the process looks as follows. First, outcome and conditions have to be selected. In this case, this means that a decision must be made as to which boundary conditions should or should not be evaluated with regard to their relevance for determining a high positive correlation between AC and INN. When the outcome and conditions have been selected, they need to be calibrated based on the raw data and the truth table is constructed (Mello, 2021). The truth table is the representation of all possible combinations of the presence or absence of conditions. Each row represents a unique combinatorial possibility. Thus, the number of rows in the truth table is determined by the number of conditions which are used in an analysis. It is calculated as 2^k with k being equal to the number of conditions in the analysis. Therefore, in this study, with five conditions, the number of truth table rows is 32 (Mello, 2021). Cases are assigned to the truth table in the row in which they hold the highest membership score (Ragin, 1987). Further, the truth table is minimized to find necessary and sufficient configurations of conditions. This is done using an algorithm. The initially common (enhanced)Quine-McCluskey algorithms (QMC/ eQMC) have been replaced by the Consistency Cubes algorithm. The latter is the default minimization algorithm in the QCA package for R, as it is superior in computational performance with identical results (Duşa, 2019; Mello, 2021). Ultimately, the findings from the QCA analysis are discussed.

Sample description

The sample on which the analysis is performed, results from the meta-analytic procedures in the earlier parts of this article. However, given the analysis of the boundary conditions, we assess the factors described in more detail in the following. The original sample for the meta-analysis has to be adapted to be able to perform QCA analysis. Some of the 145 primary studies to be analyzed with meta-analytic procedures, have to be dropped for QCA analysis, because of missing information on at least one of the boundary conditions. Therefore, the sample size for QCA analysis reduces to 72 primary studies. Descriptive statistics for the outcomes and conditions are contained in Table 22.

<u>Outcome: strong positive relationship between AC and INN (ACINN+)</u>

The outcome for the QCA analysis (n=72) is the correlation between AC and INN in the primary studies. This is available for all studies, as is central to the analysis in the MA section of this article. It ranges between -0.16 and 0.88, with a mean of 0.29 and a median of 0.28. The strong divergence in direction and strength of the relationship is reason for further analysis using QCA.

Conceptual level conditions

<u>Objective AC (objAC)</u>

This first conceptual condition measures the nature of AC. This means, whether AC was measured in a subjective (perceived) way or in an objective (archival) way. For QCA this results in a binary condition, where the study is either objective (1) or not (0). Perceived implies that individuals assessed items (questions) that make up a construct in a questionnaire on some scale (typically 1-5 or 1-7). If Cronbach alpha were reported, then a questionnaire would have been used, and hence, the measurement was subjective. Archival implies that the variable has been measured by objective means, like some measures in annual reports. 27 studies (37%) use an objective measurement.

<u>Type of innovation (qualINN)</u>

The second conceptual condition is the type of innovation. Therefore, we assess whether innovation is measured quantitatively (e.g., number of new products (Ahlin et al., 2014)) or qualitatively (e.g., ability to improve product quality (Adriansyah and Afiff, 2015)) in the primary studies. This is measured as a crisp set, where a study is either measuring INN qualitatively, coded as "1" or not, coded as "0". 31 studies (43%) use a qualitative measurement.

Temporal level conditions

Temporality of innovation (LAGGED)

on the level when considering "time", we assess, whether innovation has been measured cross-sectional or longitudinal (e.g., with allowing for a time lag). Performance effects can either be measured cross-sectional (i.e., in one point in time) versus lagged (i.e., with a time lag in between measuring an antecedent to performance and performance itself). Researchers may also have used both cross-sectional and lagged measurements. This condition is binary, as innovation is either measures in a longitudinal way (1) or not (0). 18 studies (25%) use a lagged design.

Contextual level

Firm size (SIZE)

On a contextual level, the first condition is the firm size in the primary studies. This is either large firms only, or samples including smaller firms as well. Therefore, this is a crisp set, considering the firms in the sample from SMEs (0) to large firms (1). The size of the firms is coded in categories. SMEs are considered to have 1-249 employees in Europe and 1-499 in the US or Asia. Large firms have over 250 employees in Europe and over 500 employees in the US or Asia. Depending on the location of the study sample, these coding guidelines were used to determine firm size in categories. 13 studies (18%) study large firms only.

High-tech (HIGHTECH)

The second contextual condition is the share of high-tech firms in the sample. The data is coded as having high-tech focus, or not. This is assessed via coding the share of high-tech firms in the sample of the primary studies from only high-tech (0) to only low-tech (1). This is classified by industry of the sample firms. Examples for the high-tech- industries are aircraft and spacecraft, or medical, precision and optical instruments. This may be affecting the strength of the AC effect on INN (Zou et al., 2018). 31 studies (43%) study only high-tech firms.

Calibration of sets

Outcome and conditions need to be calibrated to employ qualitative comparative analysis (QCA) (Ragin, 2008). Calibration is the process of assigning a set membership score to each case. In the case of this study, membership scores are either assigned as in a crisp or fuzzy way, where a fuzzy set was used for the outcome only. We find a solution for both options (Rohlfing, 2020). The data quality of the raw data determines the options for the calibration method. Fuzzy sets can only be derived for data on an interval or ratio level. However, crisp sets may be created on any level of data quality (Duşa, 2019). In this study, both methods of calibration are used. For all conditions, we calibrate crisp sets. For the outcome, which is not binary, we calibrate fuzzy set membership scores. The allocation of fuzzy set membership scores happens with three thresholds using the direct method. The thresholds represent full membership, full non-membership and the crossover point, respectively (Fiss, 2011). This involves overlaying the scale with appropriate criteria of what 'full membership', 'partial membership' and 'non-membership' of a set entails (Ragin, 1987, 2008). We set break points that capture differences in kind (Ragin, 1987, 2008). We follow existing literature (Linder et al., 2020) in using the 75th percentile as a full membership (0.95) threshold, the 25th percentile as a full non-membership (0.05) threshold and the median as the crossover-point (0.50) for the outcome.

TABLE 22: Description of conditions and outcome (n=72)

Outcome:	**Label**	**Outcome focus**	**Description**	**Minimum**	**Maximum**	**Median**	**Mean**	**Example**
Correlation AC-INN	ACINN+	Denotes the relationship between AC and INN in the primary studies	Strength of relationship	-0.16	0.88	0.28	0.29	Ahlin, 2014: r(AC-INN) = 0,29 Corrected R = 0,33
Conditions:	**Label**	**Condition focus**	**Description**	**Minimum**	**Maximum**	**Frequency ("0")**	**Frequency ("1")**	**Example**
Nature of AC	objAC	Denotes the nature of data used to capture AC	Objective (1) or perceived (0)	0	1	45 (63%)	27 (37%)	Belder (2015): objective measures
Type of innovation	qualINN	Denotes the type of data used to capture innovation	Quantitative (0) to only qualitative (1)	0	1	41 (57%)	31 (43%)	Lau (2015): quantity of innovation
Temporality of innovation	LAGGED	Captures time-effects of the AC-innovation relationship	Lagged, panel (1) or cross-sectional (0)	0	1	54 (75%)	18 (25%)	Torugsa (2013): time-lagged design
Context of innovation	SIZE	Captures the size of firms under study	Large firms (1), or not large firms (0)	0	1	59 (82%)	13 (18%)	Heil (2015): large firms
	HIGH-TECH	Captures the degree of knowledge intensity in the industry	High-tech (1) or not high tech (0)	0	1	41 (57%)	31 (43%)	Liu (2016): high-tech industry

The calibration of the outcomes and conditions can be observed in Table 23. The outcome, the correlation between AC and INN is calibrated as a fuzzy set using the 75th percentile as a full membership (0.95) threshold, the 25th percentile as a full non-membership (0.05) threshold and the median as the crossover-point (0.50). Therefore, full membership in the set is equal to a high positive correlation of AC to INN. For all conditions we utilize the middle between the values to calibrate the sets (0.50). These are large firm size (SIZE), high-tech (HIGHTECH), and the type of innovation (qualINN), the nature of AC (objAC), and the temporality of innovation (LAGGED). All calibrations can be found in Table 23. For crisp sets, a crossover point separates the cases into absence and presence. Given that for crisp sets, data is binary, we utilize the middle between the values to calibrate the sets. Any value between the two values characterizing the two binary values leads to the same calibration (Mello, 2021).

To gain a thorough understanding of the factors which affect the relationship between AC and INN, we run the analysis on the outcome ACINN+, representing a high positive relationship between AC and INN. We perform the analysis for the non-outcome as well. The non-outcome in Boolean logic is the part of a set which is not covered by the outcome.

Analysis for necessity

When performing QCA, the analysis of necessity of the conditions for the outcome is done first. Necessity of a condition means, that the condition is always present, when the outcome appears (Mello, 2021). For a necessary condition, the consistency of necessity for a condition has to be higher than the threshold of 0.90, which has been established as the minimum for considering a conditions necessary for the outcome (Duşa, 2019; Mello, 2021). For all five conditions we do not detect necessity for the outcome or the non-outcome. Hence, no single condition is always present, when the (non-)outcome appears.

TABLE 23: Calibration of conditions and outcome

	Label	Full Non-Membership (0.05)	Crossover Point (0.5)	Full Membership (0.95)
Outcome	ACINN+	0.11	0.29	0.45
Construct level conditions	objAC	-	0.50	-
	qualINN	-	0.50	-
Temporal level conditions	LAGGED	-	0.50	-
Contextual level conditions	SIZE	-	0.50	-
	HIGHTECH	-	0.50	-

Analysis for sufficiency

In order to analyze the sufficiency of conditions, a truth table has to be generated. This contains all possible combinations of presence and absence of conditions. It is displayed in Table 24. The number of rows is determined by the number of conditions. To allocate the cases to the rows of the truth table, given their outcome, we use an inclusion cut of consistency of 0.75 and a minimum number of cases of one. These parameters are suitable, given the research question and sample size in this particular situation (Mello, 2021). For example, the first row displays the absence of all conditions. The cases are assigned into row one and can be identified by the case number in the last column. It leads to the outcome, with an inclusion score of 0.86 and proportional reduction of inconsistency of 0.71. The most common combination of conditions is presented in row number nine, where AC is not measured objectively, INN is measured qualitatively, with no time lag in a sample of not high-tech, not large firms. For the analysis of sufficiency, we minimize the truth table (Table 24) using the QCA (Duşa, 2019) and SetMethods (Oana and Schneider, 2018) packages in RStudio (Posit team, 2022).

TABLE 24: Truth table and allocated cases for the outcome

Row-number	objAC	qualIN	LAG-GED	HIGH-TECH	Large firms	Outcome	n	Inclusion score	PRI	Cases
1	0	0	0	0	0	0	10	0.59	0.46	7,19,21,27,33,36,38,42,44,57
2	0	0	0	0	1	1	2	0.93	0.92	13,25
3	0	0	0	1	0	0	8	0.43	0.36	8,17,28,35,53,55,60,63
4	0	0	0	1	1	?	0	-	-	-
5	0	0	1	0	0	0	1	0.27	0.00	46
6	0	0	1	0	1	0	1	0.07	0.00	52
7	0	0	1	1	0	?	0	-	-	-
8	0	0	1	1	1	?	0	-	-	-
9	0	1	0	0	0	1	15	0.76	0.70	3,10,11,14,15,16,18,22,23,32,34,37,39,43,45
10	0	1	0	0	1	?	0	-	-	-
11	0	1	0	1	0	1	7	0.81	0.80	4,5,6,20,26,29,51
12	0	1	0	1	1	?	0	-	-	-
13	0	1	1	0	0	1	1	0.88	0.86	24
14	0	1	1	0	1	?	0	-	-	-
15	0	1	1	1	0	?	0	-	-	-
16	0	1	1	1	1	?	0	-	-	-
17	1	0	0	0	0	0	2	0.06	0.00	49,59
18	1	0	0	0	1	0	1	0.21	0.00	48
19	1	0	0	1	0	0	5	0.17	0.00	40,41,54,64,68
20	1	0	0	1	1	?	0	-	-	-
21	1	0	1	0	0	0	2	0.51	0.50	1,61
22	1	0	1	0	1	0	1	0.08	0.00	50
23	1	0	1	1	0	0	2	0.11	0.00	47,69
24	1	0	1	1	1	0	6	0.14	0.09	30,56,62,66,71,72
25	1	1	0	0	0	0	2	0.01	0.00	65,70
26	1	1	0	0	1	?	0	-	-	-
27	1	1	0	1	0	1	1	1.00	1.00	2
28	1	1	0	1	1	1	1	0.99	0.99	9
29	1	1	1	0	0	0	1	0.04	0	58
30	1	1	1	0	1	0	1	0.64	0.43	31
31	1	1	1	1	0	0	2	0.50	0.49	12,67
32	1	1	1	1	1	?	0	-	-	-

We report the parsimonious solutions. The parameters used are a minimum number of cases of one and minimum consistency of 0.75. Figure 10 and Figure 11 present the results of our QCA analyses of firms' AC as predictor of innovation performance, given the boundary conditions. We tested the configurations leading to the outcome: AC strongly boosting innovation (strong positive effect) and the non-outcome. The latter means not having strong positive boost on innovation (absence of strong positive effect). Black circles (●) indicate the presence of a condition, and circles with a cross-out (⊗) indicate its absence (Ragin and Fiss, 2008). Blank spaces in a solution indicate a "doesn't matter" situation in which the causal condition may be either present or absent.

Our solution in Figure 10 shows three configurations leading to the presence of a strongly positive AC-INN relationship. A configuration, as the result of QCA analysis is a combination of values for conditions, which surpass the thresholds for being considered as leading to an outcome (Duşa, 2019; Mello, 2021; Ragin, 1987). Four configurations leading to its absence are displayed in Figure 11. The two configurations leading to a strongly positive AC-INN relationship exhibit acceptable consistency (0.80). Unique coverages for these solutions indicate that each combination offers a unique contribution to the explanation of this relationship. Moreover, the combined solution configurations account for about 60% of membership in the strong AC-INN relationship. For consistency, a value of at least 0.75 is found to be high enough to warrant research attention. However, there is no minimum coverage level, as it depends on the research context. Lower coverage levels are typically expected in exploratory research and less controlled environments. Additionally, there is often a trade-off between high consistency and coverage levels. If coverage levels approach 1.00, it may indicate a selection of conditions that lacks explanatory power. (Duşa, 2019; Greckhamer et al., 2013; Mello, 2021)

For the non-outcome, we find three models of solution configurations. We report Model 1. The four configurations leading to the absence of strongly positive AC-INN relationship account for about 52% of membership in the non-outcome and also exhibit an acceptable consistency (0.89) and coverage (0.52).

A strong positive relationship between AC and INN is especially found, when AC is measured subjectively, whilst measuring INN quality. This is displayed in the first configuration. The second configuration shows, that the strong positive relationship is also present, when AC is measured subjectively, INN data is cross-sectional and large firms are assessed. The third configuration shows, that a strong AC-INN relationship is found when innovation is assessed qualitatively, on cross-sectional data from high-tech firms. All three configurations exhibit good consistency.

FIGURE 10: Configurations for strong positive AC - INN relationship (n=72)

	Solution (pars.)		
Configuration	1	2	3
objAC	⊗	⊗	
qualINN	●		●
LAGGED		⊗	⊗
SIZE		●	
HIGHTECH			●
n	23	2	9
Consistency	0.78	0.93	0.85
Raw Coverage	0.49	0.05	0.21
Unique Coverage	0.37	0.05	0.06
Overall Solution Consistency	0.80		
Overall Solution Coverage	0.60		

A negative or weak positive relationship between AC and INN is found in the following configurations. These can be observed in Figure 11. The negative or weak positive relationship can be observed when INN is measured quantitatively, with cross-sectional data on large firms. This is the first configuration. The second configuration, leading to the same relationship is described as follows. AC is measured objectively and INN quality is assessed on a sample of not-high-tech and not large firms. The third configuration is characterized by cross-sectional studies, which measure AC objectively and assess the quantity of innovation. The fourth configuration represents studies, where innovation quantity is measured, in high-tech firms. All the configurations exhibit good consistency.

FIGURE 11: Configurations for negative or weak positive AC - INN relationship (n=72)

	Solution (pars.)			
Configuration	1	2	3	4
objAC		●	●	
qualINN	⊗	●	⊗	⊗
LAGGED	⊗		⊗	
SIZE	●	⊗		
HIGHTECH		⊗		●
n	8	3	8	13
Consistency	0.88	0.98	0.86	0.86
Raw Coverage	0.20	0.08	0.20	0.31
Unique Coverage	0.05	0.03	<0.01	<0.01
Overall Solution Consistency	0.89			
Overall Solution Coverage	0.52			

Overall, our analyses reveal that the AC-INN relationship is strongly positive in studies which are distinctly different from those in which the AC-INN relationship is weak or non-positive. We can observe that all of the paths, which lead to a strong positive relationship, are characterized by (1) AC that has been measured subjectively (or "it doesn't matter), (2) INN that has been assessed qualitatively (or "it doesn't matter), (3) cross-sectional INN data (or "it doesn't matter), (4) large firms (or "it doesn't matter), (5) high-tech firms (or "it doesn't matter). Three out of four paths (path 1, 3, and 4), which lead to a negative or weak positive relationship, are characterized by (1) AC that has been measured objectively (or "it doesn't matter), (2) INN that has been measured quantitatively (or "it doesn't matter), (3) cross-sectional INN data (or "it doesn't matter), (4) large firms (or "it doesn't matter), (5) high-tech firms (or "it doesn't matter). The second path has different characteristics; however, it only holds for three studies.

Thereby, we add depth to our findings in the earlier part, and clarify which combinations of conditions result in the absence or presence of an INN effect from AC. All findings present good measures of consistency and coverage.

Step V: Discussion of and implications from MAQCA findings

This research performed a meta-analysis on the relationship between AC and INN. Many studies have assessed this relationship, finding diverging conclusions in terms of strength and direction of the relationship. The relationship between AC and INN has been investigated comprehensively in the past – in single studies as well as in meta-analyses (Maldonado et al., 2018; Song et al., 2018; Yao et al., 2020; Zou et al., 2018). According to Zahra and George (2002), AC promotes innovations and new product development and hence, contributes to the achievement of competitive advantages. Also, companies with a well-developed AC recognize environmental changes as well as new trends (Zahra and George, 2002). Additionally, an effective use of AC can determine whether a firm is able to correspond to customer needs (Teece, 2007). The results of existing studies have not been completely consistent, there are diverging conclusions in terms of strength and direction of the relationship (Marabelli and Newell, 2014; Volberda et al., 2010). One can assume an overall positive relationship between AC and INN, which our meta-analysis on 145 primary studies confirms.

Our study further clarifies conditions under which a beneficial capability such as AC leads to innovation success and under which it doesn't. Indeed, our results show that the boundary conditions of a study's design are relevant to the findings that result from it. We contribute to management and entrepreneurship research by clarifying boundary conditions for AC and drawing attention to contexts in which firms either do not benefit from absorbing more knowledge, or these benefits are not quantitatively measured. Our novel combination of methods enables us to summarize prior findings with meta-analytical data and understand inherent contradictions with the configurational perspective.

Implications for researchers

The configurations of boundary conditions which lead to the differences in direction and strength of the relationship between AC and INN are insightful. The findings we report are a step towards clarifying under which research design a certain strength and direction of the AC-INN relationship occurs. Our meta-analysis supports the findings of previous research work, which has determined the positive effect of AC on INN (Jiménez-Jiménez and Sanz-Valle, 2011; Kostopoulos et al., 2011; Leal-Rodríguez et al., 2014; Tsai, 2001). In addition, we showcase, the configurations of study conditions that result in strong or not-strong relationship between AC and INN. We show that most studies which exhibit a consistent configuration of conditions are characterized by subjective AC measurement and qualitative INN measurement. This should encourage researchers to adapt study settings which are found to exhibit a certain outcome and test whether these results hold when changing certain boundary conditions. Replication studies may be pursued this way. The multitude of research findings on the AC-INN relationship can be considered driven by the research setting to some extent. Given the complex combinations of setting, research should replicate previous findings and extend those, to test, under which conditions the results hold, and under which they do not (Ethiraj et al., 2016). MAQCA can therefore be used to understand which diverging findings occur under which conditions and be a starting point for replications. In comparison to MASEM, MAQCA is more exploratory and less restrictive on the source data, as well as better suited for smaller samples, which is a benefit, given possibly low amount of studies that assess a certain relationship (Bergh et al., 2016; Mello, 2021).

Implications for practitioners

Practitioners can gain insights from this study, as we highlight the value of AC for INN (Song et al., 2018). That means, that support towards the growth in AC helps firms in terms of INN. This is especially prominent in firms which are large and which operate in high-tech industries, as two configurations find. No strong AC-INN relation is found in a configuration where small non-high-tech firms are assessed, further reinforcing the finding. The use of objective and subjective performance measures, which has been subject to research for some time (Dess and Robinson, 1984), can affect the outcome, and should therefore be considered. When assessing research findings, practitioners need to be aware about what kind of research findings is applicable to their firm setting.

4.7. Discussion

The present study demonstrates the value of combining meta-analytic methods and QCA. MAQCA introduces the possibility to assess configurations of conditions which lead to the presence or absence of the outcome of interest from the base of on meta-analytic data/ correlations. This is helpful in many circumstances. It enables researchers to assess conflicting research findings in depth. The results that stem from the meta-analytic part of the MAQCA method provide a synthesis of research findings, which is a necessary first step to finding an agreement on relationships of constructs. The QCA analysis reveals the configurations of conditions which lead to more in-depth findings in these relationships. This is valuable in uncovering the differences in research designs, which may be responsible for differences in the results of research. Compared to a traditional meta-analysis, where differences among primary studies are investigated by performing a subgroup meta-analysis, MAQCA can serve configurations of boundary conditions that are required for a specific outcome. Therefore, boundary conditions of the research design can be assessed more in-depth. These might be measurement of constructs, temporality of measurement, characteristics of sample and more. The great value of QCA is that it conceptually entails equifinality, i.e., multiple configurations to a certain outcome, and causal complexity, i.e., multiple conditions combined in different configurations as ways to an outcome. This is not given in commonly used methods. The possibility to find configurations of conditions which are linked to the (non-)outcome adds value to second level research. We propose using MAQCA, with a meta-analysis as a baseline and QCA as a way to add depth in management and entrepreneurship research. However, there are also other meta-analytic synthesis methods, such as meta-analytic structural equation modeling (MASEM), meta-regression (MARA), or meta-synthesis.

Implications for researchers

The presented illustration of MAQCA holds several implications for researchers, in addition to the substantial implications for the AC-INN relationship, which have been discussed above. Referring to MAQCA as a research method can provide additional insights to MA studies, which has proven its worth in research areas outside of management and entrepreneurship (Moore et al., 2018; Thomas et al., 2014). Objective and subjective measurement can be compared in different sample situations, adding a level of insight. This can add to the discussion on the suitability of, for example, objective and subjective measures for organizational performance (Dess and Robinson, 1984). The need to adapt measurements to fit the sample is further highlighted from the method (Behn, 2003).

Implications for practitioners

Practitioners may further benefit from this, as understanding the differences in research can assist when assessing information for decision making (Eisenhardt and Zbaracki, 1992). They can better understand which research findings apply most to their specific situation. Resource allocation can therefore be adapted by management to the specific configurations of conditions that research has assessed, which are equivalent to the firms' situation and have been discovered from MAQCA studies. For entrepreneurs, setting up new ventures can be done more thoughtfully, given the MAQCA findings' increased specificity. Therefore, the study results can be more "realistically" presented, as multiple relationships may be described.

Limitations

As with any method, MAQCA has some limitations and particularities, which need to be considered when utilizing the method. A meta-analysis compares and summarizes single studies into one meta-analytic study even though the information as well as coding processes and results in primary, individual studies vary. Meta analyses usually include every study in a specific research area, regardless of their quality, which might lead to biased results. Also, meta-analyses mainly address broad research questions, therefore specific questions might not be possible to be answered with only a meta-analytic approach.

Furthermore, limitations are also introduced by QCA. The sample that can be fully assessed with MAQCA may be smaller than the sample they could be assessed with MA only. This is a result of the fact that the primary studies have to report data on all conditions to be assessed. This may be a subset of the studies that assess the baseline relationship. Further, QCA assesses the more extreme values for the (non-)outcome. This results in possibly less emphasis on studies, which find a relationship strength that is close to the baseline result. This limitation, however, can at the same time be considered as a strength. It highlights especially studies, which have extreme differences in their results. These are the ones, which produce the biggest debate in research. By analyzing those, MAQCA provides the differences in research design that are most influential on the results.

4.8. Conclusion

To conclude, MAQCA, as an example of a combination of QCA and a meta-analysis, provides value to explain diverging research findings. We encourage researchers to make the method their own and apply it to problems in research, where results are inconclusive. MAQCA can provide the conditions under which the diverging results can be explained by differences in research design. We generate an avenue for replications studies, where they assess research questions by adapting prominent boundary conditions that have been found to be linked to the (non-)outcome.

The MAQCA process can ultimately be condensed into five steps. First, the setting of the research question, then the identification and coding of the relevant studies. Third, the meta-analytical procedures are performed. Fourth, the QCA analysis is performed. Ultimately is the discussion of the results and implications from the findings of the MAQCA analysis.

5. General Conclusion

5.1. Summary of the thesis

New ventures are drivers of innovation, economic growth, prosperity, and wealth in the world. Therefore, they are an integral part of any economy. With their help challenges of any kind, even in terms of climate change or the supply of clean water can be tackled. Great examples of new ventures or innovation which went on to provide immeasurable value to the world are the invention of the first automobile by Carl Benz in 1886, the printing press by Johannes Gutenberg in 1450 or the invention of vaccination by Edward Jenner in 1796. Given the risk that is involved in new ventures, many new ventures fail. To optimally support and research new ventures, it is important to measure their performance, and to do so "appropriately". Furthermore, the determinants of new venture performance are important to understand. Therefore, this dissertation is researching how new venture performance is measured, what factors are linked with the success of new ventures in getting an idea to the market and how a novel combination of research methods can lead to more insightful research findings. The first research project (Chapter 2) systematically assesses the literature which uses new venture performance measures. Over 15 years, from 2007 to 2021, 255 research articles, with 489 new venture performance measures, are evaluated. Therefrom, it can be found, that a multitude of 168 different performance measures is used. These are grouped into dimensions of measures. The usage of the measures is found to be adapted to the age of the new ventures that are studied. In early stages, measures of innovation, funding and sales are more relevant. Opportunity and gestational measures are further common, in absence of accounting figures. These become more prominent with increasing age of the assessed new ventures, as data availability increases. In alignment with the lifecycle, financial market measures increase in usage with time, while funding measures decrease. The second project (Chapter 3) assesses which combinations of conditions from Timmons' model of the entrepreneurial process are linked to success and speed of getting an idea to the market. This happens on a sample of 181 new ventures from the representative PSED II dataset. We find that a combination of an attractive opportunity and high industry experience leads to success, while the lack of one of the two, in combination with a lack in resources, leads to failure. New ventures that are quick in reaching the market, are mostly characterized by an experienced team in combination with high social capital. The configurational nature and value of the

Timmons (1999) model of the entrepreneurial process is underlined. In addition, the relevance of industry experience and an attractive opportunity are essential findings. Further, the finding of a lack of resources being linked to failure, whilst the presence of resources is not linked to success. The third study (Chapter 4) shows the value of combining meta-analytic methods with qualitative comparative analysis. By doing so, researchers profit from finding the main effect in meta-analysis as well as being able to explain differences in research findings from the configurations of conditions from research design or methodology. An illustration of the benefits is given on the relationship of absorptive capacity and innovation.

Overall, this dissertation adds to research by firstly, providing an overview of new venture performance measures and their dimensions. This is added value for research, which helps researchers produce more targeted research. Secondly, the value of the elements of the Timmons (1999) model is confirmed, making one of configurational assessments of new venture performance drivers from idea to market. This assists researchers in understanding this phenomenon and the theoretically complex configurational nature of factors in new venture performance. Thirdly, MAQCA is promoted to researchers as a way to produce more insightful meta-studies to uncover reasoning behind diverging results in studies assessing correlational relationships between constructs.

5.2. Contributions to research and practice

This dissertation contributes by exploring measures of new venture performance over the lifecycle, represented by age. This is crucial because it allows us to track the progress of new ventures and understand how they evolve over time. It's also worth noting that the way new venture performance is measured differs amongst researchers. This research highlights the importance of standardized processes to ensure consistency and comparability. Practitioners may use our results to gain a better understanding of how to assess new ventures in the early stages and therefore increase effectiveness of support for new ventures and return for investors, governments, and the society.

Another research contribution worth mentioning is the use of Qualitative Comparative Analysis (QCA) to clarify the importance of different parts of the Timmons (1999) model in configurations at the gap from idea to market. By using QCA, researchers can identify which configurations of parts of the model are essential for a new venture's success and how they interact with each other. The crucial role of resources, opportunity and team are highlighted, as well as their configurational nature confirmed, answering the call for more QCA research in new venture research (Douglas et al., 2020). Practitioners may now better understand how new ventures can reach the market, what takes them there, and given where they stand, we can specifically support them in the areas in which they lack resources.

Moreover, MAQCA is a novel approach to assessing contradicting research findings. MAQCA allows researchers to analyze various factors that might influence a relationship between constructs and determine influential ones. This additionally helps practitioners, identify the critical factors to focus on and optimize the utility from support. Through the usage of MAQCA as a research method, an additional level of analysis is brought to MA studies, which has proven its worth in research areas outside of management and entrepreneurship (Moore et al., 2018; Thomas et al., 2014). This can add to the discussion on the suitability of, for example, objective and subjective measures for organizational performance (Dess and Robinson, 1984) and reminds researchers of the importance of appropriate measurement of constructs (Behn, 2003).

In summary, research plays a crucial role in improving our understanding of management and entrepreneurship. By measuring new venture performance, using QCA, and developing novel approaches like MAQCA, researchers can identify critical factors for new venture success. Practitioners can then use this knowledge to support new ventures and increase returns for investors, and society. Governments can also pursue initiatives that increase entrepreneurship by developing programs that cultivate key personality traits in individuals.

5.3. Limitations

This dissertation is not free from limitations. Each study comes with its own limitations, based on the approaches and research questions.

Systematic literature reviews are always limited to the information from primary studies. In the case of this dissertation, many primary studies lack information on the age of the new ventures they study. This is then reflected in the fact that not all primary studies that have been found using new venture performance measures can be utilized in the alignment with new venture age. In addition, the first study is limited to top journals. The results may differ when accounting for less highly rated journals. Given the expected rigor, it may be assumed, that the fit between performance measure and new venture age or lifecycle stage is less good in lower ranked publications.

The definition of a new venture is another limitation. Many studies do not provide clear-cut definitions of new ventures when researching them. This limits work on those primary studies, as it hinders comparability.

When working with qualitative comparative analysis (QCA), configurations that are found may not be generalizable to other samples. While the sample, used in Chapter 3, is representative of the United States, the results may not be applicable to any new venture in different geographical contexts. The focus on the United States, does not allow to generalize the findings directly to other regional or cultural contexts. Furthermore, the data does not capture the new ventures after reaching the market. Therefore, long term performance is not assessed.

Limitations of MAQCA are to be considered when using the method. Meta-analysis combines and summarizes studies, even though coding processes and results may vary. Subjectivity in coding processes can be an issue, and including all studies in a research area may lead to biased results. Additionally, QCA may have a smaller sample size than MA. It assesses extreme values for outcomes, which may result in less emphasis on studies with results close to the baseline. However, this can also be a strength as it highlights studies with extreme differences in results, which are influential in research design.

5.4. Avenues for future research

The limitations described above may be starting points for future research. Research on performance measurement over the new venture lifecycle could be advantageous. Tracking firms from their emergence over at least a decade, utilizing multiple measures of new venture performance would allow a more rigorous comparison of measures and be insightful. New venture performance measurement literature would further benefit from researchers assessing determinants of new venture performance. Especially the age of the new ventures and the timespan for which new venture performance measures deliver consistently significant results in new venture performance prediction. QCA can be applied to more situations in entrepreneurship research. It has the potential to uncover relationships that have not been explored (Douglas et al., 2020). Future research may also assess more relationships in the context of new ventures with MAQCA. Drivers of new venture performance, which have been found, may be assessed in terms of the boundary conditions under which they have been found. Potential conditions may be venture age, size, industry, or individual characteristics of the entrepreneurs. A replication and extension of existing meta-analysis can be a promising avenue for researchers, given the added explanatory power of MAQCA. An example is the field of success factors in new ventures (Song et al., 2008).

5.5. Conclusion

The first study in this dissertation discusses how researchers use a variety of measures to assess new venture performance and how measurement changes over the lifecycle of the venture. The study aims to assist researchers in selecting appropriate measures and provide guidance for practitioners to optimize resource allocation and support.

The second study in this dissertation examines the configurations of conditions that lead to new ventures reaching the market and the speed at which they do so. The study finds that a lack of resources hinders new ventures in their progress and highlights the importance of experience in the industry and starting a new venture to get an idea to market quickly.

The third study in this dissertation explains how MAQCA, a combination of QCA and meta-analysis, can explain diverging research findings. Researchers are encouraged to use this method to assess research questions and generate an avenue for replication studies.

Overall, these texts should contribute to the understanding of new venture creation and provide insights for both researchers and practitioners in assessing and supporting new ventures. The integration of new venture performance measures, configurations for new venture idea to market success, and the combined use of meta-analysis and QCA represent a valuable advance in management and entrepreneurship research. Together, they provide comprehensive insights that enhance our understanding of what drives new venture performance. This allows for researchers contributing to more effective strategies for fostering and sustaining new ventures.

REFERENCES

Acs, Z.J., Armington, C., 2006. *Entrepreneurship, geography, and american economic growth.* Cambridge University Press, Cambridge, pp.264.

Adriansyah, A., Afiff, A.Z., 2015. Organizational Culture, Absorptive Capacity, Innovation Performance and Competitive Advantage: An Integrated Assessment in Indonesian Banking Industry. *The South East Asian Journal of Management*, *9* (1), 70.

Aguinis, H., Pierce, C.A., Bosco, F.A., Dalton, D.R., Dalton, C.M., 2011. Debunking Myths and Urban Legends About Meta-Analysis. *Organizational Research Methods*, *14* (2), 306–331.

Aguinis, H., Ramani, R.S., Alabduljader, N., 2023. Best-Practice Recommendations for Producers, Evaluators, and Users of Methodological Literature Reviews. *Organizational Research Methods*, *26* (1), 46–76.

Ahlin, B., Drnovšek, M., Hisrich, R.D., 2014. Exploring the Moderating Effects of Absorptive Capacity on the Relationship Between Social Networks and Innovation. *Journal for East European Management Studies*, 213–235.

Albert, L.S., DeTienne, D.R., 2016. Founding Resources and Intentional Exit Sales Strategies: An Imprinting Perspective. *Group & Organization Management*, *41* (6), 823–846.

Aldrich, H., Auster, E.R., 1986. Even Dwarfs Started Small: Liabilities of Age and Size and Their Strategic Implications. *Research in Organizational Behavior*, *8*, 165–198.

Alexander, P.A., 2020. Methodological Guidance Paper: The Art and Science of Quality Systematic Reviews. *Review of Educational Research*, *90* (1), 6–23.

Ali, M., Kan, K.A.S., Sarstedt, M., 2016. Direct and Configurational Paths of Absorptive Capacity and Organizational Innovation to Successful Organizational Performance. *Journal of Business Research*, *69* (11), 5317–5323.

Almer-Jarz, D.A., Schwarz, E.J., Breitenecker, R.J., 2008. New Venture Teams: The Relationship Between Initial Team Characteristics, Team Processes and Performance. *Entrepreneurship, Sustainable Growth and Performance*, pp. 163–193.

Alvesson, M., Sandberg, J., 2011. Generating Research Questions Through Problematization. *Academy of Management Review*, *36* (2), 247–271.

Arentz, J., Sautet, F., Storr, V., 2013. Prior-Knowledge and Opportunity Identification. *Small Business Economics*, *41*, 461–478.

Bacharach, S.B., 1989. Organizational Theories: Some Criteria for Evaluation. *Academy of Management Review*, *14* (4), 496–515.

Bamford, C.E., Dean, T.J., McDougall, P.P., 2000. An Examination of the Impact of Initial Founding Conditions and Decisions Upon the Performance of New Bank Start-Ups. *Journal of Business Venturing*, *15* (3), 253–277.

Barley, S.R., 2006. When I Write My Masterpiece: Thoughts on What Makes a Paper Interesting. *Academy of Management Journal*, *49* (1), 16–20.

Barney, J., 1991. Firm Resources and Sustained Competitive Advantage. *Journal of Management*, *17* (1), 99–120.

Barney, J.B., 2020. Measuring Firm Performance in a Way That Is Consistent with Strategic Management Theory. *Academy of Management Discoveries*, *6* (1), 5–7.

Baron, R.A., Markman, G.D., 2000. Beyond Social Capital: How Social Skills Can Enhance Entrepreneurs' Success. *Academy of Management Perspectives*, *14* (1), 106–116.

Baum, J.A., Silverman, B.S., 2004. Picking Winners or Building Them? Alliance, Intellectual, and Human Capital as Selection Criteria in Venture Financing and Performance of Biotechnology Startups. *Journal of Business Venturing*, *19* (3), 411–436.

Baum, J.R., Locke, E.A., Smith, K.G., 2001. A Multidimensional Model of Venture Growth. *Academy of Management Journal*, *44* (2), 292–303.

Baumgartner, M., Thiem, A., 2020. Often Trusted but Never (Properly) Tested: Evaluating Qualitative Comparative Analysis. *Sociological Methods & Research*, *49* (2), 279–311.

Behn, R.D., 2003. Why Measure Performance? Different Purposes Require Different Measures. *Public Administration Review*, *63* (5), 586–606.

Belderbos, R., Carree, M., Lokshin, B., Fernández Sastre, J., 2015. Inter-Temporal Patterns of R&D Collaboration and Innovative Performance. *The Journal of Technology Transfer*, *40*, 123–137.

Bergh, D.D., Aguinis, H., Heavey, C., Ketchen, D.J., Boyd, B.K., Su, P., Lau, C.L.L., Joo, H., 2016. Using Meta-analytic Structural Equation Modeling to Advance Strategic Management Research: Guidelines and an Empirical Illustration via the Strategic Leadership-performance Relationship. *Strategic Management Journal*, *37* (3), 477–497.

Bhide, A., 2000. *The origin and evolution of new businesses.* Oxford University Press, Oxford.

Boeker, W., Wiltbank, R., 2005. New Venture Evolution and Managerial Capabilities. *Organization Science*, *16* (2), 123–133.

Boole, G., 1854. *An investigation of the laws of thought: on which are founded the mathematical theories of logic and probabilities.* Walton and Maberly.

Borenstein, M., Hedges, L., Higgins, J., Rothstein, H., 2006. Comprehensive Meta-Analysis, Englewood, USA.

Borenstein, M., Hedges, L.V., Higgins, J.P.T., Rothstein, H.R., 2009. *Introduction to meta-analysis.* John Wiley & Sons, Chichester.

Borenstein, M., Higgins, J.P.T., 2013. Meta-Analysis and Subgroups. *Prevention Science*, *14*, 134–143.

Brinckmann, J., Grichnik, D., Kapsa, D., 2010. Should Entrepreneurs Plan or Just Storm the Castle? A Meta-Analysis on Contextual Factors Impacting the Business Planning–performance Relationship in Small Firms. *Journal of Business Venturing*, *25* (1), 24–40.

Brinckmann, J., Salomo, S., Gemuenden, H.G., 2011. Financial Management Competence of Founding Teams and Growth of New Technology–Based Firms. *Entrepreneurship Theory and Practice*, *35* (2), 217–243.

Brockner, J., Higgins, E., Low, M.B., 2004. Regulatory Focus Theory and the Entrepreneurial Process. *Journal of Business Venturing*, *19* (2), 203–220.

Brownell, K.M., McMullen, J.S., O'Boyle, E.H., 2021. Fatal Attraction: A Systematic Review and Research Agenda of the Dark Triad in Entrepreneurship. *Journal of Business Venturing*, *36* (3), 106106.

Brüderl, J., Preisendörfer, P., Ziegler, R., 1992. Survival Chances of Newly Founded Business Organizations. *American Sociological Review*, *57* (2), 227–242.

Brush, C.G., Edelman, L.F., Manolova, T.S., 2008. The Effects of Initial Location, Aspirations, and Resources on Likelihood of First Sale in Nascent Firms. *Journal of Small Business Management*, *46* (2), 159–182.

Brush, C.G., Vanderwerf, P.A., 1992. A Comparison of Methods and Sources for Obtaining Estimates of New Venture Performance. *Journal of Business Venturing*, *7* (2), 157–170.

Busse, C., Kach, A.P., Wagner, S.M., 2017. Boundary Conditions: What They Are, How to Explore Them, Why We Need Them, and When to Consider Them. *Organizational Research Methods*, *20* (4), 574–609.

Campbell, C.A., 1992. A Decision Theory Model for Entrepreneurial Acts. *Entrepreneurship: Theory & Practice*, *17* (1), 21–27.

Carton, R., Hofer, C., 2006. *Measuring organizational performance: Metrics for entrepreneurship and strategic management research.* Edward Elgar Publishing, Cheltenham.

Carton, R.B., Hofer, C.W., 2010. Organizational Financial Performance: Identifying and Testing Multiple Dimensions. *Academy of Entrepreneurship Journal*, *16* (2), 1–22.

Castrogiovanni, G.J., 1996. Pre-Startup Planning and the Survival of New Small Businesses: Theoretical Linkages. *Journal of Management*, *22* (6), 801–822.

Chandler, G.N., Hanks, S.H., 1994. Market Attractiveness, Resource-Based Capabilities, Venture Strategies, and Venture Performance. *Journal of Business Venturing*, *9* (4), 331–349.

Chandler, G.N., Honig, B., Wiklund, J., 2005. Antecedents, Moderators, and Performance Consequences of Membership Change in New Venture Teams. *Journal of Business Venturing*, *20* (5), 705–725.

Chowdhury, F., Audretsch, D.B., 2023. Paradoxes of Accelerator Programs and New Venture Performance: Do Varieties of Experiences Make a Difference? *Small Business Economics*, 1–29.

Chrisman, J.J., Bauerschmidt, A., Hofer, C.W., 1998. The Determinants of New Venture Performance: An Extended Model. *Entrepreneurship Theory and Practice*, *23* (1), 5–29.

Coad, A., 2018. Firm Age: A Survey. *Journal of Evolutionary Economics*, *28* (1), 13–43.

Coad, A., Frankish, J., Roberts, R.G., Storey, D.J., 2013. Growth Paths and Survival Chances: An Application of Gambler's Ruin Theory. *Journal of Business Venturing*, *28* (5), 615–632.

Cockayne, D., 2019. What Is a Startup Firm? A Methodological and Epistemological Investigation into Research Objects in Economic Geography. *Geoforum*, *107*, 77–87.

Cohen, W.M., Levinthal, D.A., 1989. Innovation and Learning: The Two Faces of R & D. *The Economic Journal*, *99* (397), 569–596.

Cohen, W.M., Levinthal, D.A., 1990. Absorptive Capacity: A New Perspective on Learning and Innovation. *Administrative Science Quarterly*, *35* (1), 128–152.

Colombo, M.G., Grilli, L., 2005. Start-up Size: The Role of External Financing. *Economics Letters*, *88* (2), 243–250.

Combs, J.G., Russell Crook, T., Shook, C.L., 2005. The Dimensionality of Organizational Performance and Its Implications for Strategic Management Research, in: Ketchen, D.J., Bergh, D.D. (Eds.), Research methodology in strategy and management, vol. 2, 1 ed. Research methodology in strategy and management 1. Emerald Group Publishing Limited; Elsevier, Amsterdam, Boston, pp. 259–286.

Cooper, A.C., Gimeno-Gascon, F., Woo, C.Y., 1994. Initial Human and Financial Capital as Predictors of New Venture Performance. *Journal of Business Venturing*, *9* (5), 371–395.

Cooper, H.M., 2015. *Research synthesis and meta-analysis: A step-by-step approach,* 5th ed. Applied social research methods series, *2.* SAGE Publications, Los Angeles, pp.315.

Cooper, H.M., Hedges, L.V., Valentine, J.C. (Eds.), 2009. The Handbook of Research Synthesis and Meta-Analysis, 2nd ed. Russell Sage Foundation, New York, pp.615.

Cosh, A., Cumming, D., Hughes, A., 2009. Outside Enterpreneurial Capital. *The Economic Journal*, *119* (540), 1494–1533.

Creswell, J.W., 2014. *Research design*: Qualitative, Quantitative, and Mixed Methods Approaches, 4th ed. Sage, Los Angeles, pp.273.

Cronbach, L.J., 1951. Coefficient Alpha and the Internal Structure of Tests. *Psychometrika*, *16* (3), 297–334.

Curtin, R.T., Reynolds, P.D., 2018. Panel Study of Entrepreneurial Dynamics, PSED II, United States, 2005-2011. ICPSR - Interuniversity Consortium for Political and Social Research.

Dahlqvist, J., Davidsson, P., Wiklund, J., 2000. Initial Conditions as Predictors of New Venture Performance: A Replication and Extension of the Cooper Et Al. Study. *Enterprise and Innovation Management Studies*, *1* (1), 1–17.

Davidsson, P., 2015. Entrepreneurial Opportunities and the Entrepreneurship Nexus: A Re-Conceptualization. *Journal of Business Venturing*, *30* (5), 674–695.

Davidsson, P., Honig, B., 2003. The Role of Social and Human Capital Among Nascent Entrepreneurs. *Journal of Business Venturing*, *18* (3), 301–331.

Davis, J., Mengersen, K., Bennett, S., Mazerolle, L., 2014. Viewing Systematic Reviews and Meta-Analysis in Social Research Through Different Lenses. *SpringerPlus*, *3*, 1–9.

Davis, M.S., 1971. That's Interesting! Towards a Phenomenology of Sociology and a Sociology of Phenomenology. *Philosophy of the Social Sciences*, *1* (2), 309–344.

Davis, P.S., Pett, T.L., 2002. Measuring Organizational Efficiency and Effectiveness. *Journal of Management Research*, *2* (2), 87.

De Carolis, D.M., Litzky, B.E., Eddleston, K.A., 2009. Why Networks Enhance the Progress of New Venture Creation: The Influence of Social Capital and Cognition. *Entrepreneurship Theory and Practice*, *33* (2), 527–545.

de Mol, E., Khapova, S.N., Elfring, T., 2015. Entrepreneurial Team Cognition: A Review. *International Journal of Management Reviews*, *17* (2), 232–255.

Debrulle, J., Steffens, P., Bock, K.W. de, Winne, S. de, Maes, J., 2023. Configurations of Business Founder Resources, Strategy, and Environment Determining New Venture Performance. *Journal of Small Business Management*, *61* (2), 1023–1061.

Delmar, F., Shane, S., 2003. Does Business Planning Facilitate the Development of New Ventures? *Strategic Management Journal*, *24* (12), 1165–1185.

Denrell, J., 2004. Random Walks and Sustained Competitive Advantage. *Management Science*, *50* (7), 922–934.

Dess, G.G., Newport, S., Rasheed, A.M.A., 1993. Configuration Research in Strategic Management: Key Issues and Suggestions. *Journal of Management*, *19* (4), 775–795.

Dess, G.G., Robinson, R.B., 1984. Measuring Organizational Performance in the Absence of Objective Measures: The Case of the Privately-held Firm and Conglomerate Business Unit. *Strategic Management Journal*, *5* (3), 265–273.

Dimov, D., 2010. Nascent Entrepreneurs and Venture Emergence: Opportunity Confidence, Human Capital, and Early Planning. *Journal of Management Studies*, *47* (6), 1123–1153.

Doty, D.H., Glick, W.H., 1998. Common Methods Bias: Does Common Methods Variance Really Bias Results? *Organizational Research Methods*, *1* (4), 374–406.

Douglas, E.J., Shepherd, D.A., Prentice, C., 2020. Using Fuzzy-Set Qualitative Comparative Analysis for a Finer-Grained Understanding of Entrepreneurship. *Journal of Business Venturing*, *35* (1), 105970.

Du, Y., Kim, P.H., 2021. One Size Does Not Fit All: Strategy Configurations, Complex Environments, and New Venture Performance in Emerging Economies. *Journal of Business Research*, *124*, 272–285.

Duşa, A., 2019. *QCA with R*: A Comprehensive Resource. Springer, Cham, pp.278.

Edelman, L., Yli–Renko, H., 2010. The Impact of Environment and Entrepreneurial Perceptions on Venture-Creation Efforts: Bridging the Discovery and Creation Views of Entrepreneurship. *Entrepreneurship Theory and Practice*, *34* (5), 833–856.

Edwards, J.R., 2010. Reconsidering Theoretical Progress in Organizational and Management Research. *Organizational Research Methods*, *13* (4), 615–619.

Eesley, C.E., Lee, Y.S., 2021. Do University Entrepreneurship Programs Promote Entrepreneurship? *Strategic Management Journal*, *42* (4), 833–861.

Eisenhardt, K.M., Zbaracki, M.J., 1992. Strategic Decision Making. *Strategic Management Journal*, *13* (S2), 17–37.

Emami, A., Yoruk, E., Jones, P., 2023. The Interplay Between Market Need Urgency, Entrepreneurial Push and Pull Insights and Opportunity Confidence in the Course of New Venture Creation in the Developing Country Context. *Journal of Business Research*, *163*, 113882.

Ethiraj, S.K., Gambardella, A., Helfat, C.E., 2016. Replication in Strategic Management. *Strategic Management Journal*, *37* (11).

Eysenck, H.J., 1978. An Exercise in Mega-Silliness. *American Psychologist*, *33* (5), 517.

Fichter, K., Tiemann, I., 2018. Factors Influencing University Support for Sustainable Entrepreneurship: Insights from Explorative Case Studies. *Journal of Cleaner Production*, *175*, 512–524.

Fiss, P.C., 2007. A Set-Theoretic Approach to Organizational Configurations. *Academy of Management Review*, *32* (4), 1180–1198.

Fiss, P.C., 2011. Building Better Causal Theories: A Fuzzy Set Approach to Typologies in Organization Research. *Academy of Management Journal*, *54* (2), 393–420.

Fiss, P.C. (Ed.), 2013. Configurational Theory and Methods in Organizational Research, 1st ed. Research in the sociology of organizations, *38.2013.* Emerald, Bingley, pp.319.

Flor, M.L., Cooper, S.Y., Oltra, M.J., 2018. External Knowledge Search, Absorptive Capacity and Radical Innovation in High-Technology Firms. *European Management Journal*, *36* (2), 183–194.

Freeman, J., Carroll, G.R., Hannan, M.T., 1983. The Liability of Newness: Age Dependence in Organizational Death Rates. *American Sociological Review*, *48* (5), 692–710.

Furlan, A., 2019. Startup Size and Pre-Entry Experience: New Evidence from Italian New Manufacturing Ventures. *Journal of Small Business Management*, *57* (2), 679–692.

Furrer, O., Thomas, H., Goussevskaia, A., 2008. The Structure and Evolution of the Strategic Management Field: A Content Analysis of 26 Years of Strategic Management Research. *International Journal of Management Reviews*, *10* (1), 1–23.

Garkavenko, M., Beliaeva, T., Gaussier, E., Mirisaee, H., Lagnier, C., Guerraz, A., 2022. Assessing the Factors Related to a Start-up's Valuation Using Prediction and Causal Discovery. *Entrepreneurship: Theory & Practice*, *47* (5), 2017-2044.

Garnsey, E., 1998. A Theory of the Early Growth of the Firm. *Industrial and Corporate Change*, *7* (3), 523–556.

Garnsey, E., Stam, E., Heffernan, P., 2006. New Firm Growth: Exploring Processes and Paths. *Industry and Innovation*, *13* (1), 1–20.

Geyskens, I., Krishnan, R., Steenkamp, J.-B.E.M., Cunha, P.V., 2009. A Review and Evaluation of Meta-Analysis Practices in Management Research. *Journal of Management*, *35* (2), 393–419.

Geyskens, I., Steenkamp, J.-B.E.M., Kumar, N., 1998. Generalizations About Trust in Marketing Channel Relationships Using Meta-Analysis. *International Journal of Research in Marketing*, *15* (3), 223–248.

Gilbert, B.A., McDougall, P.P., Audretsch, D.B., 2006. New Venture Growth: A Review and Extension. *Journal of Management*, *32* (6), 926–950.

Glass, G.V., 1977. Integrating Findings: The Meta-Analysis of Research. *Review of Research in Education*, *5* (1), 351–379.

Greckhamer, T., Misangyi, V.F., Fiss, P.C., 2013. Chapter 3 the Two QCAs: From a Small-N to a Large-N Set Theoretic Approach, in: Fiss, P.C., Cambré, B., Marx, A. (Eds.), Configurational Theory and Methods in Organizational Research, vol. 38. Research in the sociology of organizations. Emerald Group Publishing Limited, pp. 49–75.

Greene, F.J., Hopp, C., 2017. Are Formal Planners More Likely to Achieve New Venture Viability? A Counterfactual Model and Analysis. *Strategic Entrepreneurship Journal*, *11* (1), 36–60.

Gruber, M., 2007. Uncovering the Value of Planning in New Venture Creation: A Process and Contingency Perspective. *Journal of Business Venturing*, *22* (6), 782–807.

Gruber, M., Heinemann, F., Brettel, M., Hungeling, S., 2010. Configurations of Resources and Capabilities and Their Performance Implications: An Exploratory Study on Technology Ventures. *Strategic Management Journal*, *31* (12), 1337–1356.

Hahn-Notter, I.G.A., 2021. *How Firms Turn Knowledge into Valuable Outputs*: Disentangling Research on Absorptive Capacity. Dissertation, 1st ed. Schriftenreihe Innovative Betriebswirtschaftliche Forschung und Praxis Series, *v.538*. Dr. Josef Kovac Wissenschaftsverlag, Hamburg, pp.200.

Hallen, B.L., Cohen, S., Park, S.H., 2023. Are Seed Accelerators Status Springboards for Startups? Or Sand Traps? *Strategic Management Journal*, *44* (8), 2060–2096.

Hamann, P.M., Schiemann, F., 2021. Organizational Performance as a Set of Four Dimensions: An Empirical Analysis. *Journal of Business Research*, *127*, 45–65.

Hanks, S.H., Watson, C.J., Jansen, E., Chandler, G.N., 1993. Tightening the Life-Cycle Construct: A Taxonomic Study of Growth Stage Configurations in High-Technology Organizations. *Entrepreneurship: Theory & Practice*, *18* (2), 5–30.

Hansen, C., Steinmetz, H., Block, J., 2022. How to Conduct a Meta-Analysis in Eight Steps: A Practical Guide. *Management Review Quarterly*, *72* (1), 1–19.

Harms, R., Kraus, S., Schwarz, E., 2009. The Suitability of the Configuration Approach in Entrepreneurship Research. *Entrepreneurship and Regional Development*, *21* (1), 25–49.

Harrison, D.A., Newman, D.A., Roth, P.L., 2006. How Important Are Job Attitudes? Meta-Analytic Comparisons of Integrative Behavioral Outcomes and Time Sequences. *Academy of Management Journal*, *49* (2), 305–325.

Haynie, J.M., Shepherd, D.A., McMullen, J.S., 2009. An Opportunity for Me? The Role of Resources in Opportunity Evaluation Decisions. *Journal of Management Studies*, *46* (3), 337–361.

Henrekson, M., Sanandaji, T., 2014. Small Business Activity Does Not Measure Entrepreneurship. *Proceedings of the National Academy of Sciences of the United States of America*, *111* (5), 1760–1765.

Henrekson, M., Sanandaji, T., 2020. Measuring Entrepreneurship: Do Established Metrics Capture Schumpeterian Entrepreneurship? *Entrepreneurship Theory and Practice*, *44* (4), 733–760.

Herrmann, A.M., Storz, C., Held, L., 2020. Whom Do Nascent Ventures Search for? Resource Scarcity and Linkage Formation Activities During New Product Development Processes. *Small Business Economics*, 1–22.

Hesse-Biber, S.N., Johnson, R.B., 2015. *The Oxford handbook of multimethod and mixed methods research inquiry.* Oxford University Press, Oxford.

Honig, B., Hopp, C., 2019. Learning Orientations and Learning Dynamics: Understanding Heterogeneous Approaches and Comparative Success in Nascent Entrepreneurship. *Journal of Business Research*, *94*, 28–41.

Hoon, C., 2013. Meta-Synthesis of Qualitative Case Studies: An Approach to Theory Building. *Organizational Research Methods*, *16* (4), 522–556.

Hopp, C., Greene, F.J., 2018. In Pursuit of Time: Business Plan Sequencing, Duration and Intraentrainment Effects on New Venture Viability. *Journal of Management Studies*, *55* (2), 320–351.

Hult, G.T.M., Ketchen, D.J., Griffith, D.A., Chabowski, B.R., Hamman, M.K., Dykes, B.J., Pollitte, W.A., Cavusgil, S.T., 2008. An Assessment of the Measurement of Performance in International Business Research. *Journal of International Business Studies*, *39* (6), 1064–1080.

Hunter, J.E., Schmidt, F.L., 1990. Dichotomization of Continuous Variables: The Implications for Meta-Analysis. *Journal of Applied Psychology*, *75* (3), 334.

Hunter, J.E., Schmidt, F.L., 2004. *Methods of meta-analysis: Correcting error and bias in research findings.* SAGE Publications, New York.

Jackson, G., Ni, N., 2013. Understanding Complementarities as Organizational Configurations: Using Set Theoretical Methods, in: Fiss, P.C., Cambré, B., Marx, A. (Eds.), Configurational Theory and Methods in Organizational Research. Research in the sociology of organizations. Emerald Group Publishing Limited, pp. 129–158.

Jain, A., 2013. Learning by Doing and the Locus of Innovative Capability in Biotechnology Research. *Organization Science*, *24* (6), 1683–1700.

Jiménez-Jiménez, D., Sanz-Valle, R., 2011. Innovation, Organizational Learning, and Performance. *Journal of Business Research*, *64* (4), 408–417.

Jin, L., Madison, K., Kraiczy, N.D., Kellermanns, F.W., Crook, T.R., Xi, J., 2017. Entrepreneurial Team Composition Characteristics and New Venture Performance: A Meta-Analysis. *Entrepreneurship Theory and Practice*, *41* (5), 743–771.

Kallmuenzer, A., Kraus, S., Peters, M., Steiner, J., Cheng, C.-F., 2019. Entrepreneurship in Tourism Firms: A Mixed-Methods Analysis of Performance Driver Configurations. *Tourism Management*, *74*, 319–330.

Kamm, J.B., Shuman, J.C., Seeger, J.A., Nurick, A.J., 1990. Entrepreneurial Teams in New Venture Creation: A Research Agenda. *Entrepreneurship Theory and Practice*, *14* (4), 7–17.

Kapoor, K.K., Dwivedi, Y.K., Williams, M.D., 2015. Examining the Role of Three Sets of Innovation Attributes for Determining Adoption of the Interbank Mobile Payment Service. *Information Systems Frontiers*, *17*, 1039–1056.

Katsikeas, C.S., Morgan, N.A., Leonidou, L.C., Hult, G.T.M., 2016. Assessing Performance Outcomes in Marketing. *Journal of Marketing*, *80* (2), 1–20.

Katz, J., Gartner, W.B., 1988. Properties of Emerging Organizations. *Academy of Management Review*, *13* (3), 429–441.

Khan, N., Li, S., Safdar, M., Khan, Z., 2019. The Role of Entrepreneurial Strategy, Network Ties, Human and Financial Capital in New Venture Performance. Journal of Risk and Financial Management, 12(1), 41. *Journal of Risk and Financial Management*, *12* (1), 41.

Kirby, J., 2005. Toward a Theory of High Performance. *Harvard Business Review*, *83* (7), 30-9, 190.

Kirca, A.H., Jayachandran, S., Bearden, W.O., 2005. Market Orientation: A Meta-Analytic Review and Assessment of Its Antecedents and Impact on Performance. *Journal of Marketing*, *69* (2), 24–41.

Klotz, A.C., Hmieleski, K.M., Bradley, B.H., Busenitz, L.W., 2014. New Venture Teams. *Journal of Management*, *40* (1), 226–255.

Kostopoulos, K., Papalexandris, A., Papachroni, M., Ioannou, G., 2011. Absorptive Capacity, Innovation, and Financial Performance. *Journal of Business Research*, *64* (12), 1335–1343.

Kraus, S., Breier, M., Dasí-Rodríguez, S., 2020. The Art of Crafting a Systematic Literature Review in Entrepreneurship Research. *International Entrepreneurship and Management Journal*, *16*, 1023–1042.

Kunisch, S., Menz, M., Bartunek, J.M., Cardinal, L.B., Denyer, D., 2018. Feature Topic at Organizational Research Methods: How to Conduct Rigorous and Impactful Literature Reviews? *Organizational Research Methods*, *21* (3), 519–523.

Lane, P.J., Koka, B.R., Pathak, S., 2006. The Reification of Absorptive Capacity: A Critical Review and Rejuvenation of the Construct. *Academy of Management Review*, *31* (4), 833–863.

Lane, P.J., Lubatkin, M., 1998. Relative Absorptive Capacity and Interorganizational Learning. *Strategic Management Journal*, *19* (5), 461–477.

Lange, J.E., Mollov, A., Pearlmutter, M., Singh, S., Bygrave, W.D., 2007. Pre-Start-up Formal Business Plans and Post-Start-up Performance: A Study of 116 New Ventures. *Venture Capital*, *9* (4), 237–256.

Leal-Rodríguez, A.L., Roldán, J.L., Ariza-Montes, J.A., Leal-Millán, A., 2014. From Potential Absorptive Capacity to Innovation Outcomes in Project Teams: The Conditional Mediating Role of the Realized Absorptive Capacity in a Relational Learning Context. *International Journal of Project Management*, *32* (6), 894–907.

Lebas, M.J., 1995. Performance Measurement and Performance Management. *International Journal of Production Economics*, *41* (1-3), 23–35.

Levie, J., Lichtenstein, B.B., 2010. A Terminal Assessment of Stages Theory: Introducing a Dynamic States Approach to Entrepreneurship. *Entrepreneurship: Theory and Practice*, *34* (2), 317–350.

Lewin, A.Y., Massini, S., Peeters, C., 2011. Microfoundations of Internal and External Absorptive Capacity Routines. *Organization Science*, *22* (1), 81–98.

Lewis, V.L., Churchill, N.C., 1983. The Five Stages of Small Business Growth. *Harvard Business Review*, *61* (3), 30–50.

Liao, J., Gartner, W.B., 2006. The Effects of Pre-Venture Plan Timing and Perceived Environmental Uncertainty on the Persistence of Emerging Firms. *Small Business Economics*, *27* (1), 23–40.

Lichtenstein, B.M.B., Brush, C.G., 2001. How Do "Resource Bundles" Develop and Change in New Ventures? A Dynamic Model and Longitudinal Exploration. *Entrepreneurship: Theory & Practice*, *25* (3), 37–58.

Linder, C., Lechner, C., Pelzel, F., 2020. Many Roads Lead to Rome: How Human, Social, and Financial Capital Are Related to New Venture Survival. *Entrepreneurship: Theory & Practice*, *44* (5), 909–932.

Lipsey, M.W., Wilson, D.B., 2001. *Practical meta-analysis.* SAGE Publications, New York.

Maldonado, T., Salaiz, A., Vera, D., Keller, R.T., 2018. Taking Stock of the Absorptive Capacity Construct and Its Dimensions in the Context of Technological Innovation: A Meta-Analytic Approach. *IEEE Transactions on Engineering Management*, *66* (2), 193–207.

Marabelli, M., Newell, S., 2014. Knowing, Power and Materiality: A Critical Review and Reconceptualization of Absorptive Capacity. *International Journal of Management Reviews*, *16* (4), 479–499.

Marttila, N., Notter, I., Schweiger, S.A., Romanova Stettler, T., Baldauf, A., 2017. Illuminating the Relationship Between Absorptive Capacity and Firm Performance: A Meta-Analysis. *Academy of Management Proceedings*, *2017* (1), 10687.

Mayer-Haug, K., Read, S., Brinckmann, J., Dew, N., Grichnik, D., 2013. Entrepreneurial Talent and Venture Performance: A Meta-Analytic Investigation of SMEs. *Research Policy*, *42* (6-7), 1251–1273.

Mello, P.A., 2021. *Qualitative comparative analysis*: An Introduction to Research Design and Application. Georgetown University Press, Washington, DC, pp.241.

Meuer, J., Rupietta, C., 2017a. A Review of Integrated QCA and Statistical Analyses. *Quality & Quantity*, *51*, 2063–2083.

Meuer, J., Rupietta, C., 2017b. Integrating QCA and HLM for Multilevel Research on Organizational Configurations. *Organizational Research Methods*, *20* (2), 324–342.

Miller, D., Friesen, P.H., 1984. A Longitudinal Study of the Corporate Life Cycle. *Management Science*, *30* (10), 1161–1183.

Miller, K.D., 2007. Risk and Rationality in Entrepreneurial Processes. *Strategic Entrepreneurship Journal*, *1* (1-2), 57–74.

Molina-Azorin, J.F., 2012. Mixed Methods Research in Strategic Management: Impact and Applications. *Organizational Research Methods*, *15* (1), 33–56.

Moore, D., Russell, A., Matthews, J., Ford, T., Rogers, M., Ukoumunne, O., Kneale, D., Thompson-Coon, J., Sutcliffe, K., Nunns, M., Shaw, L., Gwernan-Jones, R., 2018. School-based Interventions for Attention-deficit/hyperactivity Disorder: A Systematic Review with Multiple Synthesis Methods. *Review of Education*, *6* (3), 209–263.

Murphy, G.B., Trailer, J.W., Hill, R.C., 1996. Measuring Performance in Entrepreneurship Research. *Journal of Business Research*, *36* (1), 15–23.

Nardi, V.A.M., Jardim, W.C., Ladeira, W.J., Santini, F., 2020. A Meta-Analysis of the Relationship Between Customer Participation and Brand Outcomes. *Journal of Business Research*, *117*, 450–460.

Newbert, S.L., 2003. Realizing the Spirit and Impact of Adam Smith's Capitalism Through Entrepreneurship. *Journal of Business Ethics*, *46* (3), 251–258.

Oana, I.-E., Schneider, C.Q., 2018. SetMethods: An Add-on R Package for Advanced QCA. *The R Journal*, *10* (1), 507.

Oana, I.-E., Schneider, C.Q., 2021. A Robustness Test Protocol for Applied QCA: Theory and R Software Application. *Sociological Methods & Research,*

Ohlsson, A., 1994. Systematic Reviews-Theory and Practice. *Scandinavian Journal of Clinical and Laboratory Investigation*, *54* (sup219), 25–32.

Ormans, L., 2016. 50 Journals Used in FT Research Rank. *Financial Times*, September 12. https://www.ft.com/content/3405a512-5cbb-11e1-8f1f-00144feabdc0. Accessed 15 October 2021.

Parry, M.E., Song, M., 2010. Market Information Acquisition, Use, and New Venture Performance. *Journal of Product Innovation Management*, *27* (7), 1112–1126.

Paternoster, N., Giardino, C., Unterkalmsteiner, M., Gorschek, T., Abrahamsson, P., 2014. Software Development in Startup Companies: A Systematic Mapping Study. *Information and Software Technology*, *56* (10), 1200–1218.

Penrose, E.T., 1959. *The Theory of the Growth of the Firm.* Oxford University Press, Oxford.

Pfeffer, J., Salancik, G.R., 2003. *The external control of organizations*: A Resource Dependence Perspective. Stanford business classics, pp.300.

Phelps, C.C., 2010. A Longitudinal Study of the Influence of Alliance Network Structure and Composition on Firm Exploratory Innovation. *Academy of Management Journal*, *53* (4), 890–913.

Posit team, 2022. RStudio: Integrated Development Environment for R. Posit Software, PBC, Boston, USA.

Post, C., Sarala, R., Gatrell, C., Prescott, J.E., 2020. Advancing Theory with Review Articles. *Journal of Management Studies*, *57* (2), 351–376.

Powell, T.C., 2003. Varieties of Competitive Parity. *Strategic Management Journal*, *24* (1), 61–86.

Ragin, C.C., 1987. *The comparative method: Moving beyond qualitative and quantitative strategies.* University of California Press, Berkeley.

Ragin, C.C., 2008. Measurement Versus Calibration: A Set-Theoretic Approach, in: Box-Steffensmeier, J.M., Brady, H.E., Collier, D. (Eds.), The Oxford Handbook of Political Methodology. Oxford University Press, Oxford.

Ragin, C.C., Fiss, P.C., 2008. Net Effects Analysis Versus Configurational Analysis: An Empirical Demonstration. *Redesigning Social Inquiry: Fuzzy Sets and Beyond*, *240*, 190–212.

Rapp, A., Gabler, C., Ogilvie, J., 2020. A Holistic Perspective of Sales Research: Areas of Consideration to Develop More Comprehensive Conceptual and Empirical Frameworks. *Journal of Personal Selling & Sales Management*, *40* (4), 227–233.

Razmdoost, K., Alinaghian, L., Linder, C., 2020. New Venture Formation: A Capability Configurational Approach. *Journal of Business Research*, *113*, 290–302.

Reese, D., Rieger, V., Engelen, A., 2020. Should Competencies Be Broadly Shared in New Ventures' Founding Teams? *Strategic Entrepreneurship Journal*, *15* (4), 568–589.

Reynolds, P.D., 2011. Informal and Early Formal Financial Support in the Business Creation Process: Exploration with PSED II Data Set. *Journal of Small Business Management*, *49* (1), 27–54.

Reynolds, P.D., Curtin, R.T., 2007. Panel Study of Entrepreneurial Dynamics Program Rationale and Description. http://www.psed.isr.umich.edu/psed/background. Accessed 5 January 2023.

Richard, P.J., Devinney, T.M., Yip, G.S., Johnson, G., 2009. Measuring Organizational Performance: Towards Methodological Best Practice. *Journal of Management*, *35* (3), 718–804.

Robinson, K.C., 1999. An Examination of the Influence of Industry Structure on Eight Alternative Measures of New Venture Performance for High Potential Independent New Ventures. *Journal of Business Venturing*, *14* (2), 165–187.

Rohlfing, I., 2020. The Choice Between Crisp and Fuzzy Sets in Qualitative Comparative Analysis and the Ambiguous Consequences for Finding Consistent Set Relations. *Field Methods*, *32* (1), 75–88.

Rosenbusch, N., Brinckmann, J., Müller, V., 2013. Does Acquiring Venture Capital Pay Off for the Funded Firms? A Meta-Analysis on the Relationship Between Venture Capital Investment and Funded Firm Financial Performance. *Journal of Business Venturing*, *28* (3), 335–353.

Rouhani, S., Rotbei, S., Shamizanjani, M., 2017. Meta-Synthesis of Big Data Impacts on Information Systems Development. *Journal of Management Analytics*, *4* (2), 182–201.

Ruiz-Jiménez, J.M., Ruiz-Arroyo, M., Del Mar Fuentes-Fuentes, M., 2021. The Impact of Effectuation, Causation, and Resources on New Venture Performance: Novice Versus Expert Entrepreneurs. *Small Business Economics*, *57* (4), 1761–1781.

Rutten, R., 2022. Applying and Assessing Large-N QCA: Causality and Robustness from a Critical Realist Perspective. *Sociological Methods & Research*, *51* (3), 1211–1243.

Santarelli, E., Tran, H.T., 2013. The Interplay of Human and Social Capital in Shaping Entrepreneurial Performance: The Case of Vietnam. *Small Business Economics*, *40*, 435–458.

Schimperna, F., Nappo, F., Marsigalia, B., 2021. Student Entrepreneurship in Universities: The State-of-the-Art. *Administrative Sciences*, *12* (1), 5.

Schmidt, F.L., Hunter, J.E., 1999. Comparison of Three Meta-Analysis Methods Revisited: An Analysis of Johnson, Mullen, and Salas (1995). *Journal of Applied Psychology*, *84* (1), 144–148.

Schneider, C.Q., Wagemann, C., 2012. *Set-Theoretic Methods for the Social Sciences: A Guide to Qualitative Comparative Analysis.* Strategies for Social Inquiry. Cambridge University Press, Cambridge.

Schumpeter, J.A., 1934. *The theory of economic development*: An Inquiry into Profits, Capital, Credit, Interest, and the Business Cycle. Harvard economic Studies, *46.* Harvard University Press, Cambridge, pp.255.

Shane, S., Venkataraman, S., 2000. The Promise of Entrepreneurship as a Field of Research. *The Academy of Management Review*, *25* (1), 217–226.

Sharma, R., Yetton, P., Crawford, J., 2009. Estimating the Effect of Common Method Variance: The Method—Method Pair Technique with an Illustration from TAM Research. *MIS Quarterly*, *33* (3), 473–490.

Shepherd, D.A., Douglas, E.J., Shanley, M., 2000. New Venture Survival: Ignorance, External Shocks, and Risk Reduction Strategies. *Journal of Business Venturing*, *15* (5-6), 393–410.

Shepherd, D.A., McMullen, J.S., Jennings, P.D., 2007. The Formation of Opportunity Beliefs: Overcoming Ignorance and Reducing Doubt. *Strategic Entrepreneurship Journal*, *1* (1-2), 75–95.

Shepherd, D.A., Suddaby, R., 2017. Theory Building: A Review and Integration. *Journal of Management*, *43* (1), 59–86.

Shepherd, D.A., Wennberg, K., Suddaby, R., Wiklund, J., 2019. What Are We Explaining? A Review and Agenda on Initiating, Engaging, Performing, and Contextualizing Entrepreneurship. *Journal of Management*, *45* (1), 159–196.

Snyder, H., 2019. Literature Review as a Research Methodology: An Overview and Guidelines. *Journal of Business Research*, *104*, 333–339.

Söderblom, A., Samuelsson, M., Wiklund, J., Sandberg, R., 2015. Inside the Black Box of Outcome Additionality: Effects of Early-Stage Government Subsidies on Resource Accumulation and New Venture Performance. *Research Policy*, *44* (8), 1501–1512.

Song, L.Z., Song, M., Di Benedetto, C.A., 2011. Resources, Supplier Investment, Product Launch Advantages, and First Product Performance. *Journal of Operations Management*, *29* (1-2), 86–104.

Song, L.Z., Song, M., Parry, M.E., 2010. Perspective: Economic Conditions, Entrepreneurship, First-product Development, and New Venture Success. *Journal of Product Innovation Management*, *27* (1), 130–135.

Song, M., Podoynitsyna, K., Van Der Bij, H., Halman, J.I.M., 2008. Success Factors in New Ventures: A Meta-analysis. *Journal of Product Innovation Management*, *25* (1), 7–27.

Song, Y., Gnyawali, D.R., Srivastava, M.K., Asgari, E., 2018. In Search of Precision in Absorptive Capacity Research: A Synthesis of the Literature and Consolidation of Findings. *Journal of Management*, *44* (6), 2343–2374.

Spinelli, S., Adams, R., 2012. *New venture creation*: Entrepreneurship for the 21st Century, 9th ed. ed. McGraw-Hill/Irwin, New York, pp.588.

Steers, R.M., 1975. Problems in the Measurement of Organizational Effectiveness. *Administrative Science Quarterly*, *20* (4), 546–558.

Steffens, P., Terjesen, S., Davidsson, P., 2012. Birds of a Feather Get Lost Together: New Venture Team Composition and Performance. *Small Business Economics*, *39* (3), 727–743.

Stock, W.A., 1994. Systematic Coding for Research Synthesis, in: Cooper, H.M., Hedges, L.V. (Eds.), The handbook of research synthesis, vol. 236. Russell Sage Foundation, New York, pp. 125–138.

Stuart, T.E., Hoang, H., Hybels, R.C., 1999. Interorganizational Endorsements and the Performance of Entrepreneurial Ventures. *Administrative Science Quarterly*, *44* (2), 315–349.

Tashakkori, A., Teddlie, C., 2010. *Sage handbook of mixed methods in social & behavioral research,* Second Edition ed. Sage, Los Angeles, London, New Dehli, Singapore, Washington D.C., pp.893.

Teddlie, C., Tashakkori, A., 2012. Common “Core” Characteristics of Mixed Methods Research: A Review of Critical Issues and Call for Greater Convergence. *American Behavioral Scientist*, *56* (6), 774–788.

Teece, D.J., 2007. Explicating Dynamic Capabilities: The Nature and Microfoundations of (Sustainable) Enterprise Performance. *Strategic Management Journal*, *28* (13), 1319–1350.

Thiess, D., Sirén, C., Grichnik, D., 2016. How Does Heterogeneity in Experience Influence the Performance of Nascent Venture Teams?: Insights from the US PSED II Study. *Journal of Business Venturing Insights*, *5*, 55–62.

Thomas, J., O'Mara-Eves, A., Brunton, G., 2014. Using Qualitative Comparative Analysis (QCA) In Systematic Reviews of Complex Interventions: A Worked Example. *Systematic Reviews*, *3* (1), 67.

Timmons, J.A., 1999. *New venture creation*: Entrepreneurship for the 21st Century, 5th ed. McGraw-Hill, London, pp.800.

Timmons, J.A., Spinelli, S., 2009. *New venture creation*: Entrepreneurship for the 21st Century, 8. internat. ed. McGraw-Hill Irwin, Boston, pp.666.

Townsend, D.M., Busenitz, L.W., Arthurs, J.D., 2010. To Start or Not to Start: Outcome and Ability Expectations in the Decision to Start a New Venture. *Journal of Business Venturing*, *25* (2), 192–202.

Tranfield, D., Denyer, D., Smart, P., 2003. Towards a Methodology for Developing Evidence-Informed Management Knowledge by Means of Systematic Review. *British Journal of Management*, *14* (3), 207–222.

Tsai, W., 2001. Knowledge Transfer in Intraorganizational Networks: Effects of Network Position and Absorptive Capacity on Business Unit Innovation and Performance. *Academy of Management Journal*, *44* (5), 996–1004.

Tsay, R.S., 2013. *Multivariate time series analysis: with R and financial applications,* 1st ed. Wiley Series in Probability and Statistics. John Wiley & Sons, pp.520.

Unger, J.M., Rauch, A., Frese, M., Rosenbusch, N., 2011. Human Capital and Entrepreneurial Success: A Meta-Analytical Review. *Journal of Business Venturing*, *26* (3), 341–358.

Uzzi, B., 1996. The Sources and Consequences of Embeddedness for the Economic Performance of Organizations: The Network Effect. *American Sociological Review*, 674–698.

van de Vrande, V., Vanhaverbeke, W., Duysters, G., 2011. Technology In-sourcing and the Creation of Pioneering Technologies. *Journal of Product Innovation Management*, *28* (6), 974–987.

van Praag, M., Wit, G. de, Bosma, N., 2005. Initial Capital Constraints Hinder Entrepreneurial Venture Performance. *The Journal of Private Equity*, *9* (1), 36–44.

Venkatraman, N., Ramanujam, V., 1986. Measurement of Business Performance in Strategy Research: A Comparison of Approaches. *Academy of Management Review*, *11* (4), 801–814.

Venkatraman, N., Ramanujam, V., 1987. Measurement of Business Economic Performance: An Examination of Method Convergence. *Journal of Management*, *13* (1), 109–122.

Villiger, J., Schweiger, S.A., Baldauf, A., 2022. Making the Invisible Visible: Guidelines for the Coding Process in Meta-Analyses. *Organizational Research Methods*, *25* (4), 716–740.

Volberda, H.W., Foss, N.J., Lyles, M.A., 2010. Perspective—Absorbing the Concept of Absorptive Capacity: How to Realize Its Potential in the Organization Field. *Organization Science*, *21* (4), 931–951.

Watson, J., 2007. Modeling the Relationship Between Networking and Firm Performance. *Journal of Business Venturing*, *22* (6), 852–874.

Wernerfelt, B., 1984. A Resource-Based View of the Firm. *Strategic Management Journal*, *5* (2), 171–180.

West, G.P., Noel, T.W., 2009. The Impact of Knowledge Resources on New Venture Performance. *Journal of Small Business Management*, *47* (1), 1–22.

Westlund, H., Bolton, R., 2003. Local Social Capital and Entrepreneurship. *Small Business Economics*, *21* (2), 77–113.

Whetten, D.A., 1989. What Constitutes a Theoretical Contribution? *Academy of Management Review*, *14* (4), 490.

Whitesitt, J.E., 2012. *Boolean algebra and its applications.* Dover Publications, New York.

Wibbens, P.D., Siggelkow, N., 2020. Introducing LIVA to Measure Long-term Firm Performance. *Strategic Management Journal*, *41* (5), 867–890.

Wiklund, J., Shepherd, D., 2005. Entrepreneurial Orientation and Small Business Performance: A Configurational Approach. *Journal of Business Venturing*, *20* (1), 71–91.

Wise, S., Valliere, D., 2014. The Impact on Management Experience on the Performance of Start-Ups Within Accelerators. *The Journal of Private Equity*, *18* (1), 9–19.

Wood, M.S., McKelvie, A., 2015. Opportunity Evaluation as Future Focused Cognition: Identifying Conceptual Themes and Empirical Trends. *International Journal of Management Reviews*, *17* (2), 256–277.

Xie, X.-Y., Feng, W., Hu, Q., 2020. Does New Venture Team Power Hierarchy Enhance or Impair New Venture Performance? A Contingency Perspective. *Journal of Business Venturing*, *35* (6), 106059.

Yao, F.K., Jiang, K., Combs, D.R., Chang, S., 2020. Informal Institutions and Absorptive Capacity: A Cross-Country Meta-Analytic Study. *Journal of International Business Studies* (53), 1–19.

Zahra, S.A., 1996. Technology Strategy and New Venture Performance: A Study of Corporate-Sponsored and Independent Biotechnology Ventures. *Journal of Business Venturing*, *11* (4), 289–321.

Zahra, S.A., George, G., 2002. Absorptive Capacity: A Review, Reconceptualization, and Extension. *Academy of Management Review*, *27* (2), 185–203.

Zamanian, A., Myint, P.P., 2018. Measuring Entrepreneurial Performance: Is There Consistency Between Scholars?, in: 48th Decision Sciences Institute Annual Meeting (DSI 2017). Washington, DC, USA, 18-20 November 2017. 48th Decision Sciences Institute Annual Meeting (DSI 2017), Washington, DC, USA. 18 - 20 November 2017. Curran Associates Inc, Red Hook, NY, pp. 1373–1411.

Zhang, Y., Yang, J., Tang, J., Au, K., Xue, H., 2013. Prior Experience and Social Class as Moderators of the Planning-Performance Relationship in China's Emerging Economy. *Strategic Entrepreneurship Journal*, *7* (3), 214–229.

Zhao, Y.L., Libaers, D., Song, M., 2015. First Product Success: A Mediated Moderating Model of Resources, Founding Team Startup Experience, and Product-positioning Strategy. *Journal of Product Innovation Management*, *32* (3), 441–458.

Zhou, K.Z., Li, C.B., 2012. How Knowledge Affects Radical Innovation: Knowledge Base, Market Knowledge Acquisition, and Internal Knowledge Sharing. *Strategic Management Journal*, *33* (9), 1090–1102.

Zou, T., Ertug, G., George, G., 2018. The Capacity to Innovate: A Meta-Analysis of Absorptive Capacity. *Innovation*, *20* (2), 87–121.

Appendices

Appendix A: List of Articles included in Systematic Literature Review (Chapter 2)

ID	Author	Journal	Year
1	Warnick, Benjamin J.; Kier, Alexander S.; Lafrance, Emily M.; Cuttler, Carrie	Journal of Business Venturing	2021
2	Tumasjan, Andranik; Braun, Reiner; Stolz, Barbara	Journal of Business Venturing	2021
3	Xie, Xiao-Yun; Feng, Wen; Hu, Qiongjing	Journal of Business Venturing	2020
4	Kier, Alexander S.; McMullen, Jeffery S.	Journal of Business Venturing	2020
5	Boone, Sarah; Andries, Petra; Clarysse, Bart	Journal of Business Venturing	2020
6	Klyver, Kim; Steffens, Paul; Lomberg, Carina	Journal of Business Venturing	2020
7	De Mol, Eva; Cardon, Melissa S.; De Jong, Bart; Khapova, Svetlana N.; Elfring, Tom	Journal of Business Venturing	2020
8	Amezcua, Alejandro; Ratinho, Tiago; Plummer, Lawrence A.; Jayamohan, Parvathi	Journal of Business Venturing	2020
9	De Cock, Robin; Denoo, Lien; Clarysse, Bart	Journal of Business Venturing	2020
10	Taeuscher, Karl	Journal of Business Venturing	2019
11	Hmieleski, Keith M.; Sheppard, Leah D.	Journal of Business Venturing	2019
12	Vaznyte, Egle; Andries, Petra	Journal of Business Venturing	2019
13	Nagel, Hanskje; Rosendahl Huber, Laura; Van Praag, Mirjam; Goslinga, Sjoerd	Journal of Business Venturing	2019
14	Nason, Robert S.; Wiklund, Johan; McKelvie, Alexander; Hitt, Michael; Yu, Wei	Journal of Business Venturing	2019
15	Knoben, Joris; Bakker, Rene M.	Journal of Business Venturing	2019
16	Nuscheler, Daniela; Engelen, Andreas; Zahra, Shaker A.	Journal of Business Venturing	2019
17	Uy, Marilyn A.; Sun, Shuhua; Foo, Maw-Der	Journal of Business Venturing	2017
18	Wennberg, Karl; Delmar, Frédéric; McKelvie, Alexander	Journal of Business Venturing	2016
19	Kim, Phillip H.; Longest, Kyle C.; Lippmann, Stephen	Journal of Business Venturing	2015
20	Block, Joern H.; De Vries, Geertjan; Schumann, Jan H.; Sandner, Philipp	Journal of Business Venturing	2014
21	Cassar, Gavin	Journal of Business Venturing	2014
22	Coad, Alex; Frankish, Julian; Roberts, Richard G.; Storey, David J.	Journal of Business Venturing	2013
23	Boone, Christophe; Wezel, Filippo Carlo; Van Witteloostuijn, Arjen	Journal of Business Venturing	2013
24	Newbert, Scott L.; Tornikoski, Erno T.; Quigley, Narda R.	Journal of Business Venturing	2013
25	Li, Dan	Journal of Business Venturing	2013
26	Zheng, Yanfeng	Journal of Business Venturing	2012

27	Song, Michael; Wang, Tang; Parry, Mark E.	Journal of Business Venturing	2010
28	Colombo, Massimo G.; Grilli, Luca	Journal of Business Venturing	2010
29	Zheng, Yanfeng; Liu, Jing; George, Gerard	Journal of Business Venturing	2010
30	Townsend, David M.; Busenitz, Lowell W.; Arthurs, Jonathan D.	Journal of Business Venturing	2010
31	Chandler, Gaylen N.; McKelvie, Alexander; Davidsson, Per	Journal of Business Venturing	2009
32	Jennings, Jennifer E.; Jennings, P. Devereaux; Greenwood, Royston	Journal of Business Venturing	2009
33	Gilbert, Brett Anitra; McDougall, Patricia P.; Audretsch, David B.	Journal of Business Venturing	2008
34	Hmieleski, Keith M.; Corbett, Andrew C.	Journal of Business Venturing	2008
35	Zhang, Jiamin; Gu, Qian	Journal of Business Venturing	2021
36	Fultza, Andrew E.F.; Hmieleski, Keith M.	Journal of Business Venturing	2021
37	Sanchez-Ruiza, Paul; Wood, Matthew S.; Long-Ruboyianes, Anna	Journal of Business Venturing	2021
38	Sewaida, Ahmed; Parker, Simon C.; Kaakeh, Abdulkader	Journal of Business Venturing	2021
39	Yli-Renko, Helena; Denoo, Lien; Janakiraman, Ramkumar	Journal of Business Venturing	2020
40	Marvel, Matthew R.; Wolfe, Marcus T.; Kuratko, Donald F.	Journal of Business Venturing	2020
41	Gjerløv-Juel, Pernille; Guenther, Christina	Journal of Business Venturing	2019
42	Goldenstein, Jan; Hunoldt, Michael; Oertel, Simon	Journal of Business Venturing	2019
43	Oo, Pyayt P.; Allison, Thomas H. Sahaym, Arvin; Juasrikul, Sakdipon	Journal of Business Venturing	2019
44	Islam, Mazhar; Fremeth, Adam; Marcus Alfred	Journal of Business Venturing	2018
45	Ko, Eun-Jeong; McKelvie, Alexander	Journal of Business Venturing	2018
46	Anglin, Aaron H.; Short, Jeremy C.; Drover, Will; Stevenson, Regan M.; McKenny, Aaron F.; Allison, Thomas H.	Journal of Business Venturing	2018
47	Anglin, Aaron H.; Wolfe, Marcus T.; Short, Jeremy C.; McKenny, Aaron F.; Pidduck, Robert J.	Journal of Business Venturing	2018
48	Parhankangas, Annaleena; Renko, Maija	Journal of Business Venturing	2017
49	Symeonidou, Noni; Bruneel, Johan; Autio, Erkko	Journal of Business Venturing	2017
50	Kwon, Seok-Woo; Ruef, Martin	Journal of Business Venturing	2017
51	Qin, Fei; Wright, Mike; Gao, Jian	Journal of Business Venturing	2017
52	Allison, Thomas H.; Davis, Blakley C.; Webb, Justin W.; Short, Jeremy C.	Journal of Business Venturing	2017
53	Stenholm, Pekka; Renko, Maija	Journal of Business Venturing	2016
54	Du, Jun; Mickiewicz, Tomasz	Journal of Business Venturing	2016
55	Hyytinen, Ari; Pajarinen, Mika; Rouvinen, Petri	Journal of Business Venturing	2015
56	Neville, François; Orser, Barbara; Riding, Allan; Jung, Owen	Journal of Business Venturing	2014

57	Toft-Kehler, Rasmus; Wennberg, Karl; Kim, Phillip H.	Journal of Business Venturing	2014
58	Parker, Simon C.	Journal of Business Venturing	2013
59	Pe'er, Aviad; Keil, Thomas	Journal of Business Venturing	2013
60	Podoynitsyna, Ksenia; Song, Michael; Van Der Bij, Hans; Weggeman, Mathieu	Journal of Business Venturing	2013
61	Robb, Alicia M.; Watson, John	Journal of Business Venturing	2012
62	Rotger, Gabriel Pons; Gørtz, Mette; Storey, David J.	Journal of Business Venturing	2012
63	Mouri, Nacef; Sarkar, M.B.; Frye, Melissa	Journal of Business Venturing	2012
64	Bell, R. Greg; Moore, Curt B.; Filatotchev, Igor	Journal of Business Venturing	2012
65	Cruza, Cristina; Justo, Rachida; De Castro, Julio O.	Journal of Business Venturing	2012
66	Lévesque, Moren; Joglekar, Nitin; Davies, Jane	Journal of Business Venturing	2012
67	Gielnik, Michael M.; Zacher, Hannes; Frese, Michael	Journal of Business Venturing	2012
68	Chowdhury, Sanjib	Journal of Business Venturing	2011
69	McCann, Brian T.; Folta, Timothy B.	Journal of Business Venturing	2011
70	Pollock, Timothy G.; Chen, Guoli; .Jackson, Eric M; Hambrick, Donald C.	Journal of Business Venturing	2010
71	Davidsson, Per; Steffens, Paul; Fitzsimmons, Jason	Journal of Business Venturing	2009
72	He, Lerong	Journal of Business Venturing	2008
73	Jain, Bharat A.; Jayaraman, Narayanan; Kini, Omesh	Journal of Business Venturing	2008
74	Chaganti, Rajeswararao (Raj) S.; Watts, Allison D.; Chaganti, Radha; Zimmerman-Treichel, Monica	Journal of Business Venturing	2008
75	Hand, John R.M.	Journal of Business Venturing	2007
76	Aidis, Ruta; Van Praag, Mirjam	Journal of Business Venturing	2007
77	Dai, Ye; Byun, Gukdo; Ding, Fangsheng	Entrepreneurship: Theory & Practice	2019
78	Santos, Susana C.; Cardon, Melissa S.	Entrepreneurship: Theory & Practice	2019
79	McKelvie, Alexander; Wiklund, Johan; Brattström, Anna	Entrepreneurship: Theory & Practice	2018
80	Neubert, Mitchell J.; Bradley, Steven W.; Ardianti, Retno; Simiyu, Edward M.	Entrepreneurship: Theory & Practice	2017
81	Vandenbroucke, Elien; Knockaert, Mirjam; Ucbasaran, Deniz	Entrepreneurship: Theory & Practice	2016
82	Arregle, Jean-Luc; Batjargal, Bat; Hitt, Michael A.; Webb, Justin W.; Miller, Toyah; Tsui, Anne S.	Entrepreneurship: Theory & Practice	2015
83	Yamakawa, Yasuhiro; Peng, Mike W.; Deeds, David L.	Entrepreneurship: Theory & Practice	2015
84	Renko, Maija	Entrepreneurship: Theory & Practice	2013
85	Zhao, Y. Lisa; Song, Michael; Storm, Gregory L.	Entrepreneurship: Theory & Practice	2013
86	Brinckmann, Jan; Salomo, Soeren; Gemuenden, Hans Georg	Entrepreneurship: Theory & Practice	2011

87	Edelman, Linda; Yli-Renko, Helena	Entrepreneurship: Theory & Practice	2010
88	Fernhaber, Stephanie A.; Li, Dan	Entrepreneurship: Theory & Practice	2010
89	Shrader, Rod; Siegel, Donald S.	Entrepreneurship: Theory & Practice	2007
90	De Carolis, Donna Marie; Litzky, Barrie E.; Eddleston, Kimberly A.	Entrepreneurship: Theory & Practice	2009
91	Steffens, Paul; Davidsson, Per; Fitzsimmons, Jason	Entrepreneurship: Theory & Practice	2009
92	Lei-Yu Wu; Chun-Ju Wang; Cheng-Ping Chen; Lee-Yun Pan	Entrepreneurship: Theory & Practice	2008
93	West, G. Page	Entrepreneurship: Theory & Practice	2007
94	Caliendo, Marco; Künn, Steffen; Weissenberger, Martin	Research Policy	2020
95	Roche, Maria P.; Conti, Annamaria; Rothaermel, Frank T.	Research Policy	2020
96	Eiteneyer, Nils; Bendig, David; Brettel, Malte	Research Policy	2019
97	Guzman, Jorge; Kacperczyk, Aleksandra (Olenka)	Research Policy	2019
98	Doblinger, Claudia; Surana, Kavita; Anadon, Laura Diaz	Research Policy	2019
99	Söderblom, Anna; Samuelsson, Mikael; Wiklund, Johan; Sandberg, Rickard	Research Policy	2015
100	Hsu, David H.	Research Policy	2007
101	Batjargal, Bat	Research Policy	2007
102	Mann, Ronald J.; Sager, Thomas W.	Research Policy	2007
103	Howard, Michael D.; Kolb, Johannes; Sy, Valerie A.	Strategic Entrepreneurship Journal	2021
104	Leatherbee, Michael; Katila, Riitta	Strategic Entrepreneurship Journal	2020
105	Lahiri, Amrita; Pahnke, Emily C.; Howard, Michael D.; Boeker, Warren	Strategic Entrepreneurship Journal	2019
106	Haeussler, Carolin; Hennicke, Maria; Mueller, Elisabeth	Strategic Entrepreneurship Journal	2019
107	Di Lorenzo, Francesco; Van De Vrande, Vareska	Strategic Entrepreneurship Journal	2019
108	Symeonidou, Noni; Nicolaou, Nicos	Strategic Entrepreneurship Journal	2018
109	Wang, Taiyuan; Thornhill, Stewart; De Castro, Julio O.	Strategic Entrepreneurship Journal	2017
110	Greene, Francis J.; Hopp, Christian	Strategic Entrepreneurship Journal	2017
111	Chen, Jing; Thompson, Peter	Strategic Entrepreneurship Journal	2015
112	Fuller, Anne W.; Rothaermel, Frank T.	Strategic Entrepreneurship Journal	2012
113	Batjargal, Bat	Strategic Entrepreneurship Journal	2010
114	Short, Jeremy C.; McKelvie, Alexander; Ketchen, David J.; Chandler, Gaylen N.	Strategic Entrepreneurship Journal	2009
115	Hmieleski, Keith M.; Baron, Robert A.	Strategic Entrepreneurship Journal	2008
116	Grillitsch, Markus; Schubert, Torben	Strategic Entrepreneurship Journal	2020

117	Reese, Daniel; Rieger, Verena; Engelen, Andreas	Strategic Entrepreneurship Journal	2020
118	Braun, Ilija; Sieger, Philipp	Strategic Entrepreneurship Journal	2020
119	Jiang, Han; Wang, Zhiyi; Yang, Lusi; Shen, Jia; Hahn, Jungpil	Entrepreneurship: Theory & Practice	2021
120	Piening, Erk P.; Thies, Ferdinand; Wessel, Michael; Benlian, Alexander	Entrepreneurship: Theory & Practice	2021
121	Ko, Eun-Jeong; Wiklund, Johan; Pollack, Jeffrey M.	Entrepreneurship: Theory & Practice	2021
122	Linder, Christian; Lechner, Christian; Pelzel, Frank	Entrepreneurship: Theory & Practice	2020
123	Lundmark, Erik; Coad, Alex; Frankish, Julian S.; Storey, David J.	Entrepreneurship: Theory & Practice	2020
124	Luo, Xiaowei Rose; Yang, Ling; He, Xiaobin	Entrepreneurship: Theory & Practice	2020
125	Anglin, Aaron H.; Short, Jeremy C.; Ketchen, Jr., David J.; Allison, Thomas H.; McKenny, Aaron F.	Entrepreneurship: Theory & Practice	2020
126	Chadwick, Ingrid C.; Raver, Jana L.	Entrepreneurship: Theory & Practice	2020
127	Funken, Rebecca; Gielnik, Michael M.; Foo, Maw-Der	Entrepreneurship: Theory & Practice	2020
128	Uzuegbunam, Ikenna; Ofem, Brandon; Nambisan, Satish	Entrepreneurship: Theory & Practice	2019
129	Chahine, Salim; Saade, Samer; Goergen, Marc	Entrepreneurship: Theory & Practice	2019
130	Jiang, Han; Cannella, Albert A.; Jiao, Jie	Entrepreneurship: Theory & Practice	2018
131	Smolka, Katrin M.; Verheul, Ingrid; Burmeister-Lamp, Katrin; Heugens, Pursey P. M. A. R.	Entrepreneurship: Theory & Practice	2018
132	Courtney, Christopher; Dutta, Supradeep; Li, Yong	Entrepreneurship: Theory & Practice	2017
133	Chan, C. S. Richard; Parhankangas, Annaleena	Entrepreneurship: Theory & Practice	2017
134	Butticè, Vincenzo; Colombo, Massimo G.; Wright, Mike	Entrepreneurship: Theory & Practice	2017
135	Skirnevskiy, Vitaly; Bendig, David; Brettel, Malte	Entrepreneurship: Theory & Practice	2017
136	Deligianni, Ioanna; Voudouris, Irini; Lioukas, Spyros	Entrepreneurship: Theory & Practice	2017
137	Ragozzino, Roberto; Blevins, Dane P.	Entrepreneurship: Theory & Practice	2016
138	Collewaert, Veroniek; Sapienza, Harry J.	Entrepreneurship: Theory & Practice	2016
139	Roma, Paolo; Vasi, Maria; Kolympiris, Christos	Research Policy	2021
140	Bruneel, Johan; Clarysse, Bart; Bobelyn, Annelies; Wright, Mike	Research Policy	2020
141	Gimenez-Fernandez, Elena M.; Sandulli, Francesco D.; Bogers, Marcel	Research Policy	2020
142	Hoogendoorn, Brigitte; Van Der Zwan, Peter; Thurik, Roy	Research Policy	2020
143	Zhao, Bo; Ziedonis, Rosemarie	Research Policy	2020
144	Brixy, Udo; Brunow, Stephan;D'ambrosio, Anna	Research Policy	2020
145	Bertoni, Fabio; Martí, Jose; Reverte, Carmelo	Research Policy	2019
146	Roma, Paolo; Messeni Petruzzelli, Antonio; Perrone, Giovanni	Research Policy	2017

147	Protogerou, Aimilia; Caloghirou, Yannis; Vonortas, Nicholas S.	Research Policy	2017
148	Autio, Erkko, Rannikko, Heikki	Research Policy	2016
149	Kim, Jungho; Lee, Chang-Yang	Research Policy	2016
150	Colombo, Massimo G.; D'adda, Diego; Pirelli, Lorenzo H.	Research Policy	2016
151	Stucki, Tobias	Research Policy	2016
152	Bertoni, Fabio; Tykvová, Tereza	Research Policy	2015
153	Howell, Anthony	Research Policy	2015
154	Hoenen, Sebastian; Kolympiris, Christos; Schoenmakers, Wilfred; Kalaitzan-donakes, Nicholas	Research Policy	2014
155	Audretsch, David B.; Bönte, Werner; Mahagaonkar, Prashanth	Research Policy	2012
156	Criscuolo, Paola; Nicolaou, Nicos; Salter, Ammon	Research Policy	2012
157	Cumming, Douglas J.; Fischer, Eileen	Research Policy	2012
158	Helmers, Christian; Rogers, Mark	Research Policy	2011
159	Bertoni, Fabio; Colombo, Massimo G.; Grilli, Luca	Research Policy	2011
160	Gimmon, Eli; Levie, Jonathan	Research Policy	2010
161	Wagner, S.; Cockburn, I.	Research Policy	2010
162	Mohammadi, Ali; Khashabi, Pooyan	Strategic Entrepreneurship Journal	2021
163	Forti, Enrico; Munari, Federico; Zhang, Chunxiang	Strategic Entrepreneurship Journal	2020
164	Bellavitis, Cristiano; Rietveld, Joost; Filatotchev, Igor	Strategic Entrepreneurship Journal	2020
165	Chan, Chien Sheng Richard; Patel, Pankaj C.; Phan, Phillip H.	Strategic Entrepreneurship Journal	2020
166	Bischoff, Kim Marie ; Gielnik, Michael M.; Frese, Michael	Strategic Entrepreneurship Journal	2020
167	Grimpe, Christoph; Murmann, Martin; Sofka, Wolfgang	Strategic Entrepreneurship Journal	2019
168	Gafni, Hadar; Marom, Dan; Sade, Orly	Strategic Entrepreneurship Journal	2019
169	Bertoni, Fabio; D'adda, Diego; Grilli, Luca	Strategic Entrepreneurship Journal	2019
170	Drnovsek, Mateja; Cardon, Melissa S.; Patel, Pankaj C.	Strategic Entrepreneurship Journal	2016
171	Moghaddam, Kaveh; Bosse, Douglas A.; Provance, Mike	Strategic Entrepreneurship Journal	2016
172	Gerasymenko, Violetta ; De Clercq, Dirk; Sapienza, Harry J.	Strategic Entrepreneurship Journal	2015
173	Paik, Yongwook	Strategic Entrepreneurship Journal	2014
174	Hmieleski, Keith M.; Corbett, Andrew C.; Baron, Robert A.	Strategic Entrepreneurship Journal	2013
175	Park, Haemin Dennis; Steensma, H. Kevin	Strategic Entrepreneurship Journal	2013
176	Wang, Xiaodan 'Abby'; Wan, William P.	Strategic Entrepreneurship Journal	2013

177	Li, Haiyang; Zhang, Yan; Li, Yu; Zhou, Li-An; Zhang, Weiying	Strategic Entrepreneurship Journal	2012
178	Semrau, Thorsten; Sigmund, Stefan	Strategic Entrepreneurship Journal	2012
179	Boeker, Warren; Fleming, Brandon	Strategic Entrepreneurship Journal	2010
180	Colombo, Massimo G.; Grilli, Luca; Murtinu, Samuele; Piscitello, Lucia; Piva, Evila	Strategic Entrepreneurship Journal	2009
181	Hmieleski, Keith M.; Baron, Robert A.	Strategic Entrepreneurship Journal	2008
182	Eddleston, Kimberly A.; Ladge, Jamie J.; Mitteness, Cheryl; Balachandra, Lakshmi	Entrepreneurship: Theory & Practice	2016
183	Flatten, Tessa Christina; Engelen, Andreas; Möller, Timo; Brettel, Malte	Entrepreneurship: Theory & Practice	2015
184	Ahlers, Gerrit K.C.; Cumming, Douglas; Günther, Christina; Schweizer, Denis	Entrepreneurship: Theory & Practice	2015
185	Moss, Todd W.; Neubaum, Donald O.; Meyskens, Moriah	Entrepreneurship: Theory & Practice	2015
186	Allison, Thomas H.; Davis, Blakley C.; Short, Jeremy C.; Webb, Justin W.	Entrepreneurship: Theory & Practice	2015
187	Colombo, Massimo G.; Franzoni, Chiara; Rossi-Lamastra, Cristina	Entrepreneurship: Theory & Practice	2015
188	Kollmann, Tobias; Stöckmann, Christoph	Entrepreneurship: Theory & Practice	2014
189	Semrau, Thorsten; Werner, Arndt	Entrepreneurship: Theory & Practice	2014
190	Michel, Jean-Sébastien	Entrepreneurship: Theory & Practice	2014
191	Sullivan, Diane M.; Ford, Cameron M.	Entrepreneurship: Theory & Practice	2014
192	Mousa, Fariss-Terry; Reed, Richard	Entrepreneurship: Theory & Practice	2013
193	Kreiser, Patrick M.; Patel, Pankaj C.; Fiet, James O.	Entrepreneurship: Theory & Practice	2013
194	Khoury, Theodore A.; Junkunc, Marc; Deeds, David L.	Entrepreneurship: Theory & Practice	2013
195	Pollack, Jeffrey M.; Rutherford, Matthew W.; Nagy, Brian G.	Entrepreneurship: Theory & Practice	2012
196	Brettel, Malte; Engelen, Andreas; Müller, Thomas; Schilke, Oliver	Entrepreneurship: Theory & Practice	2011
197	Bonardo, Damiano; Paleari, Stefano; Vismara, Silvio	Entrepreneurship: Theory & Practice	2011
198	Chahine, Salim; Filatotchev, Igor; Zahra, Shaker A.	Entrepreneurship: Theory & Practice	2011
199	Bruton, Garry D.; Chahine, Salim; Filatotchev, Igor	Entrepreneurship: Theory & Practice	2009
200	Chandler, Gaylen N.; Lyon, Douglas W.	Entrepreneurship: Theory & Practice	2009
201	Fernhaber, Stephanie A.; McDougall-Covin, Patricia P.	Entrepreneurship: Theory & Practice	2009
202	Zimmerman, Monica A.	Entrepreneurship: Theory & Practice	2008
203	Bell, R. Greg; Moore, Curt B.; Al-Shammari, Hussam A.	Entrepreneurship: Theory & Practice	2008
204	Hanlon, Dennis; Saunders, Chad	Entrepreneurship: Theory & Practice	2007
205	Stam, Wouter; Elfring, Tom	Academy of Management Journal	2008
206	Hmieleski, Keith M.; Baron, Robert A.	Academy of Management Journal	2009

207	Batjargal, Bat; Hitt, Michael A.; Tsui, Anne S.; Arregle, Jean-Luc; Webb, Justin W.; Miller, Toyah L.	Academy of Management Journal	2013
208	Ertug, Gokhan; Kotha, Reddi; Hedström, Peter	Academy of Management Journal	2020
209	Peterson, Suzanne J.; Walumbwa, Fred O.; Byron, Kristin; Myrowitz, Jason	Journal of Management	2009
210	Baron, Robert A.; Tang, Jintong	Journal of Management	2009
211	De Jong, Ad; Song, Michael; Song, Lisa Z.	Journal of Management	2013
212	Kiss, Andreea N.; Barr, Pamela S.	Journal of Management	2017
213	Hmieleski, Keith M.; Cole, Michael S.; Baron, Robert A.	Journal of Management	2012
214	Clarysse, Bart; Wright, Mike; Van De Velde, Els	Journal of Management Studies	2011
215	Hahn, Davide; Minola, Tommaso; Eddleston, Kimberly A.	Journal of Management Studies	2019
216	Burke, Andrew; Fraser, Stuart; Greene, Francis J.	Journal of Management Studies	2010
217	Hiatt, Shon R.; Sine, Wesley D.	Strategic Management Journal	2014
218	Kulchina, Elena	Strategic Management Journal	2017
219	Fitza, Markus; Matusik, Sharon F.; Mosakowski, Elaine	Strategic Management Journal	2009
220	Geroski, P. A.; Mata, José; Portugal, Pedro	Strategic Management Journal	2010
221	Arora, Ashish; Nandkumar, Anand	Strategic Management Journal	2012
222	Vissa, Balagopal; Chacar, Aya S.	Strategic Management Journal	2009
223	Souitaris, Vangelis; Maestro, B. M. Marcello	Strategic Management Journal	2010
224	Zheng, Yanfeng; Devaughn, Michael L.; Zellmer-Bruhn, Mary	Strategic Management Journal	2016
225	Wang, Taiyuan; Bansal, Pratima	Strategic Management Journal	2012
226	Alvarez-Garrido, Elisa; Guler, Isin	Strategic Management Journal	2018
227	Dencker, John C.; Gruber, Marc	Strategic Management Journal	2015
228	Li, Haiyang; Zhang, Yan	Strategic Management Journal	2007
229	Wasserman, Noam	Strategic Management Journal	2017
230	Chatterji, Aaron; Delecourt, Solène; Hasan, Sharique; Koning, Rembrand	Strategic Management Journal	2019
231	Chahine, S., Filatotchev, I., Bruton, G. D., Wright, M.	Journal of Management	2021
232	Wang, Tang; Song, Michael	Journal of Management	2016
233	Jiang, L., Yin, D., Liu, D.	Academy of Management Journal	2019
234	Kier, A. S., McMullen, J. S.	Academy of Management Journal	2018
235	Plummer, L. A., Allison, T. H., Connelly, B. L.	Academy of Management Journal	2016
236	Lungeanu, R., Zajac, E. J.	Academy of Management Journal	2016

237	Almandoz, J.	Academy of Management Journal	2012
238	Dencker, J. C., Gruber, M., Shah, S. K.	Academy of Management Journal	2009
239	Chahine, Salim; Zhang, Yan (Anthea)	Strategic Management Journal	2020
240	Garg, S, John Li, Q, Shaw, Jd.	Strategic Management Journal	2019
241	Arend, R.J., Patel, P.C.; Park, H.D.	Strategic Management Journal	2014
242	Park, H.D.; Steensma, H.K.	Strategic Management Journal	2012
243	Yu, J., Gilbert, B.A.; Oviatt, B.M.	Strategic Management Journal	2011
244	Gruber, M., Heinemann, F., Brettel, M.: Hungeling, S.	Strategic Management Journal	2010
245	Bruton, G.D., Filatotchev, I., Chahine, S.; Wright, M.	Strategic Management Journal	2010
246	Aggarwal, V.A.; Hsu, D.H.	Strategic Management Journal	2009
247	Bolzani, Daniela; Rasmussen, Einar; Fini, Riccardo	Strategic Entrepreneurship Journal	2021
248	Stevenson, Regan; Kier, Alexander S.; Taylor, Shannon G.	Strategic Entrepreneurship Journal	2021
249	Momtaz, Paul P.	Strategic Management Journal	2021
250	Murtinu, Samuele	Strategic Entrepreneurship Journal	2021
251	Samuelsson, M., Söderblom, A., McKelvie, A.	Entrepreneurship: Theory & Practice	2021
252	Warnick, Benjamin J.; Davis, Blakley C.; Allison, Thomas H.; Anglin, Aaron H.	Journal of Business Venturing	2021
253	Momtaz, Paul P.	Journal of Business Venturing	2021
254	Abootorabi, Hooman; Wiklund, Johan; Johnson, Alan R.; Miller, Cameron D.	Journal of Business Venturing	2021
255	Rose, Stefan; Wentzel, Daniel; Hopp, Christian; Kaminski, Jermain	Journal of Business Venturing	2021

Appendix B: List of New Venture Performance Measures (Chapter 2)

Article ID	Measure term	Measure
1	Idea originality	Rated on a scale of 1 (common, mundane, or boring business idea) to 4 (rare, unusual, ingenious, imaginative, or surprising business idea).
1	Idea feasibility	Rated on a scale of 1 (low feasibility) to 3 (high feasibility), indicating the preciseness and ease of implementation into a commercial product/service.
2	Pre-money valuation	Calculated the pre-money valuation as the difference between the post-money valuation and the investment amount.
2	Investment success	Dummy variable of one if the investment results in an IPO, and zero otherwise.
2	Number of patents	Number of patent applications at the time of the financing round.
3	Return on assets (RoA)	Return on assets (RoA) in year t + 1.
4	New venture idea quality	Expert judges evaluate quality of new venture idea on the basis of customer validation, execution and design, and business model.
5	Team performance	Judges rated the quality of the idea, the clarity of the customer need, the attractiveness of the identified market, the diligence of the financial prospects, and the skills and experience of the team. The rating of each criterion was translated into a score ranging from 0 (not covered) to 5 (very good), scores of all criteria were summed and scaled to a score with a minimum of 0 and a maximum of 100. In addition, if a judge considered a submission a potential winner, (s)he could check a box, resulting in 20 extra points. The maximum score that could be obtained from an individual judge was therefore 120. the average score of evaluations was used to establish a ranking of all submissions.
6	Entrepreneurial entry	1) discontinued start-up effort? 2) still trying to start business? or 3) successfully started business? coded 1 for started, 2 for still trying, and 3 for discontinued.
7	Quality of the business idea: Early venture performance	Written business plans rated by external experts on five dimensions: innovation in products and services, customer satisfaction, cost control and expected sales growth. Each dimension was measured using a multi-item scale.
7	Funding received: Later venture performance	Categorized performance: 1) venture received no funding; 2) venture received personal funding; 3) venture received angel investments; 4) venture received venture capital investment of EUR < 100.000; 5) venture received venture capital investment EUR > 100.000 and <1.000.000; 6) venture received venture capital investment of EUR > 1.000.000.
8	Organizational exit	Organizational exit as defined by the NETS database represents a complete cessation of operations at a particular establishment and does not represent other types of exit, such as a merger or an acquisition. Thus, organizational exit equals 1 if the last year of activity reported for a startup occurs on or before 2007, the last year of observation in our data.
9	Venture survival	Dummy variable that took a value of 1 if a firm still existed as an independent venture, and 0 if a firm had ceased to exist.
9	Firm performance	Compares the entrepreneur's perception of the firm with the original business plan in a number of domains, including revenue growth, employee growth, net profit margin, and customer satisfaction.
10	Sales	Number of times a course was sold between the end of December 2015 and the beginning of April 2016.
11	Sales-per-employee	One-year lag from the time period in which participants completed the study questionnaire. Formed by dividing the sales total by the employment total for each firm within that year.
12	Start-up's total financing needs	Start-up's total financing needs defined as its total expenditures on investments and operating costs. Survey asked start-ups to indicate the amounts of (a) retained earnings, (b) founders' own means (i.e., personal savings or business deposits), and (c) external funding that were used to cover all capital investments and operating costs in the year prior to the survey. Sum of the three amounts to calculate a start-up's total financing needs.
13	Survival duration	Survival duration is measured in months from the starting date of the firm.
13	Profit	Annual profits are calculated by deducting business costs, investments and other deductions from the yearly turnover.
13	Costs	Costs that were reported by the entrepreneurs to the tax administration.
14	Sales growth rate	[(sales t+1 – sales t) / (sales t)], taken from the audited annual financial statements.
14	Employment growth rate	[(employees t+1 – employees t) / (employees t)], taken from the audited annual financial statements.
14	Profitability growth	(ros t+1 – ros t), taken from the audited annual financial statements.
15	Start-up performance	Year-on-year change in the value of each start-up's assets.
16	Growth	Absolute year-over-year change in employment
17	Venture goal progress	Incubator director/head rated each lead entrepreneur's venture goal progress using the four-item goal progress measure (1 = strongly disagree, 5 = strongly agree) adapted from Brunstein's goal progress measure (Brunstein, 1993). In all items, changed "I" to "this entrepreneur".
18	Exit	Exit defined as the complete cessation the venture as an independent unit, coded as 1 in the year when a venture exits. Otherwise, this variable is coded as 0. Ventures still active by the end of our eight-year observation period are right censored. Because selling or merging the venture may be seen as a successful outcome, we exclude ventures that were acquired or merged from our analysis and treat these ventures as censored (Gimeno et al., 1997).

Article ID	Measure term	Measure
18	Firm growth	Growth defined as the ratio between next-period and current-period size and firm growth rate as the ratio minus one (Greve, 2008).
18	Survival reference point	Altman's Z-score model of financial distress. Ventures with Z-scores below 1.8 are generally considered "near bankruptcy." We code the survival reference point as 1 for all ventures with Z-scores below 1.8 and 0 otherwise.
18	Performance aspiration point	Aspiration reference point is historical aspiration, calculated as a moving two-year average of a venture's past sales per employee performance
18	Performance above or below firms' social aspirations	Performance as the difference between the focal venture's performance and the average performance of all other firms in the same industry at the five-digit Industrial Classification level. Aspiration point variables are entered as spline functions, meaning that separate variables are entered for performance above or below a firm-specific aspiration point.
19	Number of start-up activities	To form this outcome, we used a comprehensive set of 29 activities. information came from respondents who reported at each interview whether they completed each activity and if so, when the activity occurred (month/year). On average, founders completed about 12 activities. Multiple activities could be completed in the same month. Activities: Talked with potential customers; Collected information about competitors; Purchased raw materials, inventory, supplies; Generated income; Defined market opportunities; Acquired equipment, facilities, or property; Determined regulatory requirements ; Began marketing efforts; Opened business bank account; Recruited team member; Established legal form; Developed financial projections; Filed income tax return; Finished product development; Registered business name; Established supplier credit; Hired accountant; Obtained liability insurance; Requested outside funding; Paid FICA taxes; Filed DBA name; Hired lawyer; Prepared business plan; Hired employee; Received outside funding; Joined trade association; Received loan; Paid unemployment insurance; Secured space for business
19	Achieved initial sales	Received initial revenue from the sale of goods/ services for this new business (0/1).
19	Achieved early-stage profitability	Achieved monthly revenue exceeding month expenses for more than six of the past twelve months (0/1).
19	Major work focus	Reported new business to be a major focus of work career over the next twelve months, conceptualized as making a significant commitment to the new venture (0/1).
20	Start-up valuation	Post-investment valuation of start-up at date of funding round (in million USD), i.e., the equity value of the start-up, plus the amount of funds invested. this variable discloses the post-money valuation of the start-up at its funding date (i.e., the equity value of the start-up that includes the amount of funds that are provided in that round).
20	Trademark applications	Number of US trademark applications filed by start-up until the respective funding round date.
20	Patent applications	Number of US patent applications filed by start-up until the respective funding round date.
21	Entrepreneurial forecast performance	Entrepreneurs were asked, "How much do you think your business met your expectations for growth between when the business was started and December 31, 2008?" Entrepreneurs could respond: 1) exceeded; 2) met; or 3) did not meet.
22	Survival	Set to 1 if start-up is still open at the end of the period; 0 otherwise
22	Log turnover	Log of annual credit turnover of the current account
22	Turnover growth	Growth of annual credit turnover, Sales growth is calculated by taking log-differences of annual sales.
22	Start-up size	Sales in the first year
23	Organizational mortality	The year in which the first model of producer x was mentioned in the sources, was coded as the year of entry into industry of firm x, and the year in which firm x's last model disappears from the sources' registers, was coded as its year of failure. Failure is being defined as disbanding or exit to another industry. Those firms known to have ended by a merger or an acquisition are treated as right-censored observations. While our data sources are clear about disbanding, they do not always report what happened to some firms dropped from the sample due to other reasons, 'unknown events' were in all likelihood disbandings or exits to other industries. Thus, we code them as failure events (see also Hannan et al., 1998a, Hannan et al., 1998b, Dobrev et al., 2001).
23	Product portfolio overlap at entry	Innovativeness: degree to which the product portfolio of a new entrant overlaps with those of incumbent firms. Sum of the overlap between each potential pair proportionally to their product range. If both firms exactly occupy the same niches, a value of 1 is given. This pairwise comparison is repeated with respect to each incumbent firm; subsequently, all pairwise values are summed up. Such a portfolio overlap at entry measure is computed in the year of entry of the firm.
24	Emergence	Operationalized emergence as a dummy variable, with cases assigned a value of one if they had become cash flow positive as of the final wave of data collection and zero otherwise.
25	Engagement in multilateral R&D alliances	Set to 1 when the venture is involved in a multilateral R&D alliance and 0 when it is not.
25	Market value creation (Cumulative abnormal return)	We adopt an event study methodology to retrieve the cumulative abnormal return (CAR) in the venture's stock response to the announcement of a multilateral R&D alliance. First, using an estimation period of 150 days (− 170, − 21), we estimate the

Article ID	Measure term	Measure
		market model of each venture's stock returns prior to the event date: rit = αi + βirmt + εit, where rit denotes the daily return for venture i on day t, rmt represents the corresponding daily return for the value-weighted CRSP index as the market portfolio to derive the firm-specific parameters αi and βi. The error term εit is independent and identically distributed. Second, we use the estimated coefficients from the market model to predict daily returns for venture i on day t over the event window: Rit = αi + βirmt. We adopt a two-day event window (− 1, 0)12. Third, we compute the abnormal returns (ARs) for venture i on each day of the event window: ARit = rit − Rit, where rit is the actual ex post return on the share price for venture i on day t and Rit is the predicted return on the share price for venture i on day t. Finally, the abnormal stock returns for each day in the event window are summed to arrive at the cumulative abnormal return over the event window: CARi(− 1,0) = ∑ ARit.
26	New venture growth	Self-reported approach. Following the new venture growth literature, three survey items asked for each firm's sales, employee, and market share growth on a six-point Likert scale. combined them to construct a composite growth variable.
27	Profit margin	Measured as the ratio of firm profit to firm revenue in the firm's most recent fiscal year.
28	Size: employees (n)	Firm size is measured (log of the) number of employees. the dependent variable can be interpreted as an indicator of the average yearly absolute growth of firms up to the survey date.
28	Size: sales ('000 €)	Firm size is measured by the (log of the) sales.
28	VC	One for firms that obtained venture capital. Zero otherwise.
29	Firm valuation	Total market value of the company's equity. Operationalized as the product of its shares outstanding and the price per share at the conclusion of a financing round.
30	New venture start-up	Utilized a time-lagged measure from the PSED sample which asks respondents to categorize the status of their potential venture at Time1–3 with four choices: 1 — operating business, 2 — active start-up (still actively pursuing a potential start-up), 3 — non-active start-up, 4 — abandoned idea/business. To measure actual start-up activities, all of the responses indicating the firm was operational and that we could cross-check with a reported month and year of start-up were coded as a "1." Additionally, all of the responses where the respondents reported that they had abandoned their intentions to start a new venture were coded with a "0." Those respondents indicating that they were still actively/inactively pursuing a potential start-up but had not yet done so in the last round of surveys were treated as censored observations and following standard procedure in survival analysis, were coded as "0."
31	Employment growth	Respondents were asked the number of employees working less than 10 h, from 10–35 h, and 35 or more hours. Employees working ten hours or less are computed as 1/4 FTE (full-time equivalent), employees working between 10–35 h are computed as 1/2 FTE and employees working 35 or more hours are computed as 1 FTE. We calculate the change in employment as the difference between 2004 and 1995 levels.
31	Sales growth	Sales growth is the (natural log of) slope of the sales regression line over time
32	Revenues per lawyer	Annual revenue data obtained from the British Columbia Business to Business Directory and annual data on the numbers of lawyers from the Canadian Law List.
32	Revenues per partner	Annual revenue data was obtained from the British Columbia Business to Business Directory and annual data on the numbers of partners from the Canadian Law List.
33	Relative growth in sales	Relative growth in sales from the year of IPO through the second year after IPO is our measure of growth performance. Data sourced from Compustat database.
33	Product innovation	All new and enhanced products introduced during the two years after the firm went public to reflect the overall product innovation activity of the firms during the time period of interest.
34	Sales growth	Average annual sales growth rate over the most recent three-year period. Acquired from Dun and Bradstreet
35	Startup–VC partnership performance	Survival to another funding round as a signal of partnership success. We coded follow-on funding as 1 if the focal startup received a second-round investment from its lead VC in a given year.
36	New venture performance	Assessed relative to a firm's major competitors, using seven items from Stam and Elfring (2008) that operationalize a range of growth (e.g., sales and employment growth), financial (e.g., market share, gross profits, and profit margin), and innovation metrics (e.g., product/service innovation and speed in product/service development).
37	Investor funding amount	Operationalized as a continuous outcome variable measured as the total US dollar value of funding received by each of the entrepreneurs who pitched to the investors on Shark Tank across different seasons.
37	Entrepreneur performance	Operationalized as the sales revenue reported by the entrepreneur in his or her pitch presentation. we measured sales revenue as the natural logarithm of the total USD value of the sales revenue each entrepreneur reported prior to his or her pitch.
38	Fundraising performance	Amount raised, in USD, continuous variable, measuring the amount of capital committed by backers to the campaign.
39	Firm status	Firm's status at the time of the follow-up in 2004. There are three possible outcomes: 1) having survived as an independent firm (121 firms), 2) having been acquired (27 firms), and 3) having ceased to exist (32 firms), which includes bankruptcy, having been shut down, and firms that could not be located. Having ceased to exist is used as

Article ID	Measure term	Measure
		the reference category to which the other two are compared; having survived as an independent firm is our outcome of interest.
39	Customer portfolio growth	Difference between the total number of customers in 2003 and the total number of customers in 1997, divided by the total number of customers in 1997. To ensure consistency across firms in defining an active customer, we asked respondents for the number of customers their firms sent an invoice to in the preceding year.
40	Product/service innovativeness	Startup coaches completed a five item, five-point scale that focused on the founders' product or service offering. The response scale ranged from "strongly disagree" to "strongly agree." The measure focuses on the extent to which the founders' new product or service offering is novel to the industry and advances new ideas.
41	Firm survival	Firm exit is defined as two successive years of no activity, i.e., zero employees. Because we cannot observe the exact exit time, a firm exit indicates that the firm exits within the following year.
41	Employment growth	Calculated by taking log-differences of the number of employees at time t and t – 1.
42	Failure	Value of 0 if continued to exist at the end of our observation period or 1 if failed.
43	Crowdfunding performance	Operationalized the outcome of each fundraising campaign as a dichotomous variable which was coded as 1 if successful. This operationalization is consistent with the "all-or-nothing" nature of Kickstarter.
44	VC funding	Set of binary indicator variables that were set to 1 if a startup receives any VC funding: (a) within the first two quarters, (b) between quarter three and four, or (c) between quarter five and six following a focal quarter, and set to 0 otherwise.
44	Grant	Set to 1 if a startup received a grant in that quarter, and set to 0 otherwise.
44	Patents	Continuous variable that counts the cumulative number of patent applications a startup has made since its founding. We sourced the patent data from the Patent-Edge database.
45	Total funding amount	Operationalized as the dollar amount of funding. The dependent variable only includes external funding, such as funding from venture capitalists (e.g., venture capital equity and convertible preferred stock), and funding from angel investors. It does not include any funding provided by the founders or government grants.
46	Success	If at the end of the campaign, the funds raised were greater than or equal to the funding target, a value of 1 was assigned to the success variable.
46	Funds raised	Total amount of funds raised.
47	Funds raised	Total funds raised by the end of the campaign irrespective of the funding goal set by the entrepreneur or whether the goal was met.
47	Backers	Operationalize crowdfunding performance using a continuous variable for the number of individuals that supported a campaign that we label backers.
47	Success	Captures whether the funding goal set at the beginning of the campaign was met. For campaigns that met their goal, the success variable was coded as '1' and was coded as '0' otherwise.
48	Crowdfunding success	Operationalized crowdfunding success, as a binary variable indicating whether the campaign received funding or not.
49	Internationalization propensity	Internationalization propensity was equal to 1 if the new venture engaged in international sales and 0 if it did not.
49	Internationalization intensity	International intensity was an ordinal categorical variable recording the percentage of firms' total sales generated outside the US as either below 5%, 5–25%, 26–50%, 51–75% or 76–100%.
50	Entrepreneurial founding	Respondents were asked to identify all businesses they owned since age 18 on a one-time basis. To measure the timing of founding, we used the starting month and year of each business.
50	Earnings from entrepreneurship	Followed previous studies (e.g., Chen, 2013, Fairlie, 2005, Van Praag et al., 2013) in using the sum of income from all sources to measure business earnings. For individuals who had businesses in a calendar year, earnings from entrepreneurship are computed as the natural log of the sum of reported wage, salary, and business income. If business owners go back to paid employment, we did not include those wages in their entrepreneurial earnings. To retain observations reporting zero business income, we follow Glaeser and Kerr (2009) by recoding these values as one dollar.
51	Speed of venture entry	Speed of venture entry, relates to the time taken by the entrepreneur to set up the new venture. We examine the time elapsed from 'the conception of the business idea' to 'the launch of the company' – the very initial stage of venture creation process.
52	Venture met its funding goal	On crowdfunding platforms such as Kickstarter, the venture receives $0 if campaigns fail to meet their goal. Thus, hitting the goal is a critical outcome (0/1).
53	Entrepreneurial survival	Entrepreneurial survival, is based on the respondents' answers to the following question: "What is the current status of the enterprise you started with the start-up grant?" Those who answered the option 'still in operation' were coded as, "1" for entrepreneurial survival, otherwise "0" for those who had exited.
54	Profitability	Total profit over total assets
55	Firm: Survives	The three-year survival rate of a startup (Firm: Survives), takes on the value of one if the startup remains in business three years after its entry and is zero otherwise.
55	Firm: Innovates	Firm: Innovates, takes the value of one (and zero otherwise), if any of the following conditions are true about the firm in question at the time of market entry: (i) it plans to employ new-to-the-market processes in the next three years; (ii) it plans to introduce new-to-the-market products/services in the next three years; and/or (iii) it is actively pursuing innovations.

Article ID	Measure term	Measure
56	Annual revenues 2004 to 2008 growth	Annual revenues, 2004 to 2008 growth
56	Number of employees, 2004 to 2008 growth	Number of employees, 2004 to 2008 growth
56	Salary mass 2004 to 2008 growth	Salary mass, 2004 to 2008 growth
56	After-tax net income 2004 to 2008 growth	After-tax net income, 2004 to 2008 growth
57	Entrepreneurial earnings	Venture performance based on Hamilton's (2000) definition of entrepreneurial earnings—[revenues − expenses = money taken out + retained earnings]. Firm-level performance data from the venture's annual reports (in RAMS) with individual-level tax records (from LISA). Log-transformed.
58	Financial performance	Logarithm of hourly business profits averaged over that spell. In each year, profits are defined in the PSID as the labor part of the household head's total business and farm income from the previous year. The consumer price index (CPI) was then used to express these incomes in constant 1985 dollars. After matching income data to the previous year's observations, total profits were measured in every year of each spell before being divided by the entrepreneur's (self-reported) total annual work hours. Next, hourly profits were averaged over each spell. Finally, the logarithm of spell-average performance was taken to obtain Π. As well as correcting for skewness, a log transformation factors out any tendency to under-report incomes in the data.
59	Startup failure	For each firm-year observation, startup failure was coded as 1 if the startup failed in a given year and as 0 otherwise.
59	Total assets relative to competitors	Measure firms total assets divided by the sector average assets of all other independent new ventures in the same cohort. Total assets are the sum of: fixed assets—capital equipment and property (less depreciation), cash, accounts receivable, inventory, and supplies—and intangible assets, such as copyrights, trademarks, and patents.
60	ROI	Asked for the firm's ROI in the last fiscal year
60	Customer retention rate	Firm's customer retention rate in its primary served market (Lambert, 1998, McDougall et al., 1994).
61	Firm closure	Business closed in year t
61	Return on assets	((Net income / Assets) * (Assets / Shareholders Equity))/ Leverage
61	Sharpe ratio	Share ratio with profit as our reward measure and standard deviation in profit as our variability (risk) measure.
62	Survival	We measure survival two, three and four years after CVR registration. When computing survival, the participant need not remain in the firm as an employer. If a new firm is so successful that it is acquired by another firm which then employs the entrepreneur as an employee, it is classified as a surviving firm.
62	Employment	Employment, also measured 1, 2 and 3 years after the participation year
62	Firm sales	The outcome measure is firm sales (turnover) 1, 2 and 3 years after the participation year.
62	Growth firm	Defined as growing by at least 20% in terms of employment or sales in the second and third years after receiving counselling. To assess this we use data on sales and employment for three years after participation for the 2002–3 cohorts, and for one year for the 2004–5 cohorts.
63	Shareholder returns	To measure shareholder returns, we follow Carter et al. (1998) and use monthly returns in excess of the CRSP equally weighted index, compounded annually.
63	Lagged Tobin's q	We include a lagged measure of Tobin's q to capture past firm performance.
63	ROA	Return on assets
64	IPO Success	IPO Success is a composite measure of four separate financial measures: net proceeds of the IPO offering, pre-money market valuation, the 90-day post-IPO market valuation, and the 180-day post-IPO valuation. This measurement combines both the short-term and longer-term proxies of IPO stock-market performance and is not based on restrictive assumptions about the stock-market participants described previously.
65	Sales growth	Sales growth measured as the percentage of increase in sales between 1998 and 2000.
65	Profitability	Used Return on Assets (RoA) as a measure of profitability. This continuous variable was computed as the ratio of profits to assets.
66	Performance	Ln(revenue/ COGS)
67	Venture growth	Measured with five items. The items ask business owners to indicate percent changes in sales, profit, transaction volume, income, and number of employees in the year 2007 compared to the previous year. No change in these factors was indicated by 100%. A sample item is: "Compared to 2006, have your sales increased or decreased or did they stay the same in 2007? By what percentage have they in/decreased?"
68	Revenue growth	Measured based on two consecutive years' revenue data. These two years' revenue data came from SEC database and were used to calculate the revenue growth rate. The revenue growth was calculated using the formula: revenue (t + 1) − revenue (t) / revenue (t).
69	Patent	Dichotomous variable coded "1" if the firm applied in a given year for a patent that was eventually granted, and "0" otherwise. We elect to use the year of application rather than the grant year because the time of application more closely matches the time at which the knowledge was produced.

Article ID	Measure term	Measure
70	IPO valuations	Value of the IPO firm as the natural logarithm of the firm's market capitalization at the end of the IPO's first day of trading – the total number of outstanding shares at IPO multiplied by the closing price at the end of the first trading day.
71	Sales growth	Sales growth was the change in sales from Year 1 to Year N as a percentage of the sales in Year 1. For the Australian data, sales growth could be calculated in the first year (1995). For the Swedish data only current year sales are reported. Hence, growth can only be calculated from the second year (1998). Calculated relative to other firms in the industry. Specifically, we divided by the industry median rather than the mean to reduce the impact of outliers.
71	Profitability	Return on assets (RoA) as our measure of profitability. Slightly different measures were used due to data availability. For the Australian sample, data on pre-tax ROA was available, calculated as the net profit (operating profit or loss before tax and extraordinary items) as a percentage of total assets in each year. After tax ROA was available for the Swedish sample. Calculated relative to other firms in the industry. Specifically, we divided by the industry median rather than the mean to reduce the impact of outliers.
72	Return on assets ratio (RoA)	Calculated as earnings before interests and taxes divided by total assets. Lagged by one year.
72	Firm survival status	Survival status is measured in two ways. First, all firms dropping from the public market for various reasons are treated as having a death event. The paper then distinguishes between firms experiencing merger and acquisition and firms bankrupted or delisted from the public market due to poor performance. Firm survival information is drawn from CRSP and censored in 2003. Lagged by one year.
73	Profitablity likelihood	Denotes the likelihood that an Internet IPO firm will attain profitability in each period. We use quarterly operating income before depreciation as our measure of operating profitability.
74	Sales growth	Annual growth rate in sales. Sales growth indicates development in terms of customer base. Performance data were collected from the Compustat database for all years between the year in which the venture completed its IPO and 2000.
74	Employee growth	Annual growth rate in employees. Employee growth signals the need for additional resources to meet customer demands. Performance data were collected from the Compustat database for all years between the year in which the venture completed its IPO and 2000.
74	Asset growth	Annual growth rate in assets. Asset growth indicates that the firm is investing for the future. Performance data were collected from the Compustat database for all years between the year in which the venture completed its IPO and 2000.
75	Pre-money equity valuations	Pre-money equity valuations were purchased from Recombinant Capital (Recap).
75	Round-to-round returns	Relative to other sources of pre-money values such as VentureOne and VentureXpert, one of Recap's distinctive features is that for each financing round it reports the price per share, PRICE, the number of pre-money shares outstanding, SHSPRE, and the number of shares issued in the financing, SHSISS. As a result, round-to-round returns can be computed directly, rather than having to be inferred from pre-money valuations at round k relative to post-money valuations at round k − 1. The log return of firm i between venture capital funding rounds k − 1 and k is lnRETik ≡ ln(PRICEik / PRICEi,k−1), and the excess log return lnEXRET is ln[RET − Rf], where Rf is one plus the risk-free rate over the return interval.
76	Firm size	The (log of the) number of employees (+ 1)
76	Business turnover	Annual business turnover for 1999 in five categories: Ordinal 1 = < $25,000 USD; 2 = $25,001–125,000 USD; 3 = $125,001–250,000 USD; 4 = $250,001–1,250,000 USD; 5 = > 1,250,000 USD.
76	Business financial success	Earnings from the business cover living expenses in categories. Ordinal 1 = completely insufficient, 2 = not sufficient, 3 = sufficient, 4 = more than sufficient
77	Innovation performance	Four items: (a) "the degree of newness of our firm's products/services"; (b) "the use of the latest technological innovations in our new products/services"; (c) "the speed of development of new products/services"; (d) "the number of new products/services that our firm has introduced on the market"; and (5) "the number of new products that are first-to-market (early market entrants)." For each of these items, the respondents were asked to rate the outcomes of the firm's activities involving the adoption and introduction of innovations on a 7-point Likert scale, where 1 represents "much lower than its main competitors" and 7 "much higher than its main competitors."
78	Performance	Four items referring to whether the firm was still operating as of July 2017, the number of employees, whether it had received external funding, and years of operation.
79	New venture innovation	Innovative output of the new venture: To what extent does your firm, over the coming 12 months, intend to. . . Offer customers new products/services that are extensions or modifications of existing products/services? Offer customers new products/services that are new breakthroughs and can have a high impact on the market? Develop new products/services that are extensions or modifications of existing products/services? Develop new products/services that are new breakthroughs and can have a high impact on the market?
80	Total sales	Log of sales in USD (last year)

Article ID	Measure term	Measure
80	Number of employees	Log of numbers of employees (last year)
81	Technological performance Patent filed	Patent filed (y/n)
81	Technological performance Number of patent filings	Number of patent filings
81	Market performance	Market performance comprises time to first product and number of products. Product launched takes a value of 1 when the first product is shipped for revenues. Number of products indicates the number of products the company has on the market.
82	Annual growth	Difference between sales in two consecutive years divided by sales 1 year earlier.
82	Revenue growth	Sum of revenue growth percentages divided by the number of revenue years.
83	Growth rate of employees	Ratio of the increased number of employees to the initial number of employees at the time of start-up we measure the increase in size, and divide it by age (in months) to obtain the average growth rate over the venture's life.
84	Organizational emergence	Organizations emerge: when the NE assembles some key resources for the new firm: hires employees, receives external financing, and achieves first sale
85	First three - year average annual gross profit	First Three - Year Average Annual Gross Profit: Average Gross Profit Margin * Average Sales where: Average Gross Margin (in %) = (first year gross margin + second year gross margin + third year gross margin)/3; Average Sales = (first year sales + second year sales + third year sales)/3.
86	Employment growth per year	Employment growth in terms of absolute growth per year
86	Absolute Sales growth per year	Sales growth in terms of absolute growth per year
87	Venture Start-Up	Dichotomous variable that reflects whether or not the venture was described as "an operating business."
88	Profitability	ROS average for the first three fiscal years following the IPO of a new venture
88	Sales growth	Sales growth average for the first three fiscal years following the IPO of a new venture
89	Profitability	Average return on investment (ROI), return on sales (ROS), and return on assets (ROA) of each venture during the time period of the study
89	Sales growth	Sales Growth was computed as the average annual growth rate during the period of interest.
90	Progression of new venture creation	Activities they had participated in to start their new venture from a list of 12 items adapted from prior research (Davidsson & Honig, 2003). Items were coded 0 = Have not participated and 1 = Have participated, and were summed. The higher the number the farther along the venture had progressed.
91	Sales growth	Change in sales from previous year as a percentage of sales in the previous year
91	Pretax ROA	Net profit (operating profit or loss before tax and extraordinary items) as a percentage of total assets in each year
92	Competitiveness during firm growth stage	Six-item construct, semantic differential, 7 point likert (below the industry average—above the industry average) 1. Innovation speed; 2. Ability to respond rapidly to the market; 3. Production efficiency; 4. Product quality; 5. Production flexibility; 6. R&D capability
93	Perceived performance	Composite 3-item scale: assessment of the percent of ideal performance being achieved assessing growth relative to competitors and overall performance relative to competitors on 7-point agreement scales, were then interpolated into a 0–100 range equivalent.
94	Business survival	Dummy variable, equal to one if the individual's main employment activity is self-employment with the same business started in the first quarter of 2009, zero otherwise.
94	Income	Monthly and as hourly net earned income from self-employment (in euros, inflation-adjusted to 2010 levels following the Federal Statistical Office, 2014).
94	Job creation	Number of full-time equivalent employees is a weighted sum where full-time employees are assigned a weight of 1, part-time employees and apprentices are weighted by 0.5, and others by 0.25
94	Degree of innovation	Filed at least one patent application or an application to protect corporate identity since start-up. The subjective measure is based on the question whether businesses generate new ideas, questioning existing processes.
94	Access to capital	Received a loan since start-up or access to capital was constrained; in that they wanted to borrow but did not receive a loan
95	Patents	Aggregate number of U.S. granted patents a startup applied for within three years of inception (expressed in natural logarithm)
95	Funds raised	Amount of funds a startup raised (expressed in natural logarithm)
95	VC funding	Indicator that equals one if the focal startup received VC funding within five years of its inception and zero otherwise
95	Liquidity event	Indicator that equals one if the startup either went public via an IPO or was acquired by May 2016
96	Successfully financed	Successfully financed (y/n)
96	Number of backers	Number of backers supporting project
96	New product innovativeness	Please rate the degree to which your product was ... ... challenging existing ideas in your industry.a ... very novel for your industry. ... capable of generating ideas for other products.

Article ID	Measure term	Measure
		… offering new ideas to your industry. … encouraging fresh thinking.
97	Venture-capital funding	Dummy equal to "1" if a start-up receives VC funding within 2 years after the founding date
98	Patents	Number of patent applications for firm i in year t as a proxy for innovation efforts.
98	Private financing deals	Number of annual financing deals that each startup acquired per year
98	Growth	Binary variable equaling 1 for an acquisition or IPO in year t, and 0 otherwise.
99	Average sales	Average annual sales from the year following the filing of the subsidy application until year 2011.
100	Pre-money valuation	Product of the number of outstanding shares of a firm and the share price prior to the series A round (mean = $11.9M).
101	Firm performance	Binary variable of one if the firm survived, and zero otherwise.
102	Rounds of financing	Number of rounds of financing
102	Total amount of financing	Total financing in USD
102	Exit status	Exit status in four categories: defunct (including liquidated and bankrupt firms), existing, acquired, and public (including mergers and those in registration).
102	Longevity	Survival duration in days
103	Completion of an initial public offering	Dummy variable valued as one if a firm went public, was acquired, or was liquidated during our sample period, respectively. If the firm remained private, zero.
104	Hypothesis formulation	Number of new assumptions that each team articulated about their business idea on the program's platform in a given week.
104	Hypothesis probing	Number of stakeholder interviews a team conducted each week.
104	Business idea convergence	Number of items in a given week that were either removed from a team's business-model canvas (i.e., they were deemed invalid assumptions) or added to it without being associated with a hypothesis (i.e., they were considered a fact, not an assumption).
105	Product introductions	Measured as the focal venture's count of products receiving class III device approval from the U.S. Food and Drug Administration each year.
106	Failure	Failure which equals 1 in the year a firm closed down (this reflects insolvency or the start of a prolonged period of economic inactivity).
106	Firm growth	Calculate the logarithmic 3-year turnover growth (ln(turn (t + 3)/turn (t)) × 100).
107	CVC investment	CVC investment, which equals 1 if the new venture received an investment from Intel and 0 otherwise.
108	Change in revenues	Natural logarithm of the percentage change in revenues from the previous year. Performance was calculated by taking the difference between the revenues in years t and t-1 and dividing this by the revenues in year t-1.
108	Revenue growth relative to rivals	Revenue growth relative to rivals, natural logarithm of the percentage change in revenues from the previous year. Performance was calculated by taking the difference between the revenues in years t and t-1 and dividing this by the revenues in year t-1.
109	New venture performance	Nine-item, seven-point scale (Stam & Elfring, 2008) New venture performance: Please evaluate your firm's performance in the last year by choosing a number between 1 and 7, where 1 means that your firm was much worse and 7 means that your firm was much better than major competitors. NVP1. Sales level NVP2. Market share NVP3. Sales growthNVP4. Cash flow NVP5. Ability to fund business growth from profits NVP6. Return on assets NVP7. Return on equity NVP8. Return on sales NVP9. Overall firm performance/success
110	Venture viability	When monthly revenues exceed monthly expenses for six out of 12 months; including salaries for the managers" (1 = if the monthly revenues exceed monthly expenses for six out of 12 months; including salaries for the managers; 0 = otherwise).
111	Sales	Logarithm of sales in the previous period
111	Sales growth	Sales growth at t-1 is measured by the difference between the log of sales at t-1 and the log of sales at t-2.
112	Exit status	One of four possible outcomes (IPO, Acquired, Private, and Failure). A sample firm is at risk from birth to first event. Following prior research on university start-ups, we define liquidity as an initial public offering
112	Time to VC funds	Age of the firm at the time of first funding (Time to VC Funds)
113	Profit growth	Measured as the percentage of profit growth in the second revenue year.
114	Sales	Natural log of sales
114	Survival	Survival over the five-year period. If a firm survived for the entire period of our study, it was coded as 1; if not, it was coded as 0
114	Sales growth	Sales growth via year-to-year change in sales for the years 1995–99.
115	Revenue growth	Average annual revenue growth over the two-year period immediately following the collection of the survey data.
115	Employment growth	Average annual employment growth over the two-year period immediately following the collection of the survey data.
116	Sales growth	Log of (sales in t/ sales in t-1)
117	Total amount of funding	Total amount of funding acquired, controlled for the industry of the new venture.
118	New venture performance	performance in comparison to competitors over the last 3 years in four dimensions: development of sales, market share, profit, and creation of jobs, with 1 = worse and 7 = better.
119	Fundraising success	"0" if the project failed to meet the minimum funding goal and was thus not funded, and "1" if the project was successfully funded by meeting or exceeding the funding goal

Article ID	Measure term	Measure
119	Total pledge	Measured as the ratio of the project's final pledged amount over its funding goal
120	Severity of failure	Indicates by what percentage the aspiration level (i.e., funding goal) was missed in a given crowdfunding campaign
120	Persistence of failure	Count variable that indicates how many consecutive campaigns of the same entrepreneur failed to reach the aspired funding goal before the given campaign.
121	Initiated gestational activities	Summation of 33 gestational behaviors defined in the PSED II, such as establishing supplier credits, registering legal business forms, etc. During each interview round, respondents were asked which of the 33 activities they had performed and the dates when each activity was started. We coded each gestational activity as a "1" if initiated by the end of each monthly observation, and a "0" otherwise. The activities were summed during the time when the firms were active startups.
122	New venture survival	Captures operational ventures (a) for which the founder works full-time, (b) that generate monthly revenues exceeding monthly expenses for more than 6 months within a 12-month period, and (c) the perseverance of the entrepreneur as reflected by the operational business existing for at least 5 years
123	Survival	Survival is a venture continuing operations, that is, the absence of exit. We do not distinguish between different types of exit, nor do we frame exit in terms of individual- or firm-level failure. Every 6 months, all dormant accounts were identified. If they continued to be dormant for another 6 months, it was assumed the exit took place at the start of the first 6-month period. We checked exit routes and excluded ventures that were still trading but had switched to another bank.
123	Time spent in excess of overdraft	Proportion of time a new venture spends in excess of the allowed overdraft limit each year. For example, if a venture spends 15 days in excess of the overdraft limit, then this would correspond to a value of 0.04 (i.e., 15/365).
123	Short-term revenue volatility	Standard deviation in monthly credit turnover over a 12-month period divided by the mean monthly turnover for that period.
124	Number of suppliers	Number of suppliers (i.e., business/corporate partners)
124	Number of buyers	Number of buyers (i.e., business/corporate partners)
124	Assets value	Assets value (in million yuan)
124	ROA	Return on assets
125	Success	If the campaign met its target, the success variable was coded as “1.” If the campaign missed its target, the success variable was coded as “0.”
126	Business survival	operationalized as whether the business was still in operation (coded as 1) or had been closed (coded as 0) 2 years after the first survey and 1 year after the end of the entrepreneurship program.
127	Venture progress	‘‘In the last week,’’ followed by three items ‘‘the business made good progress,’’ ‘‘it has become more likely that the business will be successful,’’ and ‘‘the business significantly developed.’’ The participants answered all items on 7-point Likert scales ranging from ‘‘not at all’’ to ‘‘absolutely.’
128	Patents (pre-/ post CVC)	"How many patents does [NAME BUSINESS] have?" (pre-/ post CVC)
128	Copyrights	"How many copyrights does [NAME BUSINESS] have?" (pre-/ post CVC)
128	Trademarks	"How many trademarks does [NAME BUSINESS] have?" (pre-/ post CVC)
129	IPO premium	Difference between the offer price and the pre-IPO book value per share expressed as a fraction of the offer price as a measure of investors' IPO valuation.
130	New venture failure risk	Altmans Z
131	Venture performance	Rate the performance of their business since its establishment in comparison to their competitors on a 7-point Likert scale (1 5 worse, 4 5 equal, 7 5 better)
132	Success	Dummy variable, equal to one if the project was able to reach the crowdfunding goal set by the project founder at the start of the project.
133	Average funding amount	Dividing the total amount of funding a campaign received by the number of funders who had pledged.
134	Success	Crowdfunding successful (0/1)
135	Success	Reached funding goal (0/1)
135	Early backers	Number of early backers (within first 1/6th of duration)
135	Early funds raised	Share of the funding goal that had been reached (within first 1/6th of duration)
135	Duration	Duration of a campaign in days
136	Subjective new venture performance	Perceived performance over the last 3 years compared with that of their main competitors in terms of sales volume, profitability, sales growth, growth in profits, and market share growth.
136	Return on equity (ROE)	Return on equity (ROE)
137	Acquisition exit	Value of one if the new venture was acquired within the first 10 years of its life and zero otherwise.
137	IPO exit	IPO exit takes a value of one if the venture experienced an IPO during the same time window, and zero otherwise.
137	Number of VCs invested in the new venture	Number of different VCs that funded the new venture during the 10 years comprising our observation
137	Total amount invested	Total dollar amount received by a company from all venture capitalists from the time of the first to the time of the last investment.
137	VC duration	Computed as the number of years that elapsed between the time of the first VC investment in the new venture until the time of the last, and it is bounded between zero and 10 years.
138	Innovativeness	Rate the current innovativeness of the company, compared with its competitors, on a 7-point Likert scale (1 = much lower than average, 7 = much higher than average).

Article ID	Measure term	Measure
138	Perceived performance	Sapienza and Gupta's multi-criterion measure of venture performance. This implies using the weighted priorities each individual holds regarding the 11 objectives used in the priority agreement scale and multiplying them with their satisfaction regarding the current performance of the venture on each of these objectives on a scale from 1 (= not at all satisfied) to 5 (= extremely satisfied). These weighted scores were then summed across all financial and nonfinancial objectives, respectively, and divided by 100. Adding these two sums and averaging them across all angels and entrepreneurs results in a weighted average, multicriterion performance measure (range 1–5).
139	Subsequent funding from VCs	New venture has received subsequent funding from VCs (1, 0 otherwise)
140	Successful exit	Define successful exit as an IPO or acquisition in which the price paid exceeded the total amount of VC received.
141	Innovation performance	Proportion relative to turnover of new or strongly improved products that the company introduced to the market and that were new to the market.
142	Innovation	General index of innovation, and this index is calculated as the average of the three items Item 1: "Do all, some, or none of your potential customers consider this product or service new and unfamiliar?" with answers all (value 2), some (value 1), or none (value 0). Item 2: "Right now, are there many, few, or no other businesses offering the same products or services to your potential customers?" with answers no (value 2), few (value 1), or many (value 0). Item 3: "Have the technologies or procedures required for this product or service been available for less than a year, between one to five years, or longer than five years?" with answers less than a year (value 2), between 1 to 5 years (value 1), or longer than 5 years (value 0).
143	Survives	Indicator set to 1 if a startup is still active and in good standing 2 (4) years after the competition
143	SBIR awards	SBIR and STTR grants a startup receives 2 (4) years after the competition
143	VC investments	VC investments a startup receives 2 (4) years after the competition
144	Innovation	Binary variable equal to 1 if the firm has introduced any kind of innovation, and to 0 otherwise
144	Turnover	Turnover amount (log)
144	Investments	Investments amount
145	Emp. growth	Year-on-year difference in the logarithm and are winsorized at the 5% threshold to reduce the impact of outliers.
145	Sales growth	Year-on-year difference in the logarithm and are winsorized at the 5% threshold to reduce the impact of outliers.
146	Subsequent professional funding	Value one if the given new venture has received any type of funding from professional investors, from seed stage to venture capital investments, zero otherwise.
146	Money pledged	Amount of money pledged (in dollars)
147	Product innovation	Constructed an ordinal variable that can take four possible values depending on the novelty of the product innovation developed and introduced into the market: 0 (=no innovation); 1 (=new to the firm); 2 (=new to the market); and 3 (=new to the world).
148	Sales growth	Log difference of sales between the year before the firm applied to the NIY Programme and realised sales during each of the three subsequent years.
149	Firm survival	Each firm in the sample has a unique identification code, if code for an existing company disappeared from the database due to either a business closure or a bankruptcy or an impaired capital case, it was regarded as an exit. If the code remained at a given year, the firm was considered as surviving until that year.
149	Profitability	Operating profit margin (operating income/total sales)
150	Total assets	Ln Total Assets
150	Cash flow/sales	Accounting ratio Cash Flow/Sales
150	Financial debt/total Aassets	Accounting ratio Financial Debt/Total Assets
151	Export yes/no	Firm has export activities yes/no
151	Export sales	Export sales, ln
152	Number of patents	Count of patents granted to the company in a given year.
152	Number of passive citations	Weights each patent by the number of forward citations.
153	Firm closure	Exit year of the firm is defined as the last year, t, that the firm reported information but not in the year t + 1, t + 2, …, 2007
153	Duration of a firm	Defined by counting the number of years the firm is in operation, excluding its initial year of operation
153	Profit rates	Calculated as the ratio of firm profits (total plant sales minus materials costs, electricity costs, expenditures on wages, etc.) to plant sales.
153	Firm's total factory productivity	Difference between the growth rate of output and the weighted average of the input factors' growth rate
153	Firm sales growth	Logarithm of the difference in firm sales between year t and year t − 1.
154	Funding size	Size of the round of venture capital funds (1,000,000 USD)
154	Patent applications	Number of patent applications filed by a biotechnology firm from foundation to the first round of investments
154	Patents granted	Number of patents granted to a biotechnology firm from firm foundation to the first round of investment
155	External financing	None/ Debt/ Equity/ both categories Entrepreneurs reported whether they used the following external financing sources to establish their business: (1) bank loans to the business, (2) home equity loan in an

Article ID	Measure term	Measure
		owner's name, (3) other bank loans in an owner's name, (4) venture funds in exchange for stock/ownership in company and (5) individual investors or companies in exchange for stock/ownership in company.
155	Patents	"Does your business own or have you applied for a patent that is essential to the business?". This question was used to compute the dummy variable 'patents' which takes the value one if the answer is YES and zero otherwise.
155	Progress	Where is your business in the start-up process? (Answers: concept in development, concept developed, prototype developed, start-up operation or product/service launched)
156	Size: employees (n)	Number of employees in 2004
156	Employment growth rate bands	Employment growth rate bands: 1: <Industry mean – std. dev. 2: (Industry mean – std. dev.; industry mean – 1/2 std. dev.] 3: (Industry mean – 1/2 std. dev.; industry mean] 4: (Industry mean; industry mean + 1/2 std. dev.] 5: (Industry mean + 1/2 std. dev.; industry mean + std. dev.] 6: >Industry mean + std. dev.
156	Product innovation	Equals to 1 if a firm introduced a product innovation
156	Share of sales from innovative products	Percentage of total sales from products new to the market and from products new to the firm introduced between 2002 and 2004
157	Sales growth	The percentage change in sales from 2008 to 2009, based on the most recent 12 month financial information as at 06/2009
157	Investments	A dummy variable equal to 1 for firms that are either actively seeking equity capital from an angel investor, or have been successful from obtaining angel capital from an equity investor, as at 06/2009
157	Patents	A dummy variable equal to 1 for firms that have applied for and/or obtained a patent as at 06/2009
158	Firm growth	Average annual change in firms' total assets
158	Firm survival	Survival indicator si of the selection equation is constructed using the information of 'inactive' firms available in FAME. Inactive firms are those that have exited the market and belong to one of the following categories: dissolved, liquidated, entered receivership or declared non-trading.
159	Likelihood of obtaining the first round of VC finance	Likelihood of the focal firm obtaining the first round of VC finance after t years from foundation, conditional on not obtaining such finance up to t (i.e. the hazard rate of VC financing). On obtaining VC, the firm enters an absorbing state and no longer contributes to the likelihood function.
159	Size	Log number of employees (in full-time equivalents and including owner–managers) and lagged by one period.
159	Patent stock	Cumulative number of patents granted to the focal firm up to t.
160	Venture survival	Non-survivors = 0; Survivors = 1
160	External investment	Funds not raised = 0; Raised funds = 1
160	Investment rounds	Continuous scale of rounds
161	Survival	Total length of the listing period on the NASDAQ as the difference between the date of delisting and the date of the IPO. This "length of listing period" is used as the duration measure in the survival analyses.
161	Cash "burn rate"	Calculated as the negative of the ratio of operating income for the current quarter to the sum of cash and short-term investments in the previous quarter.
161	Operating income	Operating Income from Compustat
161	Sales	Sales from Compustat
162	Deal CVC	Deal CVC takes the value of one if at least one of the investors in the rounds of investments is a CVC; otherwise, it equals zero.
163	Number of brand assets	Measured as the number of trademark applications filed by company i in year t.
163	VC Backing	Operationalized as a dummy taking value 1 for VC-backed startups from the year of first round of VC funding onwards, and zero otherwise.
163	Firm innovative productivity	Citation-weighted patent stock at year t
164	Successful exit	Dependent variable takes the value of 1 if, in a given year, the venture exits through IPO or M&A, 0 otherwise.
164	Equity invested	Cumulative amount of equity invested in a venture up to date (in millions of current USD)
165	Equity funding change	Captures the change from entry and at the end of Year 1 in funding amount from equity investors.
165	Debt funding change	Captures the change in amounts of money a venture borrowed during the first year in the accelerator.
165	Change in employee numbers	Difference between the numbers of full-time employees during the first year in the accelerator.
165	Change in human capital costs	Change in the total amounts of wages, salaries, and benefits paid to secure human capital during the first year in the accelerator.
165	Revenue change	Change in a new venture's total earned revenues from entry to end of Year 1 in the accelerator.
165	Profit status	Change in profit status during the first year. Profit status is based on a venture's income after all expenses and taxes and is based on a scale such that 0 = negative profit margin, 1 = profit margin between 0 and 5%, 2 = profit margin between 6 and 10%, 3

Article ID	Measure term	Measure
		= profit margin between 11 and 15%, 4 = profit margin between 16 and 20%, 5 = profit margin of 20% and above.
166	Business creation	Measured business creation before (T1) and 18 months after the training program (T3). We asked, "Are you currently the owner of a business?", coding participants' answers as "1" (yes) and "0" (no).
167	Product innovation	Dummy variable for the introduction of a new product in a given year. We identify a startup as having a product innovation when it indicates that it had a new product (or service) that is new to the market, not just new to the startup itself.
168	Funding goal reached	Measure is estimated as a binary variable that equals 1 if the project managed to raise sufficient funds to match the original goal (and proceeded to receive the funds)
168	Percentage pledged	Calculated by dividing the sum pledged by the total goal.
168	Number of backers	Number of backers funding the project
169	VCFinancing	Dummy equal to 1 if the firm has ever received VC financing.
170	Venture growth	Calculated percentage change in sales (employee) from 2011 to 2012, and from this percentage change, we subtract industry median percentage change in sales (employee) from 2011 to 2012. We then take a mean of industry-adjusted changes in sales and employee as the measure of venture growth.
171	Post money valuation	Natural logarithm of post-money valuation for the latest investment transactions
172	PFC performance	Change in value of the PFC between the initial and most recent round of funding.
173	Firm survival duration	Survival time is measured by a venture's entry and exit dates. Entry is defined as the date a start-up firm acquired its first round of financing from a VC. Exit is defined as the date a start-up firm either (1) goes out of business or (2) gets acquired by another firm but has a market valuation less than its total investment at the time of exit, which is a de facto failure. Alternatively, I include ventures that generated less than 20 percent annualized returns, which is the standard hurdle rate in the VC community, as failures. A venture that gets acquired by another firm but has a market valuation greater than its total investment at the time of exit is a financial success for both VCs and entrepreneurs alike. In this case, acquisition is an alternative exit strategy to an IPO, and the entrepreneurial business continues to operate. Hence, I do not regard this case as a failure.
173	Total investment	Measures the total amount of VC financing received
173	Time-to-funding	Measures the time between the self-reported founding date of the venture and the first round of VC financing, in months.
174	Revenue growth	Calculated as the lagged revenue percentage change over this two-year period.
174	Employment growth	Calculated as the lagged employment percentage change over this two-year period.
175	Rate of innovation/ Innovative capabilities	Number of patent applications (that were subsequently granted) within three years of last round of VC funding by a new venture / prior to first round of VC funding by a new venture
176	IPO underpricing	Calculated as the first-day closing price minus the offer price, divided by the offer price.
176	Firm size (asset)	Measured firm size by using total assets (logarithmic transformed) before IPO.
176	Current ratio	Current liabilities/Current assets
176	Operational profit	Operational profits (scaled by total assets)
177	Employment size	Measured employment size as the natural logarithm of the number of employees in a venture in a year
177	Sales	Sales as the natural logarithm of the total sales of a venture in a year
177	Profit	Profit as the natural logarithm of the total profit of a venture in year
177	Exit	We coded exit as '1' for a venture in year t if the venture appeared in the data set for year t but not for year t + 1, and as '0' (i.e., survival) otherwise. We treated all venture-year observations in 2003 (the last year of our research period) as right censored in the survival analysis.
178	Revenue	Asked our respondents to indicate, in broad categories revenue, the response categories ranged from 1 (up to €50,000) to 9 (more than €10,000,000).
178	Growth rate revenue	Revenue growth rates were grouped in seven brackets ranging from 1 (less than 5%) to 7 (more than 200%) and had to be indicated for a three-year period (or in comparison to their first 12 months of operation if the venture was younger than three years). We then divided these cumulative growth rates by three (or company age if the company was younger than three years) to obtain comparable average growth rates.
178	Profit growth rates	Profit growth rates were grouped in seven brackets ranging from 1 (less than 5%) to 7 (more than 200%) and had to be indicated for a three-year period (or in comparison to their first 12 months of operation if the venture was younger than three years). We then divided these cumulative growth rates by three (or company age if the company was younger than three years) to obtain comparable average growth rates.
178	Employment growth	Employment growth rates were grouped in seven brackets ranging from 1 (less than 5%) to 7 (more than 200%) and had to be indicated for a three-year period (or in comparison to their first 12 months of operation if the venture was younger than three years). We then divided these cumulative growth rates by three (or company age if the company was younger than three years) to obtain comparable average growth rates.
179	Revenue growth	Operationalized as proportional growth in firm sales over the prior year
180	Total factor productivity	Ln of TFP
180	Debt on assets	Debts to total assets ratio at year t − 1
180	CF on sales	Cash flow to sales ratio at year t − 1

Article ID	Measure term	Measure
181	Revenue growth	Average annual percent revenue growth for this two-year period was calculated as one-half the difference between 2004 and 2006 revenues, divided by the base year (2004) revenue
181	Employment growth	Average annual percent employment growth for this two-year period was calculated as one-half the difference between 2004 and 2006 employment divided by the base year (2004) employment
182	Business financing	Amount of monetary funds received from bank loans within the last 3 years
182	Subjective performance	Rate business's past performance from the last 3 years on a 7-point scale (1 = much worse than competitors, 4 = about the same as competitors, 7 = much better than competitors) on growth in sales, growth in market share, growth in number of employees, growth in profitability, ability to fund growth from profits, return on equity, return on total assets, and profit margin on sales. These eight items were averaged to yield a past performance score, with higher values indicating stronger performance
183	Subjective firm performance	Subjective Firm Performance (Very Unsatisfied/Very Satisfied) To what extent do you agree with the following statements? Considering the economic development of our business in relation to other businesses in our industry, we are … Considering our firm's growth in relation to our most important competitors, we are Considering the forecast for our operating result for the next years, we are … Considering our new product/service success compared to our most important competitors, we are … Considering the number of new clients compared to our most important competitors, we are … Considering our market share compared to our most important competitors, we are … Performance Goal Orientation (Applies Not At All/Applies Fully)
184	Fully funded	Variable (0/1) indicates whether a project has received the full target amount.
184	Number of investors	Counts of individual investors that invested in the project (excluding founders).
184	Funding amount	Indicates the total funding amount that was generated by the project in millions AUD.
184	Speed of investment	Uses the number of days a project needed to complete the first round of financing. Because projects are excluded from the platform after about 1 year if they are not funded, we censored this measure after 365 days.
185	Funded	Value of 1 if the loan was funded, and 0 if the loan was not funded.
185	Funding duration	Measured the length of time, in days and minutes, from which the loan was displayed on the Kiva Web site to the time it was fully funded (or the date study closed). Thus, loans funded within 24 hours of their release had a value less than 1, and those taking longer than 24 hours to fund had a value greater than 1.
186	Time to funding	Time to funding (in days)
187	Early backers	Number of backers that had supported the project between day 1 (campaign launch) and the day at which the campaign has passed one sixth of its total period.
187	Early capital	Percentage of target capital pledged between day 1 (campaign launch) and the day at which the campaign has passed one sixth of its total period.
187	Success	Dummy variable for successful campaigns equal to one if the project had met the target capital at the closure of the campaign
188	Firm performance	On a 5-point Likert scale, the respondents are first asked to indicate the degree of importance their firm attaches to several growth, financial, and nonfinancial performance criteria ((1) sales; (2) sales growth; (3) market share; (4) growth in market share; (5) net profit; (6) cash flow; (7) return on investment; (8) customer satisfaction; (9) competitive capacity; (10) feasibility of self-financed growth). Then on a second 5-point Likert scale, they are asked to indicate the extent to which they are currently satisfied with their firm's performance concerning each of the criteria. For each case, a weighted average performance index is then computed.
189	Resource access financial capital	Have you received financial support from your network contacts? [0 = no; 1 = yes]
189	Resource access information/knowledge	Have you received relevant information/knowledge from your network contacts? [0 = no; 1 = yes]
189	Resource access additional contact	Have you been introduced to additional business contacts by your network contacts? [0 = no; 1 = yes]
189	Network size	How many contacts do you currently have that you consider relevant for your founding project? [metric, in numbers]
190	Return on recent VC investment	Defined as the natural logarithm of the gross effective annual rate of return (EAR) between the firm valuation at the file date and the most recent VC valuation given within 5 years prior to the offer.
190	Total funding	Total financing an IPO firm has received from all of its VCs, in millions of December 2006 dollars.
190	Book-to-market value	BV/VCV, book value/venture capital valuation BV is the book value of equity in the year of the IPO./VC valuation, is the venture capital firm's valuation obtained within 5 years before the file date, in millions of December 2006 dollars.
190	Buy-and-hold return	BHR, the raw buy-and-hold return, is the IPO firm's buy-and-hold return using monthly returns, starting the month after the offer and ending 3 to 5 years later.
191	Network size	To assess the size of entrepreneurs' networks at a subsequent stage of early development (time two), participants were asked to list the names of people that "are currently a source of help" (January 2006). Network size was the count of people listed as sources of help for the respective time periods.

Article ID	Measure term	Measure
192	IPO value	Measured as the total value of the capital raised (the offer price * the number of shares sold in the offering) minus the underwriters' fees as presented on the cover age of the firm's prospectus
192	Return on assets (ROA)	Return on assets (ROA) was measured in the year prior to IPO
192	Sales	Measured using the total revenue as reported in the prospectus in each firm's income statement
192	Venture-capital backing	Calculated as a dichotomous measure coded 1 for VC-backing, 0 if not
192	Private financing	Private financing that IPO firms had received before going public to control for previous success in securing financial capital
192	Generated slack	Measured as sales per employee
193	Increase in firm-founding activities	Increase in firm-founding activities as the difference in firm-founding activities between the fourth and the third wave (t4 - t3) and between the third and the second wave (t3 - t2). We coded each item as a 1 if an activity as completed between waves or a 0 if the activity was not completed. These activities were based on the framework proposed by Katz and Gartner (1988). The extent of firm-founding activities is the sum of all the items in each wave. Thus, the total item scores ranged from 0 to 21 (maximum number of activities) in a particular wave.
194	Firm proceeds	Natural log of the firm's net proceeds from the IPO in United States
194	MV to BV	Ratio of market to book value for the IPO
194	Patent coverage	Number of owned and exclusively licensed patents and applications
194	Employees	Total number of employees prior to IPO
195	Amount of funding	Assessed amount of funding using the actual television episodes as well as archival data posted on the shows' websites (in USD).
196	Market performance	Operationalized market performance as the satisfaction of the respondent with the company's situation relative to major competitors during the last 3 years.
196	Profitability	Measured by a single item related to average return on sales during the last 3 years
197	Size (€m)	Sales (€m)
197	Profitability	Return on assets
197	Tobin's Q	Ratio of market value of assets to the book value of assets, where the market value is calculated as the sum of the book value of assets and the market value of common stock less the book value of common stock
197	5 year BHAR	Natural logarithm of five-year Buy-andHold Abnormal Returns (BHARs)
198	IPO Underpricing	Measured as the percentage difference between the offer price and the price at the end of the first day of trading adjusted for market movements
199	Underpricing	Percentage difference between the offer price and the price at the end of the first day of trading
200	Sales growth	Sales growth from 1997 to 1998. This was calculated using a standard growth formula ([1998 Sales—1997 Sales]/1997 Sales).
201	International sales intensity	Operationalized as foreign sales as a percentage of total sales
202	IPO value	Measured as the total value of the capital for the firm raised through the firm's IPO less the underwriters' fees as noted on the cover page of the firm's prospectus
202	Sales	Prior sales were measured using the Total Revenue reported on the firm's income statement for the fiscal year prior to the IPO date.
203	Underpricing	Measured as ([priceend - priceinitial]/priceinitial) on the first day a stock traded on a national exchange
203	Firm size	Operationalized as the natural log of revenues at the time of the IPO
204	Quantity of support	Number of types of support provided by each of the key supporters was summed across the various (key) supporters of an entrepreneur.
205	New venture performance	Self-reported measures of ten dimensions of new venture performance relative to competitors: sales growth, employment growth, market share, gross profits, net profit margin, innovation in products and services, speed in developing new products and services, quality of products and services, cost control, and customer satisfaction. Respondents used a scale ranging from 1, "much worse," to 7, "much better," to rate these items
205	Sales growth	Measured as the percent change in total sales over the previous year
206	Revenue growth	Average annual revenue growth over the two years immediately following the collection of the survey data.
206	Employment growth	Average annual employment growth over the two years immediately following the collection of the survey data.
207	Revenue growth	Revenue growth is the sum of revenue growth percentages divided by the number of revenue years
208	Survival	Survival time is measured as the age of the firm at failure or at the end of the sample (or observation) window (where right censoring is accounted for by the survival analysis estimation strategy).
208	Total sales	Total sales generated in the observation window
209	Performance-to-plan	Degree to which an executive achieved targeted net income goals for the year, calculated in terms of the percentage of net income goals met.
210	Sales growth rate	NVs sales growth rate adjusted by industry sales growth rate
210	Growth rate in profit	Profit growth rate adjusted for industry
210	Employment growth rate	Percentage change in employees
211	Gross margin	Gross margin is calculated as (revenues – variable costs)/ revenues

Article ID	Measure term	Measure
211	Subjective performance	Developed a five-item subjective performance scale, based on input from the lead founders. Sample items include "Our company has met our predefined level of sales growth" and "Our company has met our predefined level of profitability." Response options on this scale range from 1 (much lower) to 5 (much higher).
212	New venture performance	Measured new venture performance as the absolute level of sales growth over a period of 3 years after the year of IPO.
213	Firm performance	Created an overall firm performance measure by standardizing and then summing the revenue and employment growth metrics for each firm. revenue growth and employment growth. Both indices were calculated as the average annual revenue and employment growth over the one-year period
214	Sales growth	Sales growth was operationalized as total sales revenue in Euro in 2005, controlling for total sales revenue at founding.
214	Employment growth	Employment growth was operationalized as employment in 2005, controlling for total employment at founding.
215	Sales	Computed as the natural logarithm of the start-up's revenues one year after founding, adding 1 where revenues scored 0
216	Growth	Natural log of employment in 2001
216	Business planning	Prior to the business starting, did you have a formal written business plan?' (yes = 1, no = 0).
217	Firm survival	Firm survival
218	Operating return on assets	Ratio of operating profit (earnings before interest and taxes) to the book value of assets
218	Revenue	Natural log of 1+operating revenue
218	Revenue growth	Revenue growth in t relative to t-1
219	Change in company valuation	Difference between the post-money valuation of round n and the pre-money valuation of round n+1 divided by the number of month between the two rounds
220	Survival	Exit is found by identifying the moment when firms cease to report.
221	Failure	Term a firm as having failed if it ceases to exist or if it enters a 'distress sale.
221	Cash-outs	Cash-outs, defined as a favorable acquisition or an initial public offering (IPO), whichever occurred first.
222	Growth	Percentage change in sales revenues in the previous year.
222	Venture size	Log FTE
223	New venture financial performance	Return on total assets (ROTA) as a measure of new venture efficiency, and return on sales (ROS) as a measure of new venture profitability, standardized the two indicators and averaged their values, creating a composite measure of financial performance
224	ROA	ROA for the first full calendar year
225	Financial performance	Nine-item, sevenpoint scale that was validated in prior research (Stam and Elfring, 2008). The nine items included sales level (P1), market share (P2), sales growth (P3), cash flow (P4), ability to fund business growth from profits (P5), return on assets (P6), return on equity (P7), return on sales (P8), and overall firm performance/success (P9).
225	Sales	Log of sales
226	IPO or acquisition	Occurrence of an IPO or an acquisition, duration analysis
226	Cumulative investment	Cumulative investment (USDk)
227	Revenues	Sales per year
228	New venture performance	Measured by eight items. The respondent was asked to rate his or her venture's performance relative to its principal competitors over the last 3 years on return on investment, return on sales, profit growth, return on assets, overall efficiency of operations, sales growth, market share growth, and cash flow from operations.
229	Pre-money valuation	Pre-money valuation of the company at the most recent round of financing price per share in the financing round times the number of shares outstanding prior to the round.
229	Total amount of capital raised	Total amount of capital raised by the startup since founding, including all rounds of financing through the time of the survey.
230	Firm size	Number of employees
230	Firm survival	Classified each of the 100 firms in our sample as "active" or "inactive."
231	IPO Premium	Premium paid for a firm at IPO, defined as the ratio of the difference between the offer price and the book value per share over the offer price
232	Price premium	Price premium (calculated as [offer price – book value per share]/offer price)
232	Net income	Net income of the year prior to IPO
233	Number of backers	Number of backers who pledge money to the project
233	Funding amount	Total amount of funding in U.S. dollars pledged by backers
234	Idea quality	Idea quality as the combination of originality and feasibility. Operationalized "originality" using Dean and colleagues' (2006) four-point originality scale. The scale ranges from 1 (common, mundane, or boring business idea) to 4 (rare, unusual, ingenious, imaginative, or surprising business idea). Consistent with Poetz and Schreier (2012), operationalized "feasibility" using a three-point scale, ranging from 1 (low feasibility) to 3 (high feasibility).
234	Idea quantity	Two expert raters independently scored the quantity (number) of ideas generated
235	Capital received	Capital Received, which is equal to 1 if a new venture secured equity investment and 0 otherwise
236	IPO success	IPO success coded 1 for success and 0 for failure

Article ID	Measure term	Measure
236	Short-term post-IPO performance	Short-term post-IPO performance using the natural logarithm of the firms' 90-day market valuation
237	Time elapsed	Time elapsed (in days) from the filing of a bank charter application to the opening date of the bank for groups that succeeded in opening, and, for groups that failed, to the date of their withdrawal
238	Total yearly employment count	Number of full-time employees, part-time employees, mini-job and freelancers working for the firm
239	IPO valuation	Tobin's Q, which is equal to the market value of the assets over its book value
240	Return on assets	Calculate ROA (with 1-year lead vis-à-vis mediators) using the net income and total assets reported by the firm each year and calculate the industry-adjusted ROA by subtracting the industry mean.
241	Firm failure	Failure is defined as being delisted
241	RoA	Calculated absolute RoA by dividing a firm's earnings before interest by its average total assets. We then subtracted median industry RoA from a firm's absolute RoA to provide our "relative" RoA measure.
241	Tobin's q	Tobin's q was measured by dividing the total market value of a firm by its book value.
242	IPO	Binary variable that took a value of 1 if new ventures went public as of January 1, 2009, and 0 otherwise.
242	Failure	Value of 1 if new ventures were defunct and 0 otherwise.
243	International sales	Calculated as the hazard (the instantaneous rate) of a venture beginning international sales, which was coded dichotomously with 1 indicating that the venture realizes an initial foreign sale, or 0 otherwise.
243	Return on assets (RoA)	Return on assets (ROA)
244	Firm performance	Firm performance: The multidimensional firm performance construct captures four key performance dimensions. Drawing on Pelham (1999) included two items each for each firm's financial performance and growth. For each item, assessed respondent's level of satisfaction with firm performance relative to the firm's competitors
245	Percent price premium	[(offer price—book value per share)/offerprice]
245	RoA	ROA, measured at the end of the IPO year
246	Firm valuation	Most recent VC valuation for private years; market capitalization for public years (in USD M)
247	Market performance	Natural log of annual sales revenues
248	Revenue	Revenue data from administrative office of incubator
248	Investment funding received	Investment funding received data from administrative office of incubator, standardized
248	Grants received	Amount of grants received by each venture
248	Venture size	Average employment headcount during study period
249	Underpricing conformity	Deviations in absolute value from the market's average underpricing level
249	Underpricing level	Difference between the closing and opening price divided by the opening price on the first day of trading
249	VC backing	Dummy; one if at least one VC fund has invested, zero otherwise
250	TFP (productivity)	Firm-level Cobb–Douglas production function
251	Ebit	Earnings before interest and tax
251	RoA	Net earnings on total assets
251	Sales	Net revenues
251	Quick ratio	Cash and cash equivalents on current liabilities
252	Funds raised	Total amount of funds raised for the campaign
252	Number of funders	Total number of funders that contributed to the campaign
252	Success	Campaign met its target funding goal
253	Time-to-funding	Number of days between company being founded and beginning of token offering
253	Gross proceeds	Funding amount, log-transformed
253	Initial returns	Returns on the first day of trading
253	Failure	Tokens are delisted from all exchange platforms, represents a company's death
254	Sales	Annual sales revenue
254	Employees	Annual number of employees
254	Growth sales	Annual changes in sales
254	Growth employment	Annual changes in number of employees
255	Funding success	Reached funding goal: zero: funding goal not reached, one: funding goal reached
255	Amount raised	Amount of funding the campaigns had raised

Appendix C: Excerpt of PSED II questionnaire (Chapter 3)[13]

ICPSR | INTER-UNIVERSITY CONSORTIUM FOR POLITICAL AND SOCIAL RESEARCH

ICPSR 37202

Panel Study of Entrepreneurial Dynamics, PSED II, United States, 2005-2011

Richard T. Curtin
University of Michigan

Paul D. (Paul Davidson) Reynolds
Florida International University

Waves A-F Questionnaires

Inter-university Consortium for
Political and Social Research
P.O. Box 1248
Ann Arbor, Michigan 48106
www.icpsr.umich.edu

[13] As in Curtin and Reynolds (2018).

Terms of Use

The terms of use for this study can be found at:
http://www.icpsr.umich.edu/icpsrweb/ICPSR/studies/37202/terms

Information about Copyrighted Content

SECTION A: TYPE OF NEW BUSINESS

A1. What kind of business are you starting?
(Could you tell me a little more about the product or service you intend to provide?)

____

____

A2. Why do you want to start this new business? (Any other reasons)?

____

____

A3. What is the name of this new business?
[PROBE: What name can we use to refer to this new business in this interview?]
[RECORD JUST THE NAME ONLY, USE F2 FOR COMMENTS]

NAME OF BUSINESS:______________________________

A4. Has this name been registered with the appropriate government agency?

1. YES	5. NO

A5. What are the one or two main opportunities that prompted you to start this new business? (Anything else?)

____

____

A6. What are the one or two main problems involved in starting this new business? (Any other problems?)

____

____

D5. **INTERVIEWER CHECKPOINT:**

☐ 1. IF INDEPENDENT NEW BUSINESS (A10 = 1), NEW BUSINESS SPONSORED BY EXISTING BUSINESS (A10 = 4), OR SOME OTHER TYPE OF BUSINESS (A10 = 7) --> **GO TO D6**

☐ 2. OTHERS --> **GO TO D9**

D6. ([IF A10 NOT EQUAL TO 1] If this new business is affiliated with a parent company such as a distributor, multi-level marketer, franchise, or reseller please answer for the new business being created and not the established business.)

Is the product or service that this new business will sell completely developed and ready for sale or delivery, has it been tested with customers as a prototype or procedure, is it being developed as a model or procedure, or is the product or service still in the idea stage?

1. COMPLETED AND READY FOR SALE OR DELIVERY	2. PROTOTYPE/PROCEDURE TESTED WITH CUSTOMERS
3. MODEL/PROCEDURE IS BEING DEVELOPED	4. STILL IN THE IDEA STAGE; NO WORK DONE YET **GO TO D9**

D7. In what month and year did the development of this product or service begin?
[PROBE FOR SEASON IF DK MONTH]

______________/______________
MONTH YEAR

D8. [IF D6=1] In what month and year was the product or service completed and ready for sale?
[PROBE FOR SEASON IF DK MONTH]

______________/______________
MONTH YEAR

Psed2w1

Appendix D: List of Articles included in the MAQCA (Chapter 4)

ID	Author	Published in	Year	Included in Meta-analysis	Included in QCA
1	Adriansyah, A.; Afiff, A. Z.	The South East Asian Journal of Management.	2015	x	
2	Ahlin, B.; Drnovšek, M.; Hisrich, R. D.	Journal for East European Management Studies	2014a	x	x
3	Ahlin, B.; Drnovšek, M.; Hisrich, R. D.	Journal for East European Management Studies	2014b	x	x
4	Ahuja, G.; Lampert, C. M.	Strategic Management Journal	2001	x	x
5	Ali, M.; Kan, K. A. S.; Sarstedt, M.	Journal of Business Research	2016	x	x
6	Aljanabi, A. Q. R. A.; Noor, N. A. M.; Kumar, D. M.	Information Management and Business Review	2014	x	
7	Azadegan, A.; Dooley, K. J.	Journal of Operations Management	2010	x	
8	Baba, Y.; Shichijo, N.; Sedita, S. R.	Research Policy	2009	x	
9	Bapuji, H.; Loree, D.; Crossan, M.	Journal of Engineering and Technology Management	2011	x	
10	Belderbos, R.; Gilsing, V. A.; Suzuki, S.	Strategic Organization	2015a	x	x
11	Belderbos, R.; Gilsing, V. A.; Suzuki, S.	Strategic Organization	2015b	x	x
12	Bellamy, M. A.; Ghosh, S.; Hora, M.	Journal of Operations Management	2014	x	
13	Belussi, F.; Sammarra, A.; Sedita, S. R.	Research Policy	2010	x	x
14	Berchicci, L.	Research Policy	2013	x	x
15	Berchicci, L.; de Jong, J. P.; Freel, M.	Working Paper	2013	x	x
16	Berghman, L.; Matthyssens, P.; Vandenbempt, K.	Industrial Marketing Management	2012a	x	x
17	Berghman, L.; Matthyssens, P.; Streukens, S.; Vandenbempt, K.	Long Range Planning	2012b	x	x
18	Bianchi, M.; Croce, A.; Dell'Era, C.; Di Benedetto, C. A.; Frattini, F.	Journal of Product Innovation Management	2015	x	x
19	Bocquet, R.; Brion, S.; Mothe, C.	Journal of Small Business Management	2016	x	x
20	Bucic, T.; Ngo, L. V.	International Journal of Innovation Management	2013	x	x
21	Campbell, D. A.	Dissertation	2007	x	
22	Carlo, J. L.; Lyytinen, K.; Rose, G. M.	MIS Quarterly	2012	x	x
23	Cepeda-Carrion, G.; Cegarra-Navarro, J. G.; Jimenez-Jimenez, D.	British Journal of Management	2012	x	
24	Cepeda-Carrión, G.; Gabriel Cegarra-Navarro, J.; Leal-Millán, A. G.	Management Decision	2012	x	
25	Chang, S.; Gong, Y.; Way, S. A.; Jia, L.	Journal of Management	2013	x	x
26	Chang, C. H.; Chen, Y. S.; Lin, M. J. J.	R&D Management	2014a	x	x
27	Chang, C. H.; Chen, Y. S.; Lin, M. J. J.	R&D Management	2014b	x	
28	Chang, Y. C.; Chang, H. T.; Chi, H. R.; Chen, M. H.; Deng, L. L.	Technovation	2012	x	x
29	Chen, S. T.; Chang, B. G.	Contemporary Management Research	2012	x	
30	Chen, Y. S.; Lin, M. J. J.; Chang, C. H.	Industrial Marketing Management	2009	x	
31	Chen, C. J.; Lin, B. W.; Lin, Y. H.; Hsiao, Y. C.	Journal of Business Research	2016	x	x
32	Clarysse, B.; Wright, M.; Mustar, P.	Research Policy	2009	x	
33	Costa, V.; Monteiro, S.	Knowledge and Process Management	2016	x	x
34	Cruz-González, J.; López-Sáez, P.; Navas-López, J. E.	Industrial Marketing Management	2015	x	
35	Daspit, J.	Dissertation	2012	x	x
36	de Faria, P.; Lima, F.; Santos, R.	Research Policy	2010	x	x
37	De Zubielqui, G. C.; Jones, J.; Lester, L.	International Journal of Innovation Management	2016	x	x
38	del-Corte-Lora, V.; Molina-Morales, F. X.; Vallet-Bellmunt, T. M.	Technology Analysis and Strategic Management	2016	x	
39	Desyllas, P.; Hughes, A.	Research Policy	2010	x	
40	Dushnitsky, G.; Lenox, M. J.	Research Policy	2005	x	x
41	Ebers, M.; Maurer, I.	Research Policy Journal	2014	x	
42	Expósito-Langa, M.; Molina-Morales, F. X.; Tomás-Miquel, J. V.	Scandinavian Journal of Management	2015	x	
43	Fabrizio, K. R.	Research Policy	2009	x	
44	Ferreira, G. C.; Ferreira, J. J.	Revista de Administração Mackenzie	2017	x	

45	Flor, M. L.; Cooper, S. Y.; Oltra, M. J.	European Management Journal	2017	x	x
46	Forés, B.; Camisón, C.	Journal of Business Research	2016	x	x
47	Frost, T. S.; Zhou, C.	Journal of International Business Studies	2005	x	x
48	Galbreath, J.; Charles, D.; Oczkowski, E.	Journal of Business Ethics	2016	x	
49	Gao, S.; Xu, K.; Yang, J.	Asia Pacific Journal of Management	2008	x	
50	Garcia Martinez, M.; Zouaghi; F.; Sanchez Garcia, M.	Technovation	2017	x	
51	García-Morales, V. J.; Ruiz-Moreno, A.; Llorens-Montes, F. J.	Technology Analysis & Strategic Management	2007	x	
52	Garrido, I. L.; Parente, R. C.; Gonçalo, C. R.; Vasconcellos, S. L. D.	Brazilian Business Review	2017	x	x
53	Gellynck, X.; Cárdenas, J.; Pieniak, Z.; Verbeke, W.	Agribusiness	2015	x	
54	George, G.; Zahra, S. A.; Wheatley, K. K.; Khan, R.	Journal of High Technology Management Research	2001	x	x
55	Ghisetti, C.; Marzucchi, A.; Montresor, S.	Research Policy	2015	x	
56	Gilsing, V.; Nooteboom, B.; Vanhaverbeke, W.; Duysters, G.; van den Oord, A.	Research Policy	2008	x	
57	Gölgeci, I.; Swiatowiec-Szczepanska, J.; Raczkowski, K.	Technology Analysis & Strategic Management	2017	x	x
58	González, X.; Miles-Touya, D.; Pazó, C.	Industry and Innovation	2016	x	x
59	Guimaraes, T.; Thielman, B.; Guimaraes, V. C.; Cornick, M.	International Journal of the Academic Business World	2016	x	x
60	Hayton, J. C.; Zahra, S. A.	International Journal of Technology Management	2005	x	
61	Heil, S.; Enkel, E.	International Journal of Innovation Management	2015	x	x
62	Hodgkinson, I. R.; Hughes, P.; Hughes, M.	Journal of Strategic Marketing	2012	x	
63	Huang, K. F.; Lin, K. H.; Wu, L. Y.; Yu, P. H.	Journal of Business Research	2015	x	
64	Hull, C. E.; Covin, J. G.	Journal of Product Innovation Management	2010	x	
65	Hurmelinna-Laukkanen, P.	Management Decision	2012	x	
66	Hurmelinna-Laukkanen, P.; Olander, H.; Blomqvist, K.; Panfilii, V.	European Management Journal	2012	x	x
67	Hurmelinna-Laukkanen, P.; Olander, H.	Technovation	2014	x	
68	Jain, A.	Organization Science	2013	x	
69	Kapoor, R.; Klueter, T.	Academy of Management Journal	2015a	x	
70	Kapoor, R.; Klueter, T.	Academy of Management Journal	2015b	x	
71	Kim, H.; Hur, D.; Schoenherr, T.	Journal of International Management	2005	x	
72	Kim, Y. A.; Akbar, H.; Tzokas, N.; Al-Dajani, H.	International Small Business Journal	2014	x	x
73	Kostopoulos, K.; Papalexandris, A.; Papachroni, M.; Ioannou, G.	Journal of Business Research	2010	x	
74	Kotabe, M.; Jiang, C. X.; Murray, J. Y.	Journal of World Business	2011	x	x
75	Kotabe, M.; Jiang, C. X.; Murray, J. Y.	Journal of Management	2017	x	x
76	Lau, A. K. W.; Lo, W.	Technological Forecasting & Social Change	2015	x	x
77	Leal-Rodríguez, A. L.; Ariza-Montes, J. A.; Roldán, J. L.; Leal-Millán, A. G.	Journal of Business Research	2013	x	
78	Lee, S. U.; Kang, J.	Industry and Innovation	2015	x	
79	Leone, M. I.; Reichstein, T.; Boccardelli, P.; Magnusson, M.	R&D Management	2016	x	
80	Li, X.	World Development	2011	x	x
81	Li, Y.; Vanhaverbeke, W.	International Journal of Innovation Management	2009	x	
82	Li, Y.; Guo,H.; Yi, Y.; Liu, Y.	Management and Organization Review	2010	x	x
83	Li, H. L.; Tang, M. J.	Technovation	2010	x	x
84	Li, X.; Wang, J.; Liu, X.	International Business Review	2013	x	
85	Liao, T. J.; Yu, C. M. J.	The Journal of Technology Transfer	2013	x	
86	Liao, Y.; Marsillac, E.	International Journal of Production Research	2015	x	x
87	Limaj, E.; Bernroider, E. W. N.; Choudrie, J.	Information & Management	2016	x	x
88	Lin, C.; Wu, Y. J.; Chang, C.; Wang, W.; Lee, C. Y.	Technovation	2012	x	
89	Lin, C.; Chang, C. C.	Technological Forecasting & Social Change	2015	x	x
90	Lin, H.; Zeng, S.; Liu, H.; Li, C.	Journal of Business Research	2016	x	
91	Liu, X.; Huang, Q.; Dou, J.; Zhao, X.	Journal of Business Research	2017	x	x

92	Liu, Y.; Ying, Y.; Wu, X.	Thunderbird International Business Review	2016	x	x
93	Liu, R.	Working paper: "Management Learning in Business Networks: the process and the effects"	2015	x	
94	Lucena, A.; Roper, S.	European Management Review	2016	x	x
95	Maes, J.; Sels, L.	Journal of Small Business Management	2014	x	x
96	Malshe, A.	Dissertation	2005	x	x
97	McMillan, G. S.; Mauri, A.; Halmilton, R. D.	International Journal of Innovation Management	2003	x	
98	Moon, S.	Seoul Journal of Business	2014	x	x
99	Moos, B.; Beimborn, D.	International Journal of Innovation Management	2013	x	
100	Nambisan, S.	Research Policy	2013	x	
101	Nguyen, T.	Dissertation	2014	x	x
102	Nicholls-Nixon, C. L.; Woo, C. Y.	Strategic Management Journal	2003	x	x
103	Patel, P. C.; Kohtamäki, M.; Parida, V.; Wincent, J.	Strategic Management Journal	2015	x	x
104	Penner-Hahn, J.; Shaver, J. M.	Strategic Management Journal	2005	x	x
105	Phelps, C. C.	The Academy of Management Journal	2010	x	
106	Phene, A.; Fladmoe-Lindquist, K.; Marsh, L.	Strategic Management Journal	2006	x	
107	Preston, D. S.; Chen, D. Q.; Swink, M.; Meade, L.	Decision Sciences	2017	x	
108	Rakthin, S.; Calantone, R. J.; Wang, J. F.	Journal of Business Research	2016	x	
109	Ritala, P.; Hurmelinna-Laukkanen, P.	Journal of Product Innovation Management	2013	x	x
110	Roberts, N.; Dinger, M.	IEEE Transactions on Professional Communication	2016	x	x
111	Rodríguez-Serrano, M. Á.; Martín-Armario, E.	Journal of Small Business Management	2017	x	x
112	Rothaermel, F. T.; Alexandre, M. T.	Organization Science	2009	x	x
113	Ryzhkova, N.; Pesämaa, O.	International Journal of Innovation Management	2015	x	x
114	Saito, H.; Sumikura, K.	International Journal of Innovation Management	2010	x	x
115	Schildt, H.; Keil, T.; Maula, M.	Strategic Management Journal	2012	x	x
116	Sharp, B. M.	Dissertation	2009	x	x
117	Sheng, M. L.; Chien, I.	Journal of Business Research	2016	x	x
118	Shin, K.; Kim, S. J.; Park, G.	Asia Pacific Journal of Management	2016	x	x
119	Sikimic, U.; Chiesa, V.; Frattini, F.; Scalera, V. G.	Journal of Product Innovation Management	2016	x	x
120	Stam, W.	Research Policy	2009	x	x
121	Steensma, H. K.; Corley, K. G.	The Academy of Management Journal	2000	x	
122	Stock, G. N.; Greis, N. P.; Fischer, W. A.	The Journal of High Technology Management Research	2001	x	
123	Su, Z.; Ahlstrom, D.; Li, J.; Cheng, D.	R&D Management	2013	x	
124	Tomlinson, P. R.	Research Policy	2010	x	
125	Torres-Barreto, M. L.; Mendez-Duron, R.; Hernandez-Perlines, F.	R&D Management	2016	x	x
126	Torugsa, N.; Arundel, A.	The International Journal of Innovation Management	2013	x	x
127	Tsai, W.	Academy of Management Journal	2001	x	
128	Tsai, K. H.	Research Policy	2009	x	
129	Tufool, A.; Gerard, G.	Strategic Management Journal	2016	x	x
130	Tzokas, N.; Kim, Y. A.; Akbar, H.; Al-Dajani, H.	Industrial Marketing Management	2015	x	x
131	Ujari, P. U.	Dissertation	2002	x	
132	Van de Vrande, V.; Vanhaverbeke, W.; Duysters, G.	Journal of Product Innovation Management	2011	x	x
133	Vicente-Oliva, S.; Martinez-Sanchez, A.; Berges-Muro, L.	International Journal of Innovation Management	2016	x	
134	Wang, Y.; Li-Ying, J.	Technovation	2014	x	
135	Wang, Y.; Roijakkers, N.; Vanhaverbeke, W.	IEEE Transactions on Engineering Management	2013	x	
136	Watts, A. D.; Hamilton III, R. D.	R&D Management	2013	x	
137	Weng, R. H.; Huang, C. Y.	Journal of Management & Organization	2012	x	
138	Weng, R. H.; Huang, C. Y.	Technology Analysis & Strategic Management	2017	x	
139	Wu, L. W.; Lii, Y. S.; Wang, C. Y.	Journal of Business Research	2015	x	
140	Wu, J.; Wang, C.; Hong, J.; Piperopoulos, P.; Zhuo, S.	Journal of World Business	2016	x	
141	Xie, Z.; Li, J.	Journal of International Management	2015	x	

142	Xu,S.; Wu, S.; Cavusgil, E.	Journal of Product Innovation Management	2013	x	
143	Yang, X.; Sun, S. L.; Yang, H.	Industrial Marketing Management	2015	x	
144	Yu, S. H.	Technological Forecasting and Social Change	2013	x	
145	Zobel A. K.	Journal of Product Innovation Management	2017	x	x

Selbständigkeitserklärung

Ich erkläre hiermit, dass ich diese Arbeit selbständig verfasst und keine anderen als die angegebenen Quellen benutzt habe. Alle Koautorenschaften sowie alle Stellen, die wörtlich oder sinngemäss aus Quellen entnommen wurden, habe ich als solche gekennzeichnet. Mir ist bekannt, dass andernfalls der Senat gemäss Artikel 36 Absatz 1 Buchstabe o des Gesetzes vom 5. September 1996 über die Universität zum Entzug des aufgrund dieser Arbeit verliehenen Titels berechtigt ist.

Johann Josef Martin Johannes Brieler Bern, 03.09.2024